G. Chaplin (George Chaplin) Child, George Ch. Child

The great architect.

Benedicite; illustrations of the power, wisdom, and goodness of God, as manifested in his works

G. Chaplin (George Chaplin) Child, George Ch. Child

The great architect.
Benedicite; illustrations of the power, wisdom, and goodness of God, as manifested in his works

ISBN/EAN: 9783337814625

Printed in Europe, USA, Canada, Australia, Japan

Cover: Foto ©ninafisch / pixelio.de

More available books at **www.hansebooks.com**

The Great Architect.

BENEDICITE;

ILLUSTRATIONS OF THE POWER, WISDOM, AND
GOODNESS OF GOD, AS MANIFESTED IN
HIS WORKS.

By G. CHAPLIN CHILD, M. D.

TWO VOLUMES IN ONE.

NEW YORK:
G. P. PUTNAM AND SON, 661 Broadway.
1869.

[Reprinted from the London edition of John Murray, issued December, 1866.]

RIVERSIDE, CAMBRIDGE:
STEREOTYPED AND PRINTED BY
H. O. HOUGHTON AND COMPANY.

"Every advance in our knowledge of the natural world will, if rightly directed by the spirit of true humility, and with a prayer for God's blessing, advance us in our knowledge of Himself, and will prepare us to receive His revelations of His Will with profounder reverence." — Sir ROBERT H. INGLIS, *British Association*, 1847.

INTRODUCTORY NOTE.

BY HENRY G. WESTON, D. D.

THE work here offered to the American public, it is confidently believed, will be found worthy of a wide circulation. The author is an intelligent physician, at home in the various departments of natural science, who has in the treatment of his theme most happily avoided on the one hand the habit of many scientists of depreciating Revelation, and on the other the forced and strained arguments employed by some true but injudicious friends of Religion. Written in an easy and flowing style, abounding in illustrations and incidents, unincumbered by abstruse and scientific terms, the book cannot fail to interest as well as instruct. Science and Religion, Knowledge and Piety, walk together in these pages in unalloyed friendship; while the charm thrown around the train of thought continues unbroken to the close.

An occasional allusion to England and to the Established Church of that country will be noticed by the careful reader. This edition being an exact and literal reprint, these allusions are of course left untouched; they are but few in number, do not at all affect the argument, and are never offensively obtruded. A warm heart as well as a clear head is demanded for the production of a work like this, and such a heart must have a country and a church to love. Americans can understand and appreciate the feelings which find such almost involuntary utterance, and can respect in others what they cherish in themselves, — that patriotism which does not depreciate other lands while it regards with fondest affection its own God-given home.

NEW YORK, *March*, 1867.

CONTENTS.

	PAGE
INTRODUCTION. Babylon. Nebuchadnezzar and the Burning Fiery Furnace. The Song of the Three Children	7
THE HEAVENS	20
THE SUN AND THE MOON. THE PLANETS	27
THE STARS OF HEAVEN	51
WINTER AND SUMMER	72
NIGHTS AND DAYS	85
LIGHT AND DARKNESS	88
WATERS ABOVE THE FIRMAMENT	100
LIGHTNING AND CLOUDS	106
SHOWERS AND DEW	111
WELLS	122
SEAS AND FLOODS	134
THE WINDS OF GOD	158
FIRE AND HEAT	171
FROST AND COLD.—ICE AND SNOW	182
POWERS OF THE LORD	198
MOUNTAINS AND HILLS	220
THE EARTH	230
GREEN THINGS UPON THE EARTH	251
BEASTS AND CATTLE	286
FOWLS OF THE AIR	300
WHALES, AND ALL THAT MOVE IN THE WATERS	338
CONCLUDING REFLECTIONS	362

GOD MAGNIFIED IN HIS WORKS.

GOD MAGNIFIED IN HIS WORKS.

Babylon — the glory of kingdoms, the beauty of the Chaldees' excellency! — ISAIAH xiii. 19.
Her cities are a desolation, a dry land, and a wilderness, a land wherein no man dwelleth. — JEREMIAH li. 43.

IN an outlying province of the Turkish empire, where sultan and firman are often superseded by the lawless will of sheik or pacha, two famous rivers — the Tigris and Euphrates — gradually converge, and, after mingling their waters together, glide gently onward to the Persian Gulf. In the fork thus formed between them stretches a vast plain, made known to us in early Scripture History as Shinar, Chaldæa, and Babylon, as well as by other less familiar names, but to which the term Mesopotamia has been more usually applied, as it aptly designates a district "lying between rivers." The general aspect of this plain is one of desolation. Fertile strips here and there border the Euphrates' banks, and willows are still seen flourishing where the sorrowing Israelites once hung up their harps; but away from those green fringes the eye wanders over wild, dreary wastes from which the last traces of cultivation are slowly dying out. Vast tracts lie soaked in permanent swamps, while much of the remaining land is, at one period of the year, flooded by the unheeded inundations of the neighboring rivers, and, at another, baked into an arid desert by the burning rays of the sun. It need scarcely be said that population has almost disappeared from those melancholy plains; for the wandering Arab is little tempted to pitch his tent or to pasture his flocks on so sterile a soil. The doom that was so clearly foretold by the prophets has fallen upon it, and Babylon now " lies desolate in the sight of all that pass by." It has become the "habitation of the beasts of the desert." As the traveler plods onward over its unfrequented tracts, the startled wild-fowl rises with quick splash from the reedy pool, or a few scared gazelles may perhaps be descried bounding over the distant plain. The " owl " and the " bittern," the jackal and the hyena add their testimony to the exactness with which the words of Scripture have been fulfilled. More rarely a solitary lion may be seen skulking among the strange, mysterious mounds and " heaps " of stones that loom here and there above the plain.

Mournful and dreary though this land now be, it is and ever will remain one of the most interesting spots on earth. It was not always "desolate." No other place, perhaps, claims with a better title to be regarded as the scene where our first parents walked together in paradise. Such, at least, has been the common tradition; and in a well-known edition of the Bible, published in 1599, may be found a map of the Garden of Eden, of which the site of Babylon forms the centre. But, be that as it may, there can be no doubt of its former greatness and fertility, for the record is plainly written all over the soil. Everywhere it is furrowed by ruined canals, of which some tell us of departed commerce and wealth, others of skillful irrigation and abundant crops. Heaps of rubbish are to be met with in which lie hidden fragments of pottery which bear witness to the former presence of a highly cultivated people; and uncouth mounds rise strangely above the plain, in which the last relics of palaces and cities are buried together. For centuries History appeared to have lost her hold upon those great places of the past, and it is only within the last few years that some of them have been rescued from the oblivion that was slowly creeping over them. Questioned by the light of modern knowledge those mysterious stones of the plains open up to us the first page in the history of nations — transport us back almost to the dawn where antiquity begins, and bring within our sight those to whom the deluge was a recent event. They impart a substance to scenes we have often tried in vain to realize. In imagination we see Nimrod the Mighty Hunter, busy with the foundations of the city of Babel on the neighboring Euphrates' bank, and piling up the "tower that was to reach to heaven." Then it was that the patriarchal dignity of early Bible records expanded into royalty, and Babylon became the starting point in the long pedigree of kingdoms.

Babylon touched the zenith of its grandeur two thousand four hundred and fifty years ago, when Nebuchadnezzar sat upon the throne. He was the great warrior of that age. After overrunning Egypt he had returned to his capital laden with its spoil; he had chastised his rebellious subjects and treacherous allies, and he had utterly crushed the power of the Kings of Judah. The wicked and faithless Jehoiakim, blind to the warnings he received, had brought a terrible doom upon his country; for Nebuchadnezzar, not content with plundering the treasures of the temple at Jerusalem, carried the king himself a prisoner to Babylon. Among the captives on this occasion were included Daniel the Prophet and his three friends, — Ananias, Azarias, and Misael, who in the land of their exile received the Chaldean names of Shadrach, Meshach, and Abednego.

Nebuchadnezzar was no less great in the arts of peace than in those of war. He, therefore, encouraged learned men to make his capital their resort, and he also promoted the national prosperity by favoring agriculture and commerce. He dug canals in all directions to fertilize the land by irrigation. His merchants traded along the rich shores of the Mediterranean, and penetrated even to remote China. He provided for the security of Babylon by building or strengthening its walls, and he made it beautiful by adorning it with palaces. Its "hanging-gardens" were acknowledged throughout ancient times to be one of the wonders of the world, and their fame has endured up to this very hour.

At the court of such a monarch, Daniel's learning was sure to procure for him distinction, and he soon became a member of the college of Magi or wise men. His subsequent success in interpreting Nebuchadnezzar's dream, after all others had failed, raised him to the first rank in the tyrant's favor, and we are told that "he sat in the gate of the king." Nor in his prosperity did he forget his three Jewish friends, — Shadrach, Meshach, and Abednego, — who through his influence were promoted to be Governors in the province of Babylon.

The history of Nebuchadnezzar and the burning, fiery furnace — so illustrative on the one hand of perfect trust in God, and, on the other, of God's power to deliver his servants from the assaults of their enemies — is endeared to all as one of the interesting Scripture narratives by which those who watched over us in the days of childhood endeavored to attract us onward to the knowledge of our Bible. In the book of Daniel it is related how Nebuchadnezzar, after having been brought by the miraculous interpretation of his dream to acknowledge the "God of Gods and Lord of Kings," subsequently relapsed into idolatry through the corrupting influence of worldly prosperity. In the full swell of his pride he set up a golden image, and commanded that all his subjects should fall down and worship it. The Babylonian nobles were jealous of the favor shown to the three captives; and they, therefore, encouraged this wicked fancy of the king, because it seemed to open out the means of effecting their ruin. They rightly calculated that the Hebrew Governors would never forsake the God of their Fathers, nor worship the image which the king had set up. And we know that when the hour of trial did come, Shadrach, Meshach, and Abednego remained true to their faith; and were forthwith bound and cast into the burning, fiery furnace, as a punishment for their disobedience to the tyrant's will.

From the torments and dangers of this ordeal the Three Hebrews were miraculously preserved. Daniel tells us that Nebuchadnezzar himself saw them "loose and walking in the midst of the fire." " Not a hair of their heads was singed, neither were their coats changed, nor had the smell of fire passed on them." Elsewhere, in the Song of the Three Children, we are told that "they walked in the midst of the fire, praising God, and blessing the Lord." After so signal a deliverance, it is easy to conceive the fervor with which their Hymn of gratitude was poured forth. The deepest consciousness of the merciful Power of God welled up in their hearts and burst from their lips, and the whole universe was ransacked for illustrations to typify and express it. In whatever direction they turned, they beheld Nature crowded with emblems of His Greatness and Mercy, and they eagerly seized upon them as aids to bring their thoughts up to the fervor of their adoration. Shall not we also do wisely to profit by their example? Our daily obligations to God may not be so miraculous, in the ordinary meaning of the term, but they are, nevertheless, great and countless beyond our power to conceive. Let us then, in humble consciousness of the poverty and imperfection of our thanksgivings, gladly make this suggestive hymn our own; and let us on this, as on all occasions, accept with joy every aid that helps us to "bless, praise, and magnify the Lord."

God magnified in his Works.

Benedicite, omnia opera.

O ALL ye Works of the Lord, bless ye the Lord: praise him, and magnify him for ever.

O ye Angels of the Lord, bless ye the Lord: praise him, and magnify him for ever.

O ye Heavens, bless ye the Lord: praise him, and magnify him for ever.

O ye Waters that be above the Firmament, bless ye the Lord: praise him, and magnify him for ever.

O all ye Powers of the Lord, bless ye the Lord: praise him, and magnify him for ever.

O ye Sun and Moon, bless ye the Lord: praise him, and magnify him for ever.

O ye Stars of Heaven, bless ye the Lord: praise him, and magnify him for ever.

O ye Showers and Dew, bless ye the Lord: praise him, and magnify him for ever.

O ye Winds of God, bless ye the Lord: praise him, and magnify him for ever.

O ye Fire and Heat, bless ye the Lord: praise him, and magnify him for ever.

O ye Winter and Summer, bless ye the Lord: praise him, and magnify him for ever.

O ye Dews and Frosts, bless ye the Lord: praise him, and magnify him for ever.

O ye Frost and Cold, bless ye the Lord: praise him, and magnify him for ever.

O ye Ice and Snow, bless ye the Lord: praise him, and magnify him for ever.

O ye Nights and Days, bless ye the Lord: praise him, and magnify him for ever.

O ye Light and Darkness, bless ye the Lord: praise him, and magnify him for ever.

O ye Lightnings and Clouds, bless ye the Lord: praise him, and magnify him for ever.

God magnified in his Works.

O let the Earth bless the Lord: yea, let it praise him, and magnify him for ever.

O ye Mountains and Hills, bless ye the Lord: praise him and magnify him for ever.

O all ye Green Things upon the Earth, bless ye the Lord: praise him, and magnify him for ever.

O ye Wells, bless ye the Lord: praise him, and magnify him for ever.

O ye Seas and Floods, bless ye the Lord: praise him. and magnify him for ever.

O ye Whales, and all that move in the Waters, bless ye the Lord: praise him, and magnify him for ever.

O all ye Fowls of the Air, bless ye the Lord: praise him, and magnify him for ever.

O all ye Beasts and Cattle, bless ye the Lord: praise him, and magnify him for ever.

O ye Children of Men, bles ye the Lord: praise him, and magnify him for ever.

O let Israel bless the Lord: praise him, and magnify him for ever.

O ye Priests of the Lord, bless ye the Lord: praise him, and magnify him for ever.

O ye Servants of the Lord, bless ye the Lord: praise him, and magnify him for ever.

O ye Spirits and Souls of the Righteous, bless ye the Lord: praise him, and magnify him for ever.

O ye holy and humble Men of heart, bless ye the Lord: praise him, and magnify him for ever.

O Ananias, Azarias, and Misael, bless ye the Lord: praise him, and magnify him for ever.

Glory be to the Father, and to the Son, and to the Holy Ghost;

As it was in the beginning, is now, and ever shall be: world without end. Amen.

The "Benedicite" forms a part of The Song of The

God magnified in his Works.

Three Children, with whom tradition has identified Shadrach, Meshach, and Abednego. But, whether tradition be right or wrong in this instance, the Canticle has an intrinsic interest of its own, both because it has been incorporated with the Service of the Episcopal Church, and because it is one of the most suggestive and soul-stirring hymns in existence. In accordance with an injunction in King Edward the Sixth's First Book, it is customary to sing the "Benedicite" during Lent, and in some churches, we regret to think, it is never heard at any other time, while in a few it seems to be banished from the Service altogether. It is also true that Books of Common Prayer have been published in which this hymn finds no place. It is impossible, indeed, not to perceive that there is a "shyness" or even a repugnance with some in regard to it, which causes it to be sung at the times prescribed rather in obedience to custom or ecclesiastical authority, than from any feeling of its fitness for devotional use. And yet, as it cannot be denied that many find in it a valued help to adoration, the conviction rises strongly in the mind that it is equally fitted to become an aid to all. Whence comes, let us ask, this difference in the effect produced by the same thing — whence this absence of appreciation which spoils and renders distasteful to some a hymn from which others derive such heart-felt benefit? May not the cause lie either in a too literal acceptance of the words themselves, or in the want of those few grains of knowledge which alone were needed to bring home to us the force of the hymn as an exposition of the Power and Mercy of God. When sculptors and painters represent animals bellowing forth their praise from gaping mouths, they embody the literal meaning of the words, and give currency to that erroneous conception of their import which, with more or less distinctness, has found an entrance into the minds of many. It seems almost needless to remark that such a gross realization of the hymn

God magnified in his Works. 15

misses its purpose altogether. The "beasts that perish" have no knowledge of their Creator, and are not susceptible of those emotions which constitute adoration; while man is even less nobly distinguished from them by his form than he is by his moral nature, and his privilege of enjoying the perception of God and singing His praise. A literal interpretation given to the "Benedicite" clothes it with inconsistency, suggests an Æsopian fable rather than a Christian hymn, and tends to check rather than promote devotion. Every shade of such a meaning must be banished from the mind, and exchanged for another more true and elevating. It is only by the thoughts *suggested* by the wonderful perfections of animals that they can serve as aids to adoration; and it is in the same sense only that dead things — such as stars, the sea, or the wind — can be properly associated with living things as promoting with equal fitness the same end. If this interpretation be not admitted the words degenerate into extravagance, and are stripped of all their beautiful significance in the minds of thoughtful men. Invested with the same indirect meaning, the names of Ananias, Azarias, and Misael are most fitly introduced among the invocations of the hymn. They have, it is true, long passed from the scene of their trials; but, though no voice of praise may rise from the grave, their memories remain to us as symbols of God's mercy and power. In thinking of them we recall the example of men who trusted in the Lord and were not forsaken — who were ready to brave the most cruel death rather than deny their faith — and whom no tyrant could either terrify or hurt, because they were upheld by God's protection. Is there no aid to devotion in such examples, or in the thoughts that rise up in association with such names? On the contrary, no invocation in the hymn is more profitable or suggestive. Thus, by their trusting faith when living, they continue, even though dead, to praise and magnify "the power of the Lord for ever."

Though all are ready with the general admission that every thing in Nature exhibits the Power and Goodness of God, it will not be denied that a little knowledge of the way in which these are displayed would give additional distinctness to the feeling. Such knowledge, indeed, will often serve to change what is merely a tame and passive acquiescence into a fervent sentiment of adoration founded on conviction and experience. Now, if there be any truth in this remark, it is surely well worth while to turn our attention to such subjects. Physical Science and Natural History liberally reward their votaries, for every onward step is fraught with pleasure, and brings an immediate reward in the interest with which it invests the common things around us. Many of their most elevating secrets are to be learnt without that preliminary drudgery which besets the portals of some other sciences: and an amount of knowledge, so moderate as to be within the reach of every body, is all that is required to open out to us a clear view of those proofs of Power and Goodness which cluster round the verses of the "Benedicite."

It need scarcely be remarked, however, that knowledge of this kind is not to be acquired in church, but by previous preparation at home and in our walks. The offering up of praise within the sanctuary exacts our whole mind and our whole heart, and our thoughts at such moments must not be encouraged to wander away in search of illustrations of the truths we are uttering. Experience will soon bring to us the welcome proof that the thoughtful consideration of God's works which is based upon a knowledge of their nature and of the Power and Goodness they display, creates a condition of mind so impressible that every solemn allusion to them instantly and without conscious effort raises feelings of adoration in unison with the subject. The details of the wonderful perfections by which these feelings were originally developed may be absent, or even forgotten, but the deep devotional impress with which they once imbued the understanding never fades away. They who have acquired this sensibility to those hymns of praise which are ever ascending from all God's works around, have found an aid to adoration, the value of which is known and thankfully acknowledged by themselves, but which must sometimes appear like extravagance or affectation to others who have never taken any pains to cherish it. It is only by such means that our sentiments can be brought into full harmony with the spirit of the hymn. But when the words of the "Benedicite" fall upon ears thus prepared by the understanding and the heart, they speak the clearest language, and stand forth as the emblems of Power, Wisdom, and Goodness.

All Thy works praise Thee, O Lord. — Ps. cxlv.

Of the fitness of the natural objects around us to awaken feelings of devotion there can be no doubt. All things are wonderfully made and wonderfully adjusted to each other; and we alone, among created beings, have been endowed with faculties enabling us to recognize the perfections they exhibit, on purpose that we might praise God by the feelings they rouse within us. The Psalms of David are filled with beautiful illustrations to show how natural objects serve as aids to adoration, and it may be safely asserted that a Book of Praise was never yet written in which they were not thus used. If there be any skeptic who believes not in this power, let him make trial. Experience will soon convert him, and draw an answer of thankful consciousness from his own heart.

The object of this book is to offer a series of illustrations of the Beneficence and Greatness of God, as they are suggested to our minds by the words of the "Benedicite." A few of the verses, it will be noticed, are omitted, not because they are inapplicable to devotion, but because they do not come within range of that kind of illustration to which I have thought it proper to confine myself. But, within this limitation, enough and more than enough remains for the work on hand. It may, indeed, be truly said that he who undertakes to select from the many fields of Nature the most striking examples of God's Providence will find his chief difficulty to arise from the "embarrassment of riches." He is like a man wandering in a gallery where all is truth and perfection, and who has rashly engaged to single out that only which is pre-eminently the best. A feeling of this kind weighs on me now, for, while illustrations abound on every side, I fear lest I should select some examples where others ought to have been preferred, — not because they were more wonderful or more perfect, but because they were better adapted for the purpose here intended. Let me hasten to disclaim all pretension to instruct the learned or the scientific. It becomes me here rather to acknowledge with gratitude my own obligations to them. It would, indeed, be difficult to treat satisfactorily of the various matters contained in this book without seeking to profit by the labors of the Herschels, Whewell, Maury, Guillemin, Lardner, Owen, Darwin, and many others whose names are well known as the authors of standard works. I know beforehand that the subject, for its own sake, will be received with sympathy by those whose delight it is ever to be on the outlook for the suggestion of trains of thought which lead them to magnify God in His Works; but it would be even more gratifying to me if I should succeed in awakening an interest in the "Benedicite" in some who, perhaps, may not have hitherto considered the objects therein invoked under the aspect here given to them. Soon will they make the precious discovery that they cannot add a line to their knowledge of the natural objects around them without at the same time adding to the distinctness of the feeling with which they join in the words of the hymn.

While endeavoring to illustrate the effect of a little knowledge in developing that sensitiveness to the divine Power and Mercy which, while it softens the heart, beckons us onward to that worship which springs from the contemplation of natural objects, I wish carefully to guard against every appearance of desiring to elevate this means above its proper place. We are here dealing with the things that belong to the kingdom of nature, and not with those pertaining to the kingdom of grace ; and, if need be, it must often be recalled that how praiseworthy soever this meditative worship may be, it can never supersede, and must always be subordinate to, those higher motives for worship which are unfolded in the doctrines of Christianity. The one is essential and must be done ; while all that can be said of the other is that it is both fitting and profitable, and ought not to be left undone. God has graciously endowed us with faculties to comprehend His Works, and with every new appreciation of His design we seem to be taken more and more into His confidence. Shall we then neglect or throw away this inestimable privilege, or can we ever hope to employ our talents in a nobler or more elevating purpose? Experience will prove that God blesses our efforts to trace out the perfection of His Works with an immediate reward, for the pursuit is replete with rational pleasure no less than with moral improvement.

O praise the Lord with me, let us magnify His name together. — Ps. xxxiv.

THE HEAVENS.

O ye Heavens, bless ye the Lord: praise Him, and magnify Him for ever.

AMONG all the sights the eye can look upon nothing is comparable to the Heavens for the sentiment with which they charm the mind. The language they speak comes to us from remote, mysterious worlds; but, though it may be imperfectly understood, it is at least universally felt. The great and the little — the civilized man and the savage, the philosopher and the rustic — all feel their influence, and are from time to time irresistibly drawn toward them by mingled emotions of admiration, gratitude, and awe, such as none of the other features of Nature can excite in an equal degree. No wonder, therefore, that the Three Children, intent on calling up every image by which God's Goodness to men and their dependence on Him could be depicted, should first of all turn toward the Heavens. Again and again the grand features of the firmament are passed in review, and invoked with fervor. In the eager intensity of their feelings order and method are but little regarded, and they pour forth their thoughts in song as these come welling up in their minds. So may it happily sometimes be with ourselves; and in those moments when we too are drawn with desire to "bless, praise, and magnify the Lord" for the visible works of Creation, we shall surely find that the Heavens suggest to our conception the grandest symbols of His power and goodness.

So strongly, however, is the idea of the "incomprehensible" associated by many with the mysteries of the firmament, that they are habitually prone to regard the teachings of astronomers as little else than scientific guess-work. Nevertheless, the best intellects in all countries assure us, and demonstrate before our eyes, that, within certain limits, Astronomy is the most exact and perfect of sciences, and that, even when it deals with distances and magnitudes which are practically inconceivable, its conclusions, though often claiming to be approximative only, have yet no affinity whatever with guess-work. Let such skeptics think of the certainty with which sidereal events are predicted beforehand. Let them reflect on the evidence of the most exact knowledge of the heavenly bodies involved in the calculation of eclipses, in fixing the very moment when the moon's dark outline shall begin to creep over the sun's bright disk, or in predicting the instant when a planet's light shall be extinguished behind our satellite. How wonderful the tracking of a comet's wanderings — millions of miles beyond the far-off region of Uranus, and foretelling the time of its return after long years of absence! Do not these, and a thousand other equally wonderful feats, attest both the soundness of the principles on which the astronomer works, and the reasonableness of receiving his assurances with trust, even though it may be impossible for more than a few gifted minds to follow the calculations on which they are based?

Did any of our readers ever happen to bestow a glance upon the "Nautical Almanac"? It is published by the British Government at a very cheap rate, in order to facilitate its entrance into the cabin of every sea-going ship. Ostensibly it is a voluminous collection of dry figures and curious signs running on interminably page after page; but, in reality, it is a yearly record of the soundness of the teachings of Astronomy, and of the blessings they bring to man. Eclipses of the sun and moon, of Jupiter's satellites, sidereal positions and distances, and a multitude of other heavenly events and matters of the last importance to navigation, are there foretold with the most rigid exactness. Every single figure and every single sign represents an important sidereal fact, and is charged with a message from the skies for our guidance. On the trackless ocean this book is the mariner's trusted friend and counsellor, and daily and nightly its revelations bring safety to ships in all parts of the world. The acquisition of such rare and precious knowledge — this mapping out beforehand, almost to a hair-breadth, the exact order and track in which the heavenly bodies will run their course through space, and the precise relative position they will occupy at any given moment when they can be seen in any part of the world — is a fact which, if applicable to the current year only, might well fill us with astonishment. But it becomes infinitely more marvelous when we reflect that the "Nautical Almanac" is regularly published three or four years in advance, in order that the mariner, during the most distant voyages which commerce can exact, may never be without his faithful monitor. It is truly something more than a mere book — it is an emblem of the Power and Order of the Creator in the government of the Heavens, and a monument of the extent to which His creatures are privileged to unravel the laws of the Universe!

The year 1846 will ever be memorable for having witnessed one of the most striking illustrations of the truth of Astronomy. Few can have forgotten the astonishment with which the discovery of the planet Neptune was then received, or the fact that it was due not to a lucky or accidental pointing of the telescope toward a particular quarter of the Heavens, but to positive calculations worked out in the closet; thus proving that, before the planet was seen by the eye, it had been already grasped by the mind. The history of its finding was a triumph of human intellect. The distant Uranus — a planet hitherto orderly

The Heavens.   23

and correct — begins to show unusual movements in its orbit. It is, somehow, not exactly in the spot where according to the best calculations it ought to have been, and the whole astronomical world is thrown into perplexity. Two mathematicians, as yet but little known to fame, living far apart in different countries and acting independently of each other, concentrate the force of their penetrating intellects to find out the cause. The most obvious way of accounting for the event was to have inferred that some error in previous computations had occurred; and, in a matter so difficult, so abstruse, and so far off, what could have been more probable or more pardonable? But these astronomers knew that the laws of gravity were fixed and sure, and that figures truly based on them could not deceive. By profound calculations each arrives at the conclusion that nothing can account for the "perturbation" except the disturbing influence of some hitherto unknown mass of matter exerting its attraction in a certain quarter of the Heavens. So implicit, so undoubting is the faith of Leverrier in the truth of his deductions, that he requests a brother astronomer in Berlin to look out for this mass at a special point in space on a particular night; and there, sure enough, the disturber immediately discloses himself, and soon shows his title to be admitted into the steady and orderly rank of his fellow-planets. The coincidence of two astronomers, Leverrier and our countryman Adams,* arriving at this discovery through the agency of figures based on physical observation, precludes every idea of guess-work; while such was the agreement between their final deductions that the point of the Heavens fixed upon by both as the spot where the disturber lay was almost identical. "Such a discovery," says Arago, "is one of the most brilliant manifestations of the exactitude of the system of modern astronomers."

* Of Cambridge, England.

As the Heavens have irresistibly attracted the attention of mankind in all ages, Astronomy naturally came to be the Father of sciences, and it was from remotest times cultivated with considerable success by the Chaldeans on the plains of Mesopotamia. Doubtless the Three Hebrews at Nebuchadnezzar's court were well versed in the science of their day, but, whatever the amount of that knowledge might have been, it must have been extremely imperfect when measured by modern standards. Comparatively speaking they knew but little of the grandeur of the Heavens; and yet that little amply sufficed to point with its imagery the fervor of their worship. Since then, by God's blessing, the range of Astronomy has been widened, its views soar higher and probe deeper, its truths are better comprehended, its marvelous adjustments have been analyzed and traced more clearly upon the understanding. Shall we, then, with our better knowledge, find less aid in it to rouse our adoration than did the Three Children of old, and shall the more perfect view of the Heavens now vouchsafed to us fall cold and resultless upon our hearts? If this, indeed, be the case, are we not treating with neglect an aid to adoration which God himself has spread out before our eyes, and are we not in some degree frustrating that purpose of praise and glorification for which both they and we were created?

Astronomy is without question the grandest of sciences. It deals with masses, distances, and velocities which in their immensity belong specially to itself alone, and of which the mere conception transcends the utmost stretch of our finite faculties. In no other branch of science is the limited grasp of our intellect more forcibly brought home to us. Yet, though baffled in the effort to rise to the level of its requirements, our strivings are by no means profitless. Is it not truly a precious privilege to be able to trace, imperfectly though it may be, the hand of the All-mighty Architect in these his grandest works,

The Heavens.   25

and to obtain by this means a broader consciousness of his Omnipotence? In raising our wonder and admiration other sciences need the help of details and expositions, but in Astronomy the mere enunciation of a few measurements suffices to elevate our ideas of His Power to the highest point to which man's finite faculties can carry them.

The expense of suitable instruments, the preliminary study, the persevering patience, and the long night vigils that are necessary will probably always prevent the higher walks of scientific Astronomy from becoming a popular pursuit; nevertheless, we earnestly recommend all who can to seize every opportunity that may fall in their way of having a thoughtful look at the Heavens through a good telescope. Their reward will be immediate. Even were they to take their peep with feelings not more elevated than those with which folks at a fair look at a rare show, the glance would bring some profit; but, if they be prepared beforehand with their "few grains of knowledge," how useful and improving the survey becomes. The first look at the Heavens through a good telescope forms an epoch in our life. Our faith in the realities of Astronomy passes with sudden bound from theory into practice; planets and stars become henceforth distinct and solid existences in our minds; our doubts vanish, and our belief settles into conviction. We behold the mysterious Moon of our childhood mapped into brilliant mountain-peaks, and dark precipices, and softly lighted plains; we see Jupiter shining like another fair Luna, with attendant satellites moving round him in their well-known paths; or we turn with admiration to Saturn encircled by his famous ring, with outlines as distinct as if that glorious creation lay but a few miles off. Perhaps we may behold the beauteous Venus shining with resplendent circular disk, or curiously passing through her many phases in mimic rivalry of the Moon. Or, leaving these near neighbors far behind, we may penetrate more deeply into space, and mark how the brightest flashing stars are reduced to a small, round, unmagnifiable point. A few evening explorations in propitious weather will suffice to grave all these objects and many other precious recollections in our minds for ever. Then is realized, better than at any previous moment of our existence, the power of the Lord of Creation.

While Astronomy, beyond all other sciences, thus lifts up man's conception of God's glory as displayed in His works, it is no less calculated to bring home to him the "littleness" of his own world amid the great creations of the Universe. The stupendous truths at which the finger of Astronomy is ever pointing ought to keep uppermost in his heart the wholesome lesson of humility. Well may the oft-told interjection rise to his lips, Lord, what is man that Thou art mindful of him! Such thoughts, indeed, bring with them both humility and exultation. Man's habitation is in very truth a mere speck in the Universe, dwarfed and thrown into the shade by nearly all the worlds around it, and he himself is a mere atom creeping through his brief existence upon its surface. His high place in Creation is won by the loftiness of his moral nature, and, above all, by the destiny that awaits him. Apart from this revelation, man and his earth are but a grain of dust among the myriads of worlds that people the infinity of space.

Therefore shall every good man sing of Thy praise without ceasing. — Ps. xxx.

SUN AND MOON.

O ye Sun and Moon, bless ye the Lord; praise Him, and magnify Him for ever.

HERE are not a few in this world who habitually receive God's blessings so much as a matter of course that they are scarcely conscious of any active feeling of gratitude in regard to them. The very regularity and profusion with which these blessings are showered on all alike seems to have the effect of deadening the sense of individual obligation. A general admission of thankfulness may occasionally be made at church or in the closet, but there is a want of that abiding consciousness of it with which we ought to be imbued, as well as of that frequent pondering upon details which, by illustrating the dependence of every creature upon God, causes the heart to swell with grateful adoration. Such thoughts never fail to improve our moral nature by bringing the truth home to us more and more that we are indeed God's children.

It would be no easy task for a thankful mind to sum up all the blessings diffused over our planet by the Sun. It is the mainspring of animated Nature. Without its genial rays the present system of the earth's government could not endure, and life itself would soon disappear from the globe. To it we are indebted for light and warmth — the twin stimulants of vital force — for our food and clothing, for our busy days and rest-bringing nights, for months and years, and happy alternations of the seasons. Its rays, in short, are intertwined with all our wants and comforts; they gladden the eye and cheer the heart.

> I will praise the name of God with a song, and magnify it with thanksgiving. — P's. lxix.

The Sun is the central pivot of the solar system, and round it the Earth and all the other planets keep whirling in elliptical orbits. Its power and influence — its light, heat, and attraction — reach through a domain in space which it would require a line of more than 6000 millions of miles to span. With the greater part of this wide field astronomers are familiar, and it may be truly said that scarcely a man knows the roads of his own parish with more exactness than they do the highways of the skies. Not only can they map out to a nicety the paths of the planets careering through it like islands floating in a sea of ether, but they can look backward and tell the exact spot where each globe was at any moment of the remote past, or forward, and point to the place where each will be found at any given moment of the remote future.

What is the mighty power which thus maintains such order in the Heavens, which steadies the planets in their orbits, and traces out for them a route so wisely planned as to avoid all chances of collision? Two antagonistic forces — gravitation or attraction, combined with a centrifugal impulse — accomplish the wonderful task. To these faithful servants, which know neither fatigue nor slumber, God commits the safety of the Universe. Let us in imagination glance back to that far-off time when "in the beginning the Heavens and the Earth were created." Matter having been prepared sufficient, it may be, for the vast requirements of the solar system, every particle of it was endowed with the property of mutual attraction, and the force of this attraction was fixed so as to act in a certain proportion to mass and distance. In other words, the law then impressed on matter was, that attraction should increase according to mass, and diminish according to the square of the distance. The matter of the solar system may have been created in separate portions, or it may have been divided into separate portions corresponding to the size of the different planets; after which, the particles of each planet, being as yet mobile, arranged themselves in obedience to their mutual attraction into globes, just as we see the mobile particles of water coalesce into a drop, or as quicksilver runs into globules. The Sun was placed in the centre, and became the pivot of the whole system, tying to itself the different planets by the cord of its superior attraction. In accordance with the law just mentioned, this loadstone power of the Sun was the inevitable result of its superior mass.

It is obvious that in whatever corner of the Sun's domain the planets had been placed, the searching power of his attraction would have found them out, and would inevitably have destroyed them by dragging them in upon himself, had this tendency not been counteracted by some other influence. Another force, therefore, was established — the centrifugal. The Great Architect, "weighing in His hand," as the Psalmist figuratively, and yet almost literally expresses it, the mass of each orb, projected it on its course through space with exactly that force and at exactly that angle which was needed to counterbalance the attractive power of the Sun; and the obedient globe, thus seized upon by the two balanced forces, was compelled to move onward in a path representing the diagonal between both. And as these forces are permanent, the movements of the Earth and of the other planets must be permanent also; nor can any thing stop the working of this most perfect machine except the Word which created it.

The voice of the Lord is mighty in operation. — Ps. xxix.

How shall we mentally gauge the distance or estimate the size of the master-centre which thus holds all the planets in his grasp? The immensity of both confounds our efforts. When we are told that the Sun is separated from us by a chasm of nearly 92 millions of miles, that its diameter is 850,000 miles, and its circumference about 2,671,000 miles, we can realize nothing beyond a vague idea of vastness, and we are forced to look round for other standards to help our laggard faculties. From the comparatively small size of his disk when viewed from the Earth, we catch the idea how enormous that distance must be which is able thus to dwarf it down. It is 384 times as far off as the Moon. A cannon-ball fired from the earth and keeping up its velocity, would not reach it in less than 22 years. "A railway train," Brayley observes, "at the average speed of thirty miles an hour, continuously maintained, would arrive at the Moon in eleven months, but would not reach the Sun in less than about 352 years; so that if such a train had been started in the year 1512, the third year of the reign of Henry VIII., it would only have reached the sun in 1864."

The Sun's diameter is equally astounding. It exceeds by 107 times the mean diameter of the Earth. It is nearly four times greater than the radius of the Moon's orbit round the Earth; so that if the Earth were placed in the centre of the Sun, the Moon's orbit, so far from extending to the circumference of the Sun, would scarcely reach to within 187,000 miles of its surface. The locomotive just mentioned, on its arrival at the Sun, "would be rather more than a year and a half in reaching the Sun's centre, three years and a half in passing across the Sun, supposing it were tunneled through, and ten years and one eighth in going round it." "Now the same train would attain the centre of the Earth in five days and a half, pass through it in eleven days, and go round it in thirty-seven days." The bulk of the Sun is not less than 600 times as great as that of all the planets put together; and it would take 1,405,000 Earths to make a globe of equal magnitude.

Great difference of opinion prevails among astronomers respecting the physical condition of the Sun, and both its surface and encircling atmospheres are full of mysterious grandeur. Still, although not so well known as the planets, many points of interest have been partially made out. Its surface is much more rugged than that of our planet, with heights and clefts somewhat on the scale of its vast magnitude. A mountain in the Sun, however, in order to bear the same proportion to it as our highest Himalayan peaks do to our Earth, would require to attain an altitude of 600 miles: now none of its mountains have been estimated at more than 200 miles high. The mountains on the Earth have been compared to the inequalities upon the rind of an orange, while those of the Sun would in their proportion more resemble the tubercles of a pineapple.

Most astronomers consider the Sun to be an incandescent body encircled by two atmospheres. Its temperature probably varies in the different parts of its immensity, but, where most intense, it appears to transcend any thing we can conceive. Like the distances and velocities and nearly all else that relates to the heavenly orbs, the degree of the Sun's heat overtasks our power to imagine, and we should require for its comprehension some new standard of measurement. The minimum of solar temperature, indeed, seems to begin far above the point where terrestrial temperature leaves off. According to one philosopher the heat is "seven times as great as that of the vivid ignition of the fuel in the strongest blast furnace;" while another, after a careful series of experiments, estimates it at nearly 13 millions of degrees of Fahrenheit! To aid us in appreciating this temperature, or rather to show us how impossible it is for us even to conceive it, it may be borne in mind that cast-iron requires for fusion a heat which amounts only to 2786 degrees, and that the oxy-hydrogen flame — one of the hottest known — does not much exceed 14000° Fahrenheit, which is scarcely one thousandth part of the temperature here ascribed to the Sun.

Of the two atmospheres encircling the Sun, that which is nearest its surface is considered to be nonluminous, while the other floats upon it and forms the "photosphere" which we see in looking at the Sun's bright disk. From this photosphere, as well as, probably, from the surface of the Sun itself, are radiated the heat and light which are to vivify the planets of the solar system. Flame-like masses — some computed to be 150,000 miles in length — are piled upon or overlap each other, and sweep onward in constant agitation, like mountain-billows of living fire. Although the light afforded by this furnace pales that of every other luminary, its amount has been approximately ascertained, for the purpose, as we shall soon see, of serving as a standard to astronomers when estimating the distances of the stars by means of the light they evolve. Thus Wollaston calculated that 20 millions of stars as bright as Sirius, or rather more than 800,000 full moons, would be required in order to shed upon the Earth an illumination equal to that of the Sun. Another estimate makes sunlight equal to 5570 wax candles held at a distance of only one foot from an object.

Let us now turn our back upon the Sun, which for the sake of comparison may be represented by a globe two feet in diameter, and let us in imagination wing our way across the space filled by the solar system. A short flight of 37 millions of miles brings us to a world which, compared with the two-feet globe, is no bigger than a grain of mustard-seed, while it is so bathed in the Sun's dazzling rays that it is not easily distinguished when viewed from our Earth. This fussy little planet whirls round the Sun at the tremendous pace of a hundred thousand miles an hour, by which he proves his title to be called Mercury, the " swift-footed " of mythology. The Sun being so near attracts it with prodigious force, and to counteract this destructive tendency a corresponding centrifugal impulse was absolutely needed. From the strength of these two antagonistic forces its great velocity naturally results. The adjustment is perfect. At a distance of 68 millions of miles from the Sun we behold Venus, the brightest and most dazzling of the heavenly hosts. In comparative size, she may be represented by a pea. She is our nearest neighbor among the planets, and the conditions under which she exists recall many of those amid which we ourselves live.

About 92 millions of miles from the Sun we come upon another "pea," a trifle larger than the one representing Venus, and in it we hail our old familiar mother Earth. Here we shall not now linger, but passing onward some 50 millions of miles we are attracted by the well-known ruddy glow of Mars, — an appearance which may depend either on the refraction of light in its atmosphere, resembling what we ourselves often see at sunset, or on the prevailing color of its soil, which may be as highly tinted as our "old red sandstone." The comparative size is that of a pin's head. Mars is a planet that has lived down a very bad character. For ages every star-poet, astrologer, and almanac-maker had an ill word to say about him, and all sorts of evil things, including "manslaughter, byrnings of houses, and warres," were ascribed to his cross nature. But truth has at length prevailed, and he is now established as an orderly member of the solar company. His mean orbital speed is 54,000 miles an hour — nearly our own pace — but, as he takes twice as much time to run round the Sun as we do, his year is consequently twice as long. Casting a glance behind we are reminded of the distance that now separates us from the Sun by the perceptible waning of his light.

We next spread our wings for a very long flight. In.

passing through the "asteroid" zone of solar space, about 260 millions of miles from the Sun, we may chance to fall in with some worlds so small that a locomotive could travel round them in a few hours. We know not very much about them except that their ways are eccentric and mysterious. They want the smooth round outline of the old planets. Their rugged and fragmentary aspect suggests that they may be the mere ruins of some mighty parent-planet, shattered into pieces by the Word of the Architect, and skillfully stowed away in space, so as to harmonize with the nice balancings of the solar system.

At length the shores of huge Jupiter are reached at a distance of nearly 500 millions of miles from the Sun. To carry on the comparison, he is a "small orange" to the "pea" of our Earth, or to the two-feet globe that represents the Sun. His orbit is a path 3000 millions of miles long, which he accomplishes in an "annual" period of nearly 12 of our years. The Sun's light has now shrunk considerably, but four brilliant moons or satellites, one or more of which are always "full," help to afford some compensation. These moons, distant though they be from our Earth, are not without their use to man, and there is hardly a well-informed mariner that leaves our shores who cannot occasionally turn them to account in settling his position at sea. The principle is extremely simple. The exact moment when one of these moons is eclipsed behind Jupiter's disk has to be noted, by chronometer rated to Greenwich time, and by a reference to the "Nautical Almanac" it may be compared with the hour at which the same event is timed for Greenwich. The difference in time will give the longitude, 4 minutes being allowed for each degree. If the eclipse be in advance of Greenwich time, the ship is to the east of that place; and to the west of it in the contrary case. Thus the good Lord has combined the lighting up of this far-off planet with a blessing to the inhabitants of our Earth.

Before we arrive at Saturn, in our "outward-bound" course, we have to pass through a space nearly equal to the distance of Jupiter from the Sun. We are now more than 900 millions of miles distant from the central pivot. Saturn's comparative size may be represented by an orange considerably smaller than the last. His year swallows up almost thirty of our own. The Sun, though hardly giving one nineteenth part of the light which we receive, is still equal to 300 full moons, and is at least sufficient for vision, and all the necessary purposes of life. No fewer than eight satellites supplement thew aning sunlight, besides a mysterious luminous "ring" of vast proportions.

Twice as far away from the Sun as Saturn, Uranus, represented by a cherry, plods his weary way. Although he has a real diameter of 35,000 miles, he is rarely to be seen from the Earth by the naked eye. His annual journey round the Sun is 10,000 millions of miles, and he consumes what we should consider a lifetime — 84 years — in getting over it. His nights are lighted up by at least four moons that are known, but several others probably exist. The illumination received from the Sun even here is equal to several hundred moons. Our little Earth has now faded out of sight.

Only a few years ago Uranus was the last planetary station of our system, but the discovery of Neptune in 1846 gave us another resting-place on the long journey into space. Here, at a distance of 2862 millions of miles from the Sun, we may pause awhile before entering upon the more remote exploration of the starry universe. We are approaching the frontier regions of our system, and the Sun's light and the power of his attraction are gradually passing away. Between the shores of our sun-system and the shores of the nearest star-system lies a vast, mysterious chasm, in the adjacent recesses of which may still lurk some undiscovered planets, but into which, so far as we yet know, the wandering comets alone plunge deeply. We stand on the frontier of the Sun's domain, and we are in imagination looking across one of those broad gulfs which, like impassable ramparts, fence off the different systems of the Universe from each other. It seemed needful that the Great Architect should interpose some such barrier between the contending attractions of the giant masses of matter scattered through space — that there should be a sea of limitation in which forces whose action might disturb each other should die out and be extinguished. In it the light-flood of our glorious Sun gets weaker and weaker, and its bright disk wastes away by distance until it shines no bigger than a twinkling star. And the strong chain of its attraction, which held with firm grasp the planets in their orbits, after dwindling by fixed degrees into a force that would not break a gossamer, is finally dissipated and lost.

It has been already stated that the Earth and its fellow-planets are kept steady in their orbits by the exact adjustment of centrifugal and centripetal forces. They are in the position of the stone whirled round in a sling. If let go from the centre, they would fly off into space; if surrendered to the sole influence of the Sun's attraction, they would inevitably be dragged into the vortex of its flames. As a curiosity in Astronomy, calculations have been made to show the time which each planet would require for its fall into the Sun. Thus it appears that while Mercury, the nearest, would require a fortnight, Uranus, at a distance of 1820 millions of miles, would be nearly 15 years in falling; while our Earth would take $64\frac{1}{2}$ days before it crashed into the Sun.

Such calculations, however, have not always had a merely speculative interest. There was a time, not so very remote, when the possibility, or rather the certainty, of our Earth dashing headlong into the Sun seemed to be only too well established. Weak minds were terrified, and even the soundest astronomers were perplexed at the alarming import of their own deductions. A hundred years have scarcely elapsed since the astronomer Halley startled the world by announcing the existence of a flaw in the construction of the solar system, by which the certain though distant ruin of our Earth was involved. He was led to this supposed discovery by a comparison of the eclipses of his own time with those recorded by Ptolemy in the second, and by Albutegnius in the ninth century. From this comparison it appeared to be established that the mean velocity of the Earth in her orbit was increasing. The philosophers of that day were puzzled, nor was the cause of this circumstance explained until Laplace demonstrated that it was due to a diminution in the eccentricity of the Earth's orbit round the Sun, produced by certain perturbing influences in the planets. This orbit, as our readers know, is elliptical, and, as it was proved that this ellipsis tended to change into a "round" or circle, at the rate of about 41 miles annually, it followed that a perfectly circular orbit would be established in the course of 37,527 years.

But the conclusion to which this discovery led was frightful. The sure effect would be to draw the Earth nearer and nearer to the Sun, until at length the centripetal would so overbalance the centrifugal force, that our globe would fall helplessly into it. It is true, the lease of existence thus given to the Earth, even on the most unfavorable estimate, was a long one; but its direful ending appalled contemplation, and concentrated upon the question the whole intellectual strength of astronomers. Never was the surpassing construction of the solar system made more strikingly manifest than when Laplace demonstrated that this "weak point" had not been overlooked by the Great Architect. In a way which cannot be here explained, but which has received the assent of all succeeding astronomers, he showed that the alteration in its orbit which the Earth is now undergoing can only continue up to a certain point, and that, when this point is reached, other planetary influences will come into play, which, by gradually undoing the work that has been done, will ultimately bring back the Earth once more into her old ellipsoid orbit. And when the limit is again reached in the latter direction, the "influences" will again change, and a new progress toward circularity will recommence. Thus, so far from leading to the destruction of our Earth, this regular oscillation specially provides for its unlimited endurance; nor can any thing stop the perfect machinery of our solar system, except the Word of the Almighty Artificer who created it.

He hath made the round world so sure that it cannot be moved. —Ps. xciii.

In gazing at our fellow-planets, as on a clear night they stand out with preëminent brightness among the twinkling stars, who has not longed to penetrate the mystery of their being, and to know whether they, like our own Earth, are worlds full of life and movement? The vast distance that intervenes between us forbids us to expect a direct solution of the question, for no instruments we can make, or even hope to make, will bring their possible inhabitants within the range of vision. We are reduced, therefore, to survey them with the sifting force of intellect, and to rest contented with such circumstantial proof as is derived from a knowledge of their general structure, and the analogies subsisting between them and our Earth.

Among our nearest neighbors, Venus is nearly the size of our Earth; and Mercury and Mars, though considerably smaller, would still form worlds which, to our ideas, would not in their magnitude be so very different from our own. All the planets revolve in elliptical orbits round the Sun, and the time consumed in this journey constitutes their year. Their polar axis is not "straight up and down," but leans over or is "inclined" to the plane of their orbit, so that each pole is turned toward the Sun at one period of the year, and away from it at another. This arrangement insures the regular alternation of seasons and a variety of climates on their surface. The orbital inclination of Mars, for example, is much the same as that of the Earth, and therefore the relative proportion of his seasons must have a close resemblance to our own. It might be expected under these circumstances that ice would accumulate toward the poles in winter time, as on the Earth, and accordingly glacial accumulations have not only been observed by astronomers, but it has been remarked that they occasionally diminish by melting during the heats of summer, while they increase in winter.

Again, the planets, like the Earth, turn round on their axes with perfect regularity, and those just mentioned do so in very similar periods of time. Hence all have their days and nights. These divisions represent in our minds intervals mercifully set apart by Providence for the welfare of living creatures — times designedly arranged to regulate alternate labor and rest in beings whose requirements in this respect would seem to be analogous to our own. Diurnal rotation, moreover, insures to each planet a determinate amount of light and heat from the Sun, which is necessary to the well-being both of animals and plants; and it is measured out to them with a regularity equal to that with which we ourselves receive it. One can see no other purpose that could be served by diurnal rotation except the distribution of light and heat; and, if the axes of the planets had been "inclined" very differently to what is actually the case, this purpose would not have been so efficiently accomplished. The amount of light and heat received by the more distant planets must be necessarily small in comparison with our own supply; thus at Neptune it is a thousand times less than at our Earth. Still it is easy to conceive that by a corresponding increase in the sensibility of the retina nearly every purpose of vision may be adequately fulfilled. Even on our own Earth there are animals which see with an amount of light which to us is little else than darkness.

The next point of analogy is that most of the planets, if not all, are surrounded with atmospheres which distribute and refract the light, while they retain and intensify the heat, just as on our Earth. In some of them, indeed, as in Venus, the soft twilight is as visible to astronomers, as our own twilight is to ourselves. Earth has its atmosphere often charged with clouds, Jupiter is belted round with them; from which may be inferred the existence of an atmosphere and of water. An atmosphere must necessarily give rise to currents of wind. From the vast size of Jupiter, and the velocity with which his surface moves round at the equator, there must likewise be trade-winds of much greater force than our own. One effect of those stormy trades would be to give a streaky character to the clouds encircling tropical districts — a theory with which the appearance of Jupiter's famous belts exactly corresponds. The main divisions of the surface into land and water can be distinguished and mapped out in Mars, while chains of mountains are to be descried in Mercury and Venus.

Analogy carries the argument still further. Planets, like our Earth, have their moons, whose number and size are in some degree proportionate to the distance of the planet from the Sun, or, in other words, to the urgency with which supplemental "lamps" are needed. Mercury and Venus, lying near the Sun, bask in his light, and have no proper satellites, although they must act as moons to each other. Our Earth has one. Mars, though lying more remote from the Sun than we are, has none. Jupiter, five times more distant from the Sun than our Earth, has four satellites disposed with such careful design that some of them are always shining. Farther off, in the darker regions of the solar system, Saturn's night is broken by the light of eight satellites, some of which are always full, as well as by his wonderful luminous "ring"; while Uranus has not fewer than four moons, and probably may have more over which distance has hitherto cast obscurity. As regards Neptune, his enormous distance must continue to make the number of his satellites a question of extreme difficulty. One, however, has already been discovered, and improved telescopes will probably reveal more. As corroborative evidence I need do no more in this place than merely allude to the recent results of spectrum analysis, or the chemical examination of the light itself which they transmit; from which it appears that not only the Sun and planets, but even the stars, actually contain substances with which we are familiar here on Earth.

That those planetary globes, with their continents and oceans so analogous to our own in the plan of their physical conditions and so vastly surpassing them in extent of surface, should be void and barren and destitute of life in every form, seems scarcely consistent with our knowledge of the ways of the Creator. All over our globe, except, perhaps, among the polar snows or in the desert, we see life abounding. Space is everywhere economized by Nature, and thriftily allotted out to living creatures. To promote the spread of life the most dissimilar spots have inhabitants expressly constructed for them, so that every place may become a home in which something living may exist. The abundance of Nature — the profusion of life — is proverbial, and forces itself on our notice in every direction. Is it likely that those vast orbs — with masses and densities so wonderfully modified and adjusted in accordance with what we perceive to be the requirements of living creatures — with years and months, days and nights, seasons and climates — with atmospheres and twilights, trade-winds and currents — with clouds and rains, continents and seas, mountains and polar snows — with sun, moon, and stars, and, in short, with all the elements that make up the conditions of a habitable globe — is it likely that those glorious works of the Creator should have been formed to lie waste, sterile, and unprofitable? Or even if we could bring ourselves to think that those masses, whose united bulk dwarfs our Earth to insignificance, had been created solely as make-weights to keep this little atom of Earth in its place, why should they have been provided with a complicated system of moons revolving round them to give them auxiliary light? The Sun's light they share in common with ourselves; but for what conceivable purpose should deserts void of life have been supplied with those wonderful lamps to light them up in the absence of the Sun? Our own Moon, we know, was made "to rule the night," to give light to something that could profit by it; has the same beautiful machinery been repeated, and even more extensively than here, for the sake of globes where nothing living exists to which it can be of use? Not less wonderful, and for a purpose not less obvious, is the way in which the size and density of the different planets have been modified to harmonize with the probable strength and power of objects existing upon them. The very conditions that would be incompatible with our organization may, from the adjustments of creative wisdom, be exactly suited to the beings called on to inhabit them. All life, even if it be essentially the same in principle, may not everywhere assume the same phase of outward existence, nor need we attempt to set limits in this respect to the Lord of Life. The spaces lie there furnished and ready — the Word only was required to people them with a life which may be different, but which, so far as we can understand the conditions, need not be very different, from life such as we see existing around us. Reflection upon these and other points seems to reverse the question with which we set out, and to make the difficulty consist in believing, not that life in some shape exists upon our fellow-planets, but that they can be destitute of it. Such inquiries have an interest which goes beyond their mere astronomical import, for they touch our conceptions of God's greatness. Is there any one who does not long to be able reasonably to cherish the thought that, far away from this tiny speck of Earth, in the remote realms of space, we behold worlds inhabited by beings who, it may be, are privileged like ourselves to know their Creator, and to bless, praise, and magnify Him for ever?

We turn toward our nearest neighbor in the solar system with a sentiment bordering on familiar affection. We speak of it emphatically as "our Moon." The Sun we share with other planets, but this beauteous orb belongs exclusively to ourselves. Although we transmit to each other but little warmth, we yet cheer up the darkness of each other's nights by liberally reflecting the rays which each receives from the Sun. Like loyal friends we give and we take to our mutual advantage; and, as the Earth is the larger reflecting body of the two, we repay with interest the light we borrow. To young and old the Moon is ever interesting and beautiful. The infant questions it with delighted eye, and stretches out its tiny arms to play with or to catch it. From moonland have descended some of the mysterious legends of childhood. The boy soon learns to recognize "the man in the moon," and the familiar face roots itself in his imagination for life. Its gentle light is associated with many pleasures. We welcome its first curved streak in the west as a sign that our gloomy nights are past; we watch it to "the full" with ever-increasing admiration, and we part from it at last with regret and hope. Our very dogs salute it with their bark; a notice they bestow on no other celestial object. Floating in the clear sky, or poised among the fleecy, tinted clouds, silvering the water or piercing through the trees — in every phase and aspect it is beautiful. Like an enchanter it casts the charm of picturesqueness over the meanest objects, and masses which look hard or ugly in the garish light of the Sun mellow into beauty when touched by the power of the moonbeam.

The Moon's journey round our Earth — the lunar month — is accomplished in a little more than twenty-nine days and a half. When interposed between the Earth and Sun she is invisible, because her dark side is turned toward us; but during nearly all the rest of her circuit she reflects a portion of the light received from the Sun, and cheers our nights with brightness. The actual amount of light thus transmitted is small when compared with that which floods in upon us from the Sun, being scarcely equivalent to the 300,000th part; and it has been calculated that were the whole heavens covered with full moons, it would not equal the light of the Sun. The distance from the centre of the Earth to the centre of the Moon is 238,793 miles. An express train would easily clear the distance between the two globes in 300 days.

Unlike the active Earth, which rotates on its axis every twenty-four hours, the Moon turns herself round only once in twenty-seven days seven hours and forty-four minutes. Every body must have observed that the well-known features of "the man in the moon" never change; in other words, the same hemisphere of our satellite is always presented toward us. That this peculiarity is the result of the coincidence in point of time which exists between her axial rotation — constituting her day — and her orbital rotation round the Earth, which constitutes our month, may be easily illustrated by experiment. Thus, if a person move slowly round a circular table, keeping his face, which we may suppose to represent the Moon, always directed toward the centre of the table, where we may suppose the Earth to be placed, he will find that in making one complete circle his face has rotated or turned round once also. Such is precisely the relation between Earth and Moon during the course of the month, and thus it may be easily understood why we always see the same side of the Moon, notwithstanding her rotation.

As the Moon revolves only once on her axis in the course of a month, it follows that during half of that time each hemisphere is turned toward the Sun, and during the other half it is turned away from it:—the whole period forming one long day and one long night. The Lunarians, therefore, if any exist, must be subject to a very singular climate. During their long "half-month" day the surface must be scorched by a Sun whose fierceness is tempered by no atmosphere; and this must be succeeded by a "half-month" night, in which the Sun is altogether absent, and the darkness is broken only by starlight. During the day the temperature will far transcend the hottest tropical climate, while in the night it will sink far below the greatest cold of the arctic regions.

He who once fairly surveys the Moon through a good telescope will never afterward forget its aspect. It charms and fascinates the eye, and, though resembling so many other things, it is yet always so specially its own individual self. A good pictorial chart gives an idea which wonderfully approaches Nature, and it is as easy to follow upon it the various localities in the Moon, as it is to follow upon a map the various features of the land. If we look at the full Moon we take, as it were, a bird's-eye view from a great height, which levels inequalities. Its disk presents a smiling, brilliant yet softly lighted surface—a sunny land, from which all gloom is banished. But both before and after the full Moon, when we see its features more in profile, a different tale is told. Here and there softly shaded plains are still to be noticed, but the chief part of the surface appears to have been fashioned by the most violent volcanic forces. It is scarred and rent, convulsed and burnt into an arid, cindery ruin. Serrated craters, some more than a hundred miles wide, are thickly dotted about, and inclosed within them are levels from whose centre cones of igneous origin shoot up. The brightest peaks, the darkest precipices, the most jagged ridges crowd this rugged picture. To many minds the idea has suggested itself that some scathing doom has blighted the surface of our satellite, for nowhere else can Nature match this aspect of desolation. Fancy rather than science has tried to deal with such a scene. Some have conjectured that it might be an Earth burnt up and destroyed by the outpouring of God's wrath. Others have supposed that it is a comparatively recent world — a globe in a state of chaos — whose crust has not yet been sufficiently worn down by the hand of Time to fit it for the abode of living creatures. Destitute of life it certainly appears to be at present, nor do its physical conditions seem to fit it for ever becoming the abode of that kind of life which we see existing on our own globe. Amid these conjectures let us fall back with thankfulness upon what is certain. Cosmically considered it performs its part in upholding the balance of our solar system; and, in reference to ourselves, we know that it was created by Our Father "to rule the night," and in other ways to shed blessings on His children.

Many of the mountains in the Moon have been measured by ingenious mathematical processes, and at least one has been found to attain a height of 26,691 feet, which, though not quite equal to that of our highest Himalayan or Andean peaks, is yet proportionately higher, since the Moon's diameter is little more than a fourth of that of the Earth. As the rays of the Sun fall obliquely upon them they are seen in profile — being bright on the side next the Sun, and in dark shadow on the side turned away from it. Their peaked and jagged outline is best displayed along the inner margin of the crescent Moon. Mountains in the Moon present in miniature an exact counterpart of the effects which sunlight produces on the mountains of the Earth. In alpine districts the rays are first caught by the loftiest peaks, then the side next the

Sun is brightened, while the side turned away from it still remains in shade. Lastly the western slope becomes illuminated, and the eastern in its turn passes into darkness. In the Moon the mountains may be observed to undergo changes in their lighting up which are precisely of the same nature.

From the absence of those effects that would necessarily result from the refraction of light, astronomers conclude either that the Moon has no atmosphere, or that, if it exist, it must be as attenuated as the air in the vacuum of an air-pump. For the same and for other reasons it is also to be inferred that water is equally wanting. During the long moon-day of half a month, the Sun's rays beat fiercely upon its surface, and would certainly send up clouds of vapor if any water existed for them to act upon. The result would be to cover the Moon with a nebulous screen impenetrable to vision, — a condition which is plainly inconsistent with the fact that whenever the Earth's atmosphere is clear, we always see the Moon with the same unvarying brightness. According to Dr. Lardner, however, there might possibly be ice, for " in the absence of an atmosphere, the temperature must necessarily be not only far below the point of congelation of water, but even that of most other fluids," and he points to the fact that, even under the burning Sun of the tropics, the rarefied condition of the atmosphere existing at a height of 16,000 feet upon the Andes produces a cold which converts all vapor into snow and ice. On the other hand, it seems clear that, if ice existed in the Moon, some amount of vapor could hardly fail to be produced by the long-continued action of the Sun, and we know that in the tropics clouds hang round even the highest peaks. If there were a cloud even 200 yards in extent, it would be visible to us by telescope. Thus all arguments tend to prove that the Moon is destitute of water.

The Earth and our satellite, as has been said, mutually

interchange their good offices, and shine upon each other as moons. A curious illustration of this is seen when the dim outline of the rest of the Moon fills up the hollow of the bright crescent, or when, in popular phrase, "the young Moon has the old one in her arms." We all know it is the reflected rays of the Sun which makes the crescent visible, but how is it that we are able to see the rest of the Moon upon which the Sun is not shining? It is by what is termed "earth-shine," or by means of those rays which in our quality of moon we send across to her. The "earth-shine" on the Moon is pale and shadowy, but we must recollect that the rays which bring it to us have traveled many a weary mile. They sprang originally from the fountain of the Sun, and had to speed across some 92 millions of miles before they reached our shores. They were then the young and joyous rays that dazzled our eyes by their brightness. The Earth next caught them up, and cast them, softened into mild moonlight, across the 238,000 miles of space that separates us from our satellite. And lastly, these enfeebled remnants of light, after having brightened up Luna's rugged surface, were sent back once more across the wide gulf to the Earth, bringing with them to our eyes the dim image of the Moon they had left behind.

Some may be inclined to ask, — How happens it that this earth-shine is not seen at other phases of the Moon? It arises from the circumstance that the crescent Moon always coincides with the period when our fully illumined disk is turned toward it. We are then at the "full." Our lamp-power, therefore, is at its highest, and is strong enough to produce the earth-shine. But when the Moon is about half full, not only is our lamp-power diminished from our "phase" in relation to the Moon having been changed, but the more extensive illumination of the Moon herself by the direct rays of the Sun obscures and, as it were, "puts out" the more feeble earth-shine that was previously visible.

From the comparative nearness of the Moon, and the perfection gradually imparted to optical instruments, many have been bold enough to anticipate that we shall some day see in it the familiar objects of every-day life, or even the Lunarians themselves, if any do exist. This rather unreasonable expectation has been from time to time encouraged by premature announcements. Thus, on one occasion, it was given out that a town had been plainly distinguished in the Moon; on another, that a fortification with roads and canals were equally discernible. But these supposed discoveries have never received subsequent confirmation. On the contrary, Mädler, of Berlin, has pointed out that it is in the highest degree improbable we shall ever be able to observe objects so small as the human figure. The extreme distance, he remarks, at which a man is visible to the unassisted eye is a German league. Now, to bring an object in the Moon to that apparent distance would require a magnifying power of 51,000, while with all our modern skill in instrument-making, we do not as yet possess any power which magnifies more than 6000 times.

Scripture as well as experience and common sense tells us that the Moon was made "to rule the night;" but some have objected to the obvious meaning of the expression, if not to the perfection of the work itself, on the ground that the "lamp" is only occasionally lighted up. The observations of Laplace certainly sanctioned the opinion that the Moon might possibly have been placed in the heavens in such a position as to be always "full" to us; but this advantage could only have been purchased at the cost of the loss of light that would have arisen from increased distance. As things are actually regulated, more or less moonlight brightens our Earth on most nights of the year, and few months pass over without our practically experiencing the advantage of the light which has been placed by Our Father in the heavens for our use.

In arctic regions the Moon and the stars alone break through the darkness of the long winter's night, and all who have read the story of polar voyages will recollect the thankfulness with which moonlight is welcomed and appreciated. The Arab of the desert steers on emergency by the light and position of the Moon. Over the pathless seas the Moon is the navigator's friend and counsellor. It places in his hand a certain scale for measuring the longitude and fixing the spot where the ship may be. When we think of the fleets of noble vessels, the wealth of merchandise, and the thousands of lives whose safety is dependent on its teachings, we may form some estimate of the value of this blessing. "Without the Moon's aid," an astronomer observes, "our ships, instead of fearlessly traversing the ocean from pole to pole, would probably even now be incapable of performing long voyages, and would content themselves with exchanging commodities and intelligence between well-known and neighboring shores."

Of old the Moon played a more important part than she now does in the notation of time; but, among many Eastern peoples, the Moon still indicates the seasons, while its different phases serve as an almanac to mark particular days. Among the Jews the new Moon was associated with certain religious ceremonies, and men were stationed on the hill-tops to give the earliest notice of its approach. Some Orientals are also accustomed to indicate the seasonal stages of vegetable life by the epithets they apply to the Moon: — thus there is the rice-moon, the wild-strawberry moon, the leaf-falling moon, and there is likewise an ice-moon. We have, at least, our glorious Harvest-moon. Nor is the Moon unrecognized in our Church festivals; for Easter is always celebrated on the Sunday following the first full Moon which happens on or after the 21st March, or vernal equinox.

The Heavens declare the glory of God; and the firmament showeth His handiwork. — Ps. xix.

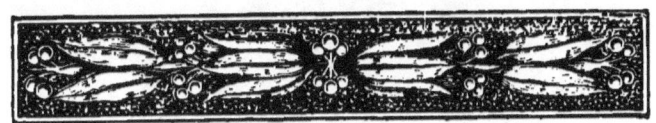

THE STARS OF HEAVEN.

O ye Stars of Heaven, bless ye the Lord: praise Him, and magnify Him for ever.

HE who turns his thoughts starward will speedily find his power of distinct conception strained to its utmost effort; for as the distances, magnitudes, and movements with which we are familiar upon Earth are dwarfed by those of the Solar system, so do the latter in their turn shrink into insignificance when compared to the distances, magnitudes, and movements of the Stellar Universe. Miles now become useless, and no longer speak to us with their old intelligible meaning; and the other familiar aids that helped us on in the comprehension of Solar measurements are scarcely more serviceable. The locomotive with its 30 miles an hour, the cannon-ball with its flight of 500 miles an hour, are all too slow to mete out distances such as are now to occupy us. Nothing but light itself, cleaving through space with a velocity of 192,000 miles a second — or, according to Foucault's latest estimate, 186,000 miles a second — can supply us with a standard capable of representing the remoteness of the more distant, visible stars.

In the immensity of the plans and natures revealed by Astronomy we miss those homely illustrations of providential design which are so often impressed upon us in our daily experience among the familiar objects around us. But, on the other hand, we behold in their mightiest development the laws governing that Universe of worlds which peoples the realms of space, and among which our spot of Earth occupies so humble a position. In presence of this grand view the physical details of our little globe seem almost too petty to be remembered. The Omnipotence and Infinity of God confront us with all the vividness which our finite understanding can conceive, and we bow our heads in heartfelt adoration.

By the Word of the Lord were the Heavens made, and all the hosts of them by the breath of His mouth. — Ps. xxxiii.

The "Hosts of Heaven" are truly called innumerable, and, as we glance upward on a clear, starry night, the twinkling points that meet our gaze in all directions seem to defy enumeration. Yet, strange though it may appear, the sum of all the stars that can be distinguished by the naked eye in both hemispheres under the most favorable circumstances does not exceed 6000, and of these considerably less than a half belongs to our own northern division. But, when the telescope is turned toward the sky, stars come forth in myriads from the dark depths of the firmament; and, as each additional light-grasping power is given to the instrument, a new region of the heavens is joined on to those that have been already explored; and every new stratum of space thus added is found to be studded with stars in an ever-increasing ratio. It is difficult to estimate the number which may thus be brought into view, but astronomers compute it to be not less than 100 millions. To a superficial observer the stars seem scattered about as if by chance, but a more careful inspection reveals that some fixed law of distribution, which we cannot as yet unravel, reigns supreme among them. "Suppose," says Dr. Nichol, "a number of peas thrown at random on a chess-board, what would you expect? Certainly that they should be found occupying irregular or random positions; and if, contrary to this, in far more than average numbers, arranged by *twos* upon each square, it would be a most natural inference that here there is no random *scattering.*" Appearances, indeed, have convinced some most eminent astronomers that our own solar system — in its entirety — has been planted in the midst of a cluster of stars, of which the exterior rim is composed by the encircling stellar hoop of the Milky Way. Lying beyond the Milky Way are other clusters, which may represent similar systems, but which, at all events, display a certain, recognizable, general structure; and the same may be said of the still more remote nebulæ, whenever it has been possible by the aid of the telescope to resolve them with any degree of fair distinctness into their proper forms. In picturing the distant regions of space Dr. Nichol observes: "Mystery, indeed, heavy, almost oppressive, hangs over all the perspective; but the shapes strewn through that bewildering territory have nothing in common with the fantastic creations of a dream. It is the essence of these nebulæ that they are not formless, but, on the contrary, impressed indelibly by system on the grandest scale; clearly as a leaf they have an organism; something has seized on their enormous volumes, and molded them into a wonderful order." Thus every thing bears the mark of order impressed upon it by the Almighty hand. That noble gift of God to man — the telescope — has magnified Him by driving away every semblance of chance from the firmament, and by exhibiting in its place design and established law. Up there as down here the idea of irregularity or chance is but the suggestion of our own ignorance. How far into space our view has been carried by the power of the telescope we shall immediately endeavor to point out.

Certain groups of stars, named Binary and Multiple, are interesting to us in many respects, and in none more so than from their exhibiting the harmony and order amid which they exist. The telescope reveals to us that two or more stars are sometimes linked together in the relation of sun and planet, or rather as coördinate suns revolving round each other, or round a common centre. These Binary stars display the evidence of design and power as convincingly as is done by the members of the solar system. The same law of gravity with which we are so familiar on Earth, is proved to be in full operation among them, and their orbital revolutions in obedience to it have, in some instances, been observed and calculated upon the same principles as those by which the movements of the planets are determined. With more perfect instruments and a sufficient allowance of time for the collection of data, their movements may, at some future day, be chronicled with as much accuracy as the other sidereal events of the almanac. Yet so well are the orbital movements of some stars understood, even now, that a "perturbation" or deviation from the usual path has been detected in the bright Sirius, of the same nature as happened in the famous case of Uranus; and calculations indicating the position in which the "perturbator" would be found were made on the same principle as those which led to the discovery of the planet Neptune. Nay more — the disturbing mass which caused the star to stagger in its path has been seen through an American telescope, in the very quarter to which the finger of science had already pointed, and the discovery has since then been amply confirmed. We shall immediately have to consider the distance of the field in which this scrutiny was held. "When a branch of science," says Guillemin, "scarcely known two centuries ago, and cultivated steadily for less than a hundred years, arrives at such results, what may we not hope for in the future progress of sidereal astronomy?"

Binary and Multiple stars — being suns — are probably attended by their planetary systems, giving rise to cosmical conditions of extreme interest. The inhabitants of those earths — if there be any — will frequently see two suns, or two sunrises and sunsets on the same day. Occasionally there will be no night, from the continuance of one of the suns above the horizon; or one sun may be rising while another is setting. It often happens too that the stars are of different colors, from which the most singular and beautiful appearances will arise. "It may be easier suggested in words," says Sir John Herschel, "than conceived in imagination what a variety of illumination two stars, a red and a green, or a yellow and blue one, must afford a planet circulating round either, and what charming contrasts and grateful vicissitudes — a red and a green day, for instance, alternating with a white one and with darkness — must arise from the presence or absence of one or other or both, from the horizon."

The most striking wonders of the Firmament are comprised in the distances, magnitudes, and velocities of the stars, and it may well excite both our astonishment and our gratitude that we, the humble dwellers upon an atom of earth, should be privileged to gauge them with even approximative accuracy. Yet the principle on which astronomers have succeeded in measuring the distance of a few of the nearest stars is none other than that by which the surveyor maps out an estate or a county. It is an ordinary problem of triangulation. There is no doubt as to the truth of the principle employed, and there is no mystery in the process — the difficulty lies in the inevitable imperfection of the instruments with which the necessary measurements must be made. But every new improvement in the measuring power of instruments cancels a certain amount of previous error; and even now there is among astronomers — working separately and independently — so wonderful an agreement in regard to the vast distances involved, that it is impossible to suppose either that such coincidence is accidental, or that there can be any very material amount of error in the estimates thus formed.

Has my reader ever heard of the parallax of the stars? The most unlearned need not be dismayed at the scientific look of the expression, for the principle involved in it is in reality most easy to understand. It will, indeed, largely repay a few minutes of attention, for it is the ladder by which we shall best climb to a clear conception of those truths of the stellar universe which illustrate so grandly the Power of the Creator. And even where the conclusions to which it leads baffle the efforts of our finite faculties, the definite basis on which they rest will at least banish every idea of guess-work from our thoughts.

It is easy to understand that parallax movement is that *apparent* shifting of bodies which arises from changing our own position. We cannot stir a step without producing examples of it. If we pace up and down the street opposite to any object on the other side — as a door or a lamp-post — the angular direction or parallax of the object changes at every moment. If we sail down a river and fix our eyes on some church-spire at a distance from its bank, we find that the direction in which we see it is always altering. At first the spire appears in advance of us, then on our sides, and lastly it lies behind. If instead of limiting our attention to one object we look at several that can be easily observed together, we find that as we move they move, or rather seem to move, and the angles formed by their lines of direction are displaced relatively to each other and to us. One cannot look out of a railway carriage without being amused by the way in which objects seem to move about. Trees, houses, and churches are never for a moment at rest. Things that are in line "open out," as sailors would say; near objects are moving backward, the more distant are moving forward. In this apparent change of position we have an example of parallax movement. In all these cases the line from which our observations are made is the "base;" and if the angle subtended by the objects from the extremities of this base be given, the distance may be easily calculated.

In all instances of this parallax shifting it must have been remarked that the effect of a change of our position in altering the direction of objects is greater when they are near than when they are distant. A few paces will sensibly alter the angular position or direction of the door or lamp-post on the opposite side of the street. But if we look at a church some miles off, or at ships anchored in the offing, we find that we require to move much more than a few paces — in other words, we require to increase considerably the length of the base — before we can make any sensible change in the angle or direction in which we see them. In proportion, therefore, as the distance of objects increases, so must we lengthen out the base from which we survey them in order to obtain parallax displacement. It follows, too, that if in observations taken from a short base line objects appear to have changed much, we may infer that they are near; but, if the base require to be long in order to produce an effect, we may equally infer that they are distant.

Such is the plain and certain principle which astronomers applied to measure the distance of the stars; but the great difficulty was to find a base line long enough to give parallax displacement to objects so remote. Stations in this country were obviously too near for such a purpose. Simultaneous observations were therefore made from Greenwich and the Cape of Good Hope, — the distance between the two stations of course representing the "base," — and from these the most interesting and important results were obtained. For it was found that, though a distinct parallax movement could be traced in the planets, none whatever could be detected in the stars. And it followed, therefore, that while the planets were comparatively near, the distance of the stars was such that a still longer base was needed to bring them within the grasp of parallax.

The line from Greenwich to the Cape having failed,

astronomers next had recourse to the base represented by the diameter of the Earth's orbit. As our globe revolves annually round the Sun, it is obvious that it must occupy a very different position in space at one period of the year from what it does at another. On the 1st January it is at one extremity of its ellipse, on the 1st July it is at the point exactly opposite, and the length of a line drawn from the one station to the other is 190,600,000 miles. Could it be doubted that a base line was at last obtained long enough to insure a parallax for any conceivable distance?

It may well be imagined with what astonishment the fact broke upon astronomers that, even from this enormous base, the keenest scrutiny could not detect the slightest displacement among the stars! Not one apparently changed its position. The result perplexed philosophers, for it forced the conclusion upon them either that the Copernican doctrine of the Earth's orbital movement round the Sun was an error altogether, or else — what seemed almost as difficult to believe — that the base line yielded by the Earth's orbital diameter was but an inappreciable point in relation to the inconceivable distance of the stars. For generations, therefore, "to discover the parallax of the stars" was one of the grand astronomical problems; but while the chief observers strove earnestly for the prize, the best among them failed to carry it away. The triumph was reserved for our own time.

In truth, however, this want of success in demonstrating the parallax of the stars was no reproach to the older astronomers, for it depended on causes over which they had no control. To accomplish this grand object instruments of great delicacy were essential; and instruments have only been brought to the requisite degree of perfection within the last few years. But, be it remarked, what those old philosophers could not register with the hand they yet saw clearly with the head; and, therefore, with perfect faith in the truth of the Copernican theory of the world's movement in space and in the ultimate solvability of the problem, they never lost heart, nor ceased to strive for its accomplishment. At length in 1839 the long-looked-for discovery was made almost simultaneously by two observers of equal merit;—the British astronomer, Henderson, at the Cape, having succeeded in measuring the parallax of a star known as a Centauri, while Bessel had already been equally fortunate in regard to 61 Cygni. It is pleasing to think that these astronomical triumphs, after being scrutinized and tested in almost every great Observatory possessed of instruments sufficiently fine for the purpose, have stood their ground and been substantially confirmed.

The difficulty of the feat becomes at once obvious when we consider the small sum of the stellar displacement obtained, which, even in the case where it was greatest, did not quite amount to one second of a degree. But the conclusion that was to be drawn even from so inconsiderable a parallax was astounding; for, when the necessary allowances had been made, it was proved that the distance of the nearest of those stars from the Earth was nearly 20 billions of miles. How can we get into our minds some idea of so great a distance? The standard of miles seems utterly vague and profitless. Do we succeed better when we are assured that it is equal to 206,000 times the space separating our planet from the Sun; or 211,330 radii of the Earth's orbit; or that a ray of light darted from its surface could not reach our eye under three years and seven months, though it traveled with its usual speed of 192,600 miles a second? "Such then," says Sir John Herschel, "is the length of the sounding-line with which we first touch bottom in the attempt to fathom the great abyss of the sidereal Heavens."

"First touch bottom!" Let us pause, and take breath. Let us try soberly to realize the fact that this flight, through which our imagination has carried us on the wings of a ray of light, has landed us only at the threshold of the starry universe. So far as is yet known this famous star of the Centaur is our nearest neighbor. Of the thouands of others whose parallax astronomers have tried to measure, there are not more than a dozen where it has been detected, and all of them lie at various distances beyond. The well-known Sirius — the very star whose perturbations, as we have seen, have already been calculated and accounted for by visible demonstration — which from being the brightest among stars was conjectured to be also the nearest, has been proved by parallax measurement to be at least six times the distance of α Centauri; from which it follows, that every ray of that dazzling orb that now meets our eye set out on its journey toward us some twenty-two years ago. One of the most distant stars that has as yet been gauged is the beauteous Capella. In expressing its enormous distance we may discard all other standards of measurement save that which light supplies; and even a ray of light, with its speed of 192,000 miles each second, would take 72 years to reach our Earth. As for stars placed at greater distances the base line of the Earth's orbit, seconded by the most perfect modern instruments of measurement, fails as yet to demonstrate with reliable accuracy any sensible amount of parallax. In relation to those distant orbs, a base line of 190,600,000 miles shrinks into a mere point.

The belt of measurable parallax, therefore, proves to be but a comparatively shallow layer of the firmament. All "the Hosts of the stars" lie farther off in regions which no parallax can reach. A longer base line than 200 millions of miles would be needed to continue the survey, and unfortunately the resources of Astronomy do not as yet supply any that are available. We say "as yet," for it is not impossible that a longer base may at some distant future day be found, if, as is almost certain, our Sun itself is moving in an immense orbit round *something* in space, and carrying along with it the whole solar system. The diameter of the Sun's orbit may then afford a base line of immensity sufficient to conquer the difficulties of distant stellar parallax. Of the interval which would necessarily elapse between the observations made on such a base no one can now imagine the duration.

At that depth in the firmament, therefore, where Capella lies — representing a space to pass through which light would require 72 years — we come to the limit of parallax. With it ends the means which enable star-measurements to be placed on a reliable basis, and all beyond is subject to the greatest uncertainty. Are, then, our estimates of the distances of stars sunk farther away in space than Capella to be absolute guess-work? By no means, thought the illustrious Sir W. Herschel, for when parallax can plumb no longer, light still affords a line which measures immensity with at least a rough approximation. It is true that this method sets out with the hardy assumption that the size and illumination of the different stars are the same; whereas we know with certainty that both are subject, like the planets, to much variation. Nevertheless it may, perhaps, be assumed with considerable probability, that in the multitude of stars examined there must at least be some to which such a method will apply, and which therefore may serve, in the absence of all other means, as a rough measure of the depths of space beyond Capella to which the eye of man can penetrate. All are familiar with the fact that light diminishes as we recede from it, in proportion as the square of the distance increases. If, for example, one luminous body be twice as far removed as another equally luminous body, it will give four times less light; if it be ten times as far off, it will give a hundred times less light, and so on in proportion. Now it has just been shown that the distance of α Centauri, an average star of the

1st magnitude, is in round numbers 20 billions of miles, while it shines with an amount of brightness which, by means of an instrument called a photometer, can be measured, and adopted as a standard from which to set out. A star of the 6th magnitude, just visible to the naked eye, is found to have a light 100 times less bright than α Centauri; and, therefore, it must be ten times more distant, supposing the luminous surface to be the same in both. We have now got a second standard of measurement, according to which it may be assumed that a star having a brightness which we can just discern is 200 billions of miles distant. Here we are, for a moment, necessarily brought to a stop, for our unaided sight is unable to force its way farther into space; and here, therefore, our survey must have come to an end but for that wonderful "tube," by means of which the regions lying beyond have been fathomed to an extent that almost overwhelms. It fortunately happens that astronomers can "scale" a telescope, according to what is termed its "space-penetrating" power. When, therefore, it is said to have a space-penetrating power of 50, it means that we can see with it 50 times farther than with the naked eye — 50 times as far, therefore, as the distance lying between us and the star of the 6th magnitude which has just been measured. Sir W. Herschel, whose name will ever be remembered in connection with this subject, penetrated into space 75 times farther than the distance which separates us from a star of the 6th magnitude, by which he brought stars thus deeply sunk in space to shine with a brightness equal to stars of that class. Now, what was the stupendous import thereby implied? A star of the 6th magnitude is at least 10 times more distant than α Centauri, its distance, therefore, is 200 billions of miles; and the star 75 times more distant than the star of the 6th magnitude must have a distance of not less than 15,000 billions of miles! How is this distance to be expressed by an intelligible standard? It is equal to 170 million times the distance of the Sun from the Earth — the unit being 92 millions of miles. Told off by terrestrial standards these figures sound vaguely and seem to stupefy the ear, nor indeed can any other measure than light rise to the level of such distances. It is astounding to think that the few straggling rays of light which at length found rest in Herschel's eye might have left their native sun 2656 years ago, although they had been traveling at the rate of 192,000 miles a second ever since. The messenger arrives only now, but he speaks of an old event. "It is within the scope of physical possibility," says Dr Lardner, "that those stars may have changed their conditions of existence, and consequently of appearance, or even have ceased to exist altogether more than 2000 years ago, although we actually see them at this moment."

But even those distances, stupendous though they be, do not represent the full depth of that fathoming of space which has possibly been effected by modern instruments. What shall we say of the Nebulæ — those "wisps" of cloudy light that faintly gleam down upon us through the telescope from the remotest corners of the Universe to which we can force our vision? As the more perfect instruments of recent days conquered their secret, one after another, and resolved the hazy cloudlets into clusters of bright stars, the conclusion naturally arose that, with every new increase of penetrating power, we should only behold a repetition of the process. There do, however, appear to be some Nebulæ which cannot be so resolved, and which show no indications of condensing into stars; and "spectrum analysis" — that potent discovery of yesterday, which is able to extract from a ray of light its history by passing it through a prism — comes to the support of the telescope by declaring that such distant glimmers are due to vast volumes of luminous gaseous matter. But, making allowance for these, there still remain many Nebulæ of true stars — suns like the rest, heat-giving, and light-giving, and animated as our little Earth is by the same universal principle of gravitation. A certain cluster of stars was estimated by Sir W. Herschel to be 700 times the distance of a star of the 1st magnitude — therefore, at least 700 times 19 billions of miles! But, observes Guillemin, "if this cluster were removed to five times its actual distance, that is to say to 3500 times the distance of Sirius, the large Herschelian telescope of 40-feet focus would still show it, *but only as an irresolvable Nebula.* It is, then, extremely probable that, among the many Nebulæ indecomposable into stars, beyond the Milky Way, in the depths of the heavens, many are as distant as that of which we speak. *Doubtless many are more so.* Now to reach us, light-rays must have left stars situated at such a distance more than 700,000 years ago!"

On such a subject I prefer to transcribe words recently written by an astronomer, and they at least claim our attention as the latest conjectural opinions of science. That such calculations are but the roughest of wide approximations — that they are liable to error of a magnitude which in any other branch of physics except universe-measurement would make them utterly valueless, is a point admitted by none more readily than by astronomers themselves. Still, after every deduction for probable error has been made, more than enough of solid truth remains to leave our highest conceptions hopelessly stranded behind, and it would even mock our power of belief did not reason tell us that such conclusions are in perfect accordance with the attributes of Omnipotence. When we have touched the verge of this uttermost range, Infinity, boundless as ever, still lies beyond. The idea of God extinguishes in our mind every suspicion that there can be any limit to space, magnitude, or power, in relation to His works. The mighty universe we have been considering is but the stepping-stone to what is farther on; and although our imagination fails to grasp it, our reason assures us that it must be so. There is no such thing as taking from or adding to The Illimitable.

The distance of the stars is likewise impressively brought home to us by the impossibility of magnifying them. It is easy to magnify terrestrial objects, and even when the telescope is pointed at the planets, as Venus or Jupiter, they can be made to look bigger than the full Moon. But with regard to the stars the telescope fails to increase their size, for they are absolutely "unmagnifiable." Viewed by the highest powers they still remain mere specks of light; and, although their comparative brightness is increased, no one star is really made larger than another. When, therefore, the "magnitude" of a star is mentioned it refers to its brightness, and not to the size of its nucleus. As the telescope cuts off the external rays, its effect, indeed, is rather to diminish than enlarge, and Herschel used to affirm that the more he magnified the more the nucleus appeared to shrink to a point. But as the faithful telescope, by virtue of its construction, cannot help magnifying the image of the star presented to it, and yet fails to give it any appreciable size, we are driven to infer that even the nearest stars are so remote that their apparent magnitude is too minute to be perceived by the eye, though magnified, as was done by Sir W. Herschel, six thousand times.

This result appears all the more astonishing when we consider the vast magnitude which the stars must really possess. As they do not form any distinguishable disk, it is of course impossible to calculate their size from their known distance and apparent diameter, as may be done in the case of the Moon; but astronomers possess other means by which their magnitude may be at least roughly estimated. It has been already mentioned that, as we recede from a luminous surface, the quantity of light received from it diminishes as the square of the distance increases. By applying this principle, the Sun furnishes us with a means of measuring the magnitude of stars, always assuming, as may be done when the trial is extended over a great number, that the average intensity of the luminous surface is nearly the same in both. We know that the Sun, being of a known size and at a known distance, gives a certain amount of light as determined by the photometer. Supposing that the Sun were to be moved away from us in the direction of a Centauri, his light would diminish in the proportion in which the square of the distance increased; and, accordingly, before he had got much more than half way, he would have dwindled to the size of a Centauri. If the Sun were to be farther removed, his brightness would go on diminishing until at the distance of a Centauri — 19 billions of miles — he would shine as a star of the 2d magnitude, or like the Pole-star. Thus it appears, that in order to enable the Sun to shine with a light equal to that of a Centauri at the same distance as that star, he would require to be twice his actual size; and, therefore, the magnitude of a Centauri may be roughly estimated as double that of our Sun.

In contemplating "the Stars of Heaven" by the aids which Astronomy holds out to us, our thoughts are carried away from the small things of this Earth, and, borne onward by the faculties bestowed on us by God, we reach our highest practical perceptions of His Power as Creator and Ruler of the Universe. We cannot, it is true, comprehend The Infinite, but Astronomy stations us nearer to its frontier than any other science, and we are only stopped in our conceptions by that barrier which subdues all human intellect, and beyond which it is not intended that we should pass.

Not less marvelous are the stars in their velocities. We speak of them as the "fixed" stars, and so they are to us for all practical purposes; yet some, if not all, have a movement through space. Binary stars, as we have seen, circulate in orbits round each other, or round a common centre, with a regularity and speed which in some instances has been calculated. The star 61 Cygni — the same whose parallax has been measured — rushes through space with the enormous velocity of 177,000 miles an hour; while Mercury, the swiftest of our planets, does not exceed 100,000 miles in the same time. A star in the constellation of Ophiuchus, and another in the Scorpion, are moving on so rapidly as to leave neighboring stars behind them. There is a triple star in Cassiopeia journeying through the heavens at the rate of 125,000 miles an hour. Arcturus is the most rapid star-traveler yet discovered, moving onward at a pace equal to 54 miles per second, or three times faster than our Earth in its orbit. Thus every thing connected with the stars — distance, magnitude, and motion — is equally gigantic and marvelous in its scale.

Having glanced at the distances, magnitudes, and velocities of stars, let us pause for a moment to consider their number and the vast space they must necessarily occupy in the domain of creation. In an area of the Milky Way not exceeding one tenth part of the moon's disk Herschel computed that there were at least 20,000 stars, and by the most moderate estimate the number of stars that can be counted in the firmament by telescopic aid does not fall short of 100 millions! Clusters and Nebulæ that have not yet been resolved lie beyond. There is little doubt that most of those twinkling points are suns dispensing light and heat to earths or planets like our own; and, indeed, no bodies shining by reflected light would be visible at such enormous distances. From the superior magnitude of those stars that have been measured, as compared to our Sun, it may be assumed that the average diameter of their solar systems must exceed our own; but, taking it as nearly equal, it would give a breadth of at least 6000 millions of miles as the field in space occupied by each. Every star or sun-system is, moreover, probably begirt with a gulf or void like that encircling our own, in which the antagonistic or disturbing attractions of surrounding suns waste themselves out and are extinguished; hence, the distance of each star from its nearest neighbor is probably not less than that which intervenes between our Sun and the nearest star. Now this distance, as we have seen, cannot be less than 19 billions of miles. How inconceivably vast, therefore, must be the space required to give room for so many and such stupendous solar systems. The mind absolutely reels under the load of conceptions so mighty, Yet Infinity still lies beyond!

Among those great Hosts of heaven where is the home of our Earth and Solar system? A probability lying nearer to certainty than conjecture suggests that our Sun, with its planetary system, forms a unit in a cluster of stars, similar to other clusters which we see gathered together in the far-off regions of the firmament. The space occupied by our cluster may in shape be compared to a millstone, of which the Milky Way forms the outer rim; while nearly in the centre of this gigantic assemblage of stars, and about half-way between the two sides of "the millstone" rests our Sun and its planets — "an atom in the luminous sand" of the firmament.

Still, we must not say *rests*, for there is absolutely nothing on Earth or in the firmament which is without movement. That our Sun — like all his fellow-stars — is traveling through space with a speed which though not yet determined is certainly immense, is a point on which astronomers are agreed. The most recent calculations assign to it a rate of four miles per second. Whither are we hurrying, round what are we moving? These are problems of which the solution is left to future observers, yet even now calculations tend to indicate that we are hastening on with rapid strides in the direction of the constellation Hercules. Who has not looked on clear nights at the twinkling Pleiades, and tried, perhaps, to count their sparkles as they glitter like diamonds on a field of black. Their name recalls to us a heathen fable, but they have an interest far more lasting and reasonable if it be true, as astronomers conjecture, that among them is fixed the pivot which is central to the centre, and round which our Sun with its system careers in an orbit whose length it is as impossible for us to conceive as the distance of the stars themselves.

If Astronomy were altogether silent on the subject, it would still be a hard matter for a reflecting mind to believe that the masses which fill up space, the aggregate sum of which dwarfs our Earth into less than an atom or a speck, can have been created for no other purpose than to shed a glimmer of star-light on our dark evenings. "For what purpose," says Sir John Herschel, "are we to suppose such magnificent bodies scattered through the abyss of space? Surely not to illumine our nights, which an additional moon of the thousandth part of the size of our own would do much better — not to sparkle as a pageant void of meaning and reality, and to bewilder us among vain conjectures. Useful, it is true, they are to man, as points of exact and permanent reference; but he must have studied Astronomy to little purpose, who can suppose man to be the only object of his Creator's care, or who does not see, in the vast and wonderful apparatus around us, provision for other races of animated beings."

Though placed at such inconceivable distances from our Earth, stars are yet near enough to contribute to the happiness and safety of mankind. During the Sun's absence they bestow an illumination which, though feeble, is highly useful. When the Moon has forsaken the long polar night they cast a dim twilight over the snow. In the deserts of the East, stars have served to guide the traveler since those ancient days when Astronomy began to be cultivated on the plains of Chaldea. The pilots of antiquity learnt to steer by the stars before the loadstone was discovered; and, in these days of science, Sun, Moon, and Stars may be said to cover the firmament with lamps and sign-posts. Familiarity with the fact has long dulled within us the feeling of surprise; still it is a wonderful thing to think that, in the most lonely spots of the trackless ocean, the position of a ship can be told with accuracy by questioning the aspects of the heavenly bodies. By means of Sun, Moon, and Stars, aided by a chronometer keeping Greenwich time, or by the "Nautical Almanac," both latitude and longitude may be certainly determined. To these aids every ship that sails upon the wide ocean is daily indebted for safety, nor could any thing bring home to us more strikingly how even the most remote works of Our Father are made by his providence to subserve the welfare of His children.

With what just propriety of thought has light been called the "voice" of the stars. Through light alone comes all the knowledge we possess concerning them. Had light been created with less marvelous properties than those it actually possesses, even their existence would have been unknown to us. Can any thing be conceived more suggestively true than the expressions with which the Heavens are described by the Psalmist?

There is neither speech nor language, but their voices are heard among them.
Their sound is gone out into all lands, and their words unto the ends of the earth!

In the "speechless" voice of light the stars proclaim to us from the depths of space the existence of innumerable other worlds which, like our own, share the Creator's care. Silently they tell us of distances, magnitudes, and velocities which transcend our power to conceive. With mute argument stars prove to us that, in those far-off regions, gravitation — the power that brings the apple to the ground — still reigns supreme, and with suggestive whispers of probability they persuade us that, like our own bountiful Sun, they bathe attendant worlds in floods of brightest light, deck them in colors of beauty, and shower countless blessings on the life of myriads of beings.

He who by thoughtful contemplation has familiarized his mind with the wonders of the Heavens will feel his whole spirit imbued with the glory of the Great Architect, by whose Almighty Word they were called into existence. To him Sun, Moon, and Stars, silent though they be, will speak a language which he will ever deeply feel even though he may not always comprehend. Nor will they fail, when solemnly invoked in the Service of the Church, to stir up responsive adoration in his heart, for they symbolize to him more than any other visible objects the Wisdom and Power of the Creator.

Whoso is wise will ponder these things, and they shall understand the loving-kindness of the Lord. — Ps. xcvii.

WINTER AND SUMMER.

O ye Winter and Summer, bless ye the Lord : praise Him, and magnify Him for ever.

THE great Architect has appointed that the earth, like its fellow-planets, should make an annual journey round the sun in a path which is not far from circular. During this time the earth is separated from the central luminary of our system by a mean distance of 92 millions of miles, which has been designedly fixed as securing to it the reception of that exact amount of heat and light which is best suited to the requirements of all the beings found upon it. Any other distance than this would, in fact, have been incompatible with the order of life we see established around us. But, besides this general arrangement as to distance, there are certain modifications in connection with it which affect most remarkably the local distribution of heat over the globe, giving rise to seasonal variations — to Winter and Summer, and to differences of climate. In looking at an astronomical diagram it will be remarked that the sun is placed, not in the centre, but in one of the foci of the ellipse which the earth's orbit describes round it; and the result of this necessarily is that the earth is nearer to the sun at one period of the year than it is at another. The conclusion is naturally suggested that this period of "nearness" must coincide with Summer, and that of distance with Winter; but, strange though it may appear, it is exactly the reverse. On the 1st January the earth is about one thirtieth part nearer the sun than it is on the 21st June.

Winter and Summer.

It is clear, therefore, that the cold of Winter and the heat of Summer must depend on other causes acting with power sufficient to overbalance the effect which this relative nearness or distance of the sun ought naturally to produce. Such a cause is found in the inclination of the earth's axis to the plane of its orbit. The effect of this arrangement can be easily illustrated by an impromptu orrery. Let a card placed near the centre of a round table represent the sun; a ball of worsted will be the earth, and a knitting-needle thrust through its centre will form its axis and poles. The rim of the table conveniently traces the earth's orbit round the sun, while the flat surface forms the imaginary "plane," on a level with which the centre of the sun and earth are supposed to be arranged. The earth's axis, it must be recollected, is not perpendicular to this plane — not straight up and down — but is inclined toward, or leans upon, it at an angle of $23\frac{1}{2}$ degrees. If we now apply the centre of the worsted ball, or earth, against the rim of the table at the point farthest removed from the sun, giving the knitting-needle, or axis, an inclination toward the sun to the amount specified; and if we then slide it round the rim, taking care not to alter the direction of the inclination, and to make the needle always maintain the same parallel throughout, we have a rough imitation of the orbit which the earth describes in its annual journey round the sun.

But let us draw attention more particularly to the point of this arrangement on which the alternation of Summer and Winter depends. If, on starting from that part of the rim of the table which is farthest from the "sun," the upper or north "pole" of the worsted ball be inclined toward that luminary, it will be found that on arriving at the side of the table exactly opposite — and nearest to the sun — the same "north pole" is now inclined away from it. Exactly the reverse of this has, of course, happened to the "south pole;" it inclined at first from, but now inclines toward the sun. The necessary effect of these changes of position is to place that side of the earth, which for the time being leans toward the sun, in a more favorable position for receiving light and heat than the side which is inclined away from it. The result thus produced upon the temperature much more than compensates for the heat either gained or lost on account of the comparative nearness or distance of the earth in relation to the sun at the two periods of the year, and it therefore rules the seasons. In the hemisphere which is inclined toward the sun there is Summer; while, in that which is inclined away from it, there is Winter. Every body knows that when it is Summer in England it is Winter at the Antipodes.

When we consider the forethought with which the conditions of animal and vegetable life have been adjusted to the distance of the earth from the sun — to their respective sizes and densities — to the length of the earth's orbit — to the velocity with which it travels, and to the nicely poised inclination of its axis — we cannot fail to be deeply impressed with the admirable design of the Creator and the excellence of His Power. All these elements had to be adjusted, one with the other, in order to establish Winter and Summer, and the least deviation in any of them from the condition which actually exists would have spoilt the harmonious working of the whole. The beauty and necessity of these arrangements have been happily illustrated by Dr. Whewell: "The length of the year or interval of recurrence of the seasons is determined by the time which the earth employs in performing its revolution round the sun: and we can very easily conceive the solar system so adjusted that the year should be longer or shorter than it actually is. We can imagine the earth to revolve round the sun at a distance greater or less than that which it at present has, all the forces of the system remaining unaltered. If the earth were removed toward the centre by about one eighth of its distance, the year would be diminished by about a month, and in the same manner it would be increased by a month on increasing the distance by one eighth. We can suppose the earth at a distance of eighty four or one hundred and eight millions of miles, just as easily as at its present distance of ninety-six millions: we can suppose the earth with its present stock of animals and vegetables placed where Mars or where Venus is, and revolving in an orbit like one of theirs; on the former supposition our year would become twenty-three, on the latter, seven of our present months. Or we can conceive the present distances of the parts of the system to continue what they are, and the size, or the density of the central mass, the sun, to be increased or diminished in any proportion; and in this way the time of the earth's revolution might have been increased or diminished in any degree; a greater velocity, and consequently a diminished period, being requisite in order to balance an augmented central attraction. In any of these ways the length of the earth's natural year might have been different from what it now is: in the last way without any necessary alteration, so far as we can see, of temperature. Now, if any change of this kind were to take place, the working of the botanical world would be thrown into utter disorder, the functions of plants would be entirely deranged, and the whole vegetable kingdom involved in instant decay and rapid extinction. That this would be the case, may be collected from innumerable indications. Most of our fruit-trees, for example, require the year to be of its present length. If the Summer and the Autumn were much shorter, the fruit could not ripen; if these seasons were much longer, the tree would put forth a fresh suit of blossoms to be cut down by the Winter. Or if the year were twice its present length, a second crop of fruit would probably not be matured, for want, among other things, of an intermediate season of rest and consolidation, such as the Winter is. Our forest-trees, in like manner, appear to need all the seasons of our present year for their perfection; the Spring, Summer, and Autumn, for the development of their leaves and consequent formation of their proper juice, and of wood from this; and the Winter for the hardening and solidifying the substance thus formed."

As a general rule it may be said that temperature falls in proportion to increase of latitude; at first slowly, and then more rapidly. Our daily experience of midday sun and sunset teaches us that oblique rays give much less heat than those that are more nearly vertical; and as the earth is round, and as rays from the sun, therefore, fall on it all the more obliquely the greater the distance is from the Equator, it follows that in high latitudes, where the globe from its shape curves in rapidly toward the poles, the temperature will fall with accelerated ratio.

Such is the cosmical arrangement by which the general supply of heat is meted out to the earth, but there are many circumstances which modify this distribution, so as to produce great differences of climate in places that are on nearly the same latitude. Thus, in proceeding northward from the tropics, the mean annual temperature falls much more quickly in America than in Europe. For example, the cities of Madrid and Philadelphia are both situated at nearly 40 degrees of latitude; but the mean annual climate of the former is 9° higher than that of the American city. In comparing places farther to the north the difference is still more striking.

We have space in this chapter to notice only very briefly some of the causes which modify climate. The reader will find many additional observations bearing on this subject in those sections of this book wherein Mountains, Winds, Ice and Snow, the Sea, and the Green things upon the earth are considered.

The great equalizer and mitigator of extremes of heat

and cold is the ocean. A maritime climate is for the most part moderate in its seasonal changes, in comparison to an inland climate on the same latitude. In Winter, the sea being warmer than the land, tempers the winds which blow toward it; while, in Summer, as its temperature is lower than the heated surface of the shore, it imparts fresh coolness to the breezes. Warm or cold ocean currents, if they be extensive, have much influence on climate. Thus the great Gulf Stream, laden with the heat of the Tropics, by laving the shores of Western Europe, and more especially those of our own islands, sensibly moderates the rigor of the Winter; while, on the other hand, the cold current from the Greenland Sea and Baffin's Bay, which streams past Newfoundland and the Atlantic shore of North America, materially lowers the climatic temperature of those countries.

As a general rule, the effect of a deep inland or continental position in temperate regions is to give what is called an "extreme" character to the climate, — that is, to make it colder in Winter and hotter in Summer than other places on the same parallel of latitude which are surrounded by or near the sea. To illustrate this point, the climate of Warsaw in nearly 52° 13' may be contrasted with that of Dublin in 53° 21'. Warsaw lies on the great plain of Central Europe. In Winter, the surface over a wide tract around loses its temperature under the influence of the long nights and keen frosts, while there is no neighboring sea to mitigate the cold. Had the ocean been near, as its temperature does not fall under 40° Fahrenheit, it would have corrected this rigor; but, instead of the comparatively warm sea, there is an extensive land surface, which, being cooled down far below the freezing point, imparts to the air passing over Warsaw much of its own intense rigor. Dublin, on the other hand, by having a maritime position, enjoys during the Winter a far milder climate, although it lies more than a degree farther north.

The temperature of its coldest month does not fall below a mean of 37°, while that of Warsaw sinks to 27 degrees. In Summer, however, the same physical conditions produce exactly the contrary effect. The sandy plains round Warsaw get baked in the sun, and the air in passing over them is heated as in an oven; but round Dublin there are no scorched plains, and the sea that encircles Ireland tends still further to cool the temperature. Hence, while the mean of the hottest month at Warsaw is 70°, that of Dublin is only 60°. Thus Warsaw is 10 degrees colder than Dublin in Winter, and 10 degrees hotter in Summer.

To similar causes is to be attributed the extreme character of the climate throughout the greater part of North America. At New York, for example, the thermometer in Summer often rises to above 100° in the shade; while during the Winter of 1866 it fell to 15° below zero, and marked 28° in places more inland. The explanation of this excessive rigor is that most of this vast continent lies far from the sea, while it stretches in unbroken continuation into the frozen regions. In the same way Central Asia chiefly owes its "extreme" climate to its distance from the ocean.

Although there be no Winter or Summer within the tropics and in certain adjacent districts in the sense in which we understand them, there is nevertheless a division of the year into "wet and dry" periods, which, in their influence on the functions of animal and more especially of vegetable life, have effects analogous to those produced by the warm and cold seasons of higher latitudes. In the wet season vegetation is most vigorous; but, after the dry season has continued for some time, the grass withers and dries up, the deciduous leaves fall, the growth of plants is arrested, and the vegetable world reposes very much as in the Winter of more northern climes. The analogy between these seasons is still more strikingly shown by the torpor into which some animals fall during the dry season, just as elsewhere they pass into a state of hibernation during the Winter. Thus when that reptile-looking fish, the Lepidosiren of the river Gambia, perceives that the waters are falling on the approach of the dry season, and that food is becoming scarce, it buries itself in the mud, and there awaits in a dormant state the return of the rains. Sir J. E. Tennent has noticed other animals in Ceylon which become torpid during the dry season in the mud of the great water-tanks, and more extended observation will probably add to the list.

Nowhere, from the force of contrast, is Summer more brilliantly joyous or its approach welcomed with greater delight, than in polar regions, where amid perennial frost and snow Winter seems to be enthroned for ever. The long, continuous night, after passing through a tedious dawn, at length opens into that bright, brief interval in which Spring, Summer, and Autumn are blended into one. In rays of warmth the sun sends forth the signal, and Nature promptly answers to the call. As heat increases, the solitude once more shows signs of life and movement. The frozen lumps and ledges covering the sea begin to strain and crack and split asunder, and glacier masses breaking loose from their icy cables yield themselves up to the current and the wind. Food is no longer absolutely wanting, and many creatures that have been slumbering through the Winter now shake off their torpor. Torpor enforced, but merciful! As Winter approached, supplies of food ran short and then became exhausted, so God in kindness sent them sleep. Hunger was extinguished in lethargy. It was needful to husband the forces of vitality until the time of abundance should again come round; so the heart was made to beat, and the lungs to breathe, at the lowest rate that was compatible with existence. The expenditure of fuel to maintain animal warmth was thus brought down to its minimum, and the lamp of life was sparingly fed with the fat which Nature had providentially stored up in the body when food was plenty. But now, called forth by light and warmth, the bear creeps from its lair of snow, and seals and walruses begin to gambol round the rocks where lately solid ice sealed up the surface of the deep. Myriads of migratory waterfowl from the warm South whiten the in-shore cliffs. Then the Esquimau, rousing himself from the enforced idleness of the long night, sallies forth to hunt and fish, and to gather up supplies of food in snow-built safes against the never-distant Winter. The short, thick grass and moss spread their carpet of green over every sheltered spot from which the snow has melted, and the rest of the scanty but often brightsome flora of remotest North puts on with marvelous rapidity its Summer aspects.

Diversity of climate and season — of Winter and Summer — over the globe has produced for man's advantage a corresponding variety of animal and vegetable life. Man himself has an organic strength which enables him to exist in every clime; but other animals, and all plants, have a more limited geographical distribution, and are endowed with constitutions which fit them for thriving in certain regions only. By means of commerce, however, the short-comings of one climate are supplemented by the riches of another, and all the most useful productions growing upon the earth are thus most widely scattered. This necessary interchange, moreover, becomes a means of knitting the whole world in bonds of mutual dependence.

We may rest assured that nothing in Nature has been established without benevolent design, and even the difficulties arising from the proverbial uncertainties of climate, as well as the impediments encountered in the cultivation of the soil, are not without their use. Every thing shows that we are here as in a training school, and surrounded by circumstances which, by demanding the energetic exercise of our faculties, tend to preserve and strengthen them. In man's contests with the so-called faults of climate, he is, for the most part, reasonably victorious. His prudent foresight, his ingenious contrivances, his dexterous wielding of science to avert evils and improve opportunities, are continually showing how abundantly the Creator has supplied him with all means needful for his welfare, in whatever quarter of the world his lot may happen to be cast.

Diversity of climate circumscribes within limits more or less narrow many of the most useful of our food-producing plants, but this unavoidable evil has sometimes been lessened or obviated in a way which affords another instance of the kind forethought of Our Father. One of the most useful articles of vegetable diet is sugar, and Nature has taken care that many substances in common use shall contain a fair proportion of it. At the same time, there are certain plants in which it exists so abundantly that we are accustomed to resort to them for our large supplies. Of these the chief is the well-known "cane." But the sugar-cane flourishes only in the tropics and adjacent regions; and therefore all sugar from this source consumed in extra-tropical countries must be brought to them by commerce. Many a wide district, however, lying far in the interior of continents, is unfavorably situated for thus receiving its supplies, and it might either have been deprived of that article altogether, or at least have been inadequately provided with it, had not Providence, with kind intent, created other sugar-producing plants constitutionally suited to different climates, for the purpose of distributing the gift more generally over the world. Thus we find that, from the "cane" region to the Mediterranean, the supply of sugar is maintained by several plants, among which may be mentioned the date-palm and the fig. Beyond this, in climates corresponding to southern Europe, there are the sorghum and maize, from which much sugar is now manufactured in France and America. Farther to the north the beetroot in the field and the maple in the forest extend the system of sugar-producing plants almost to the confines of the arctic circle. In another article of diet, which from its importance we are accustomed to call the "staff of life," a similar providential succession is observed. Farinaceous food is tropically represented by the rice-plant in great abundance; in proceeding northward rice is associated with the maize or Indian corn; that is succeeded by wheat; and lastly, we have oats and barley flourishing almost up to the North Cape. The same representative system is observed in regard to many other important vegetable principles with more or less distinctness. In this manner, then, the difficulties opposed by climate to the wide distribution over the globe of some of the most valuable products of the vegetable kingdom have been entirely surmounted. It is clear that, according to the laws which regulate the vegetable kingdom, it was impossible for the same useful plants to flourish everywhere; but Providence has created duplicates, as it were, to yield abundantly the same products, and has adapted them by their constitution to take up their position in the different climatic belts of the world, in order that no extensive region should be without them.

With all their imputed faults of climate, we have no occasion in these favored islands* to envy the plantal glories of warmer regions. In absolute beauty who shall say that we are not on an equality, whilst the great charm arising from the well-marked progression of the seasons is more especially our own. Nothing is more frequently debated than the comparative attractions of the different periods of the year, and certainly no season — not even excepting Winter — need be without its admirers. The never-ending contrasts which every season spreads before us unquestionably contribute much to enhance our enjoyment. Never do "green things" seem so green or flowers

* Great Britain.

so bright as when our first glimpses of them are caught through the opening portals of the Spring. Then do we feel more than at any other time the great value of this seasonal alternation. How gladly the eye wanders over and reposes upon the "universal garb" of Nature. To the beauties of Summer and Autumn we are led up as it were through an avenue which, by gradually preparing us for what is to follow, lessens in some degree the keenness of our relish. The banquet is more varied, but the freshness of the appetite is wanting.

Though Winter may yield in beauty to other seasons, it is yet universally felt to have special attractions of its own. There is much to admire in the cheery, ruddy glow of the sun, in the noble and picturesque though naked forms of the woods, in the hoar-frost on the grass, in the sparkle of the ice-gemmed trees, the stalactites of crystal, and the wreaths of snow. Even in Winter's gloomiest moods the comforting thought is ever rising to our mind, that the stillness we see round is not death but needful repose spread over Nature in mercy, and that the woods will soon again be clothed in green, and vocal with the songs of birds.

Winter has yet another aspect by which it is endeared to us. At Christmas-time it is crowned by the great Festival of the Church and of the family. Then, while Nature slumbers in wood and field, Winter is brightly and lovingly awake around the hearth, gladdening millions of hearts with warm affection. Families that were scattered by the various calls of life once more gather together to enjoy the present, glance at the past, and treasure up new associations for the future. Then shops put on their gayest looks, and young and old press eagerly forward in search of the little gifts that are to make others happy. Streets and railway stations are thronged with bustling groups hurrying on to claim from expectant friends the cordial welcome of the season. Here and there, too, may be seen the "knotless threads" and waifs of the world drawn onward by the social influence of the season toward some genial home, where, for a time, the sense of loneliness will be forgotten. At Christmas the Church and the Home seem to draw closer to each other, and the thoughts awakened by the solemn festival mingle with and temper the current of family rejoicing. Christmas is pre-eminently the season of "good-will toward men." Under its kindly impulses the mind softens with sympathy, and, while keenly alive to the blessings that fall to its own lot, is more heedful, perhaps, than at other times of the plaints of the less fortunate. The parish work-house is for the day made radiant with merry faces, and Charity enters through its gloomy gates to spread the feast in honor of the Anniversary. In the good soil which Christmas thus prepares in the heart old friendships revive and new affections quickly strike their roots; while animosities, curbed by the gentle influences of the season, shrink out of sight, or are swept away altogether in the gush of better feelings.

The lot is fallen unto me in a fair ground: yea, I have a goodly heritage.—Ps. xvi.

NIGHTS AND DAYS.

O ye Nights and Days, bless ye the Lord: praise Him, and magnify Him for ever.

WE have already alluded to the earth's orbital movement round the sun, from which our year results; and we have now to direct attention to that other movement of the earth by which, in turning upon its axis every 23 hours 56 minutes and 4 seconds, it gives rise to the division of time into Nights and Days. How perfect the working of that machine must be by which this division is meted out may be inferred from a calculation by Laplace, which demonstrated that "it was impossible that a difference of one hundredth of a second of time should have occurred between the length of the day in the earliest ages, and at the present time!"

Reverting for a moment to our impromptu orrery, it is obvious that if the ball of worsted, representing the earth, were to be held steady during its solar orbit, so as not to turn round on its axis, one hemisphere of its surface would be directed toward the sun for one half of its circuit, and the remaining hemisphere during the other half. In other words, a whole year would be divided into one long day and one long night. During the day the sun would always be above the horizon, and the accumulation of heat which would thus accrue would far transcend the hottest tropical climate. In the other hemisphere, turned away from the sun, there would be a constant loss of heat from radiation, and as no compensatory rays would be received from that luminary, the temperature would sink below that of the frozen regions. It is clear that such an arrangement would be incompatible with the conditions under which life now exists upon our globe. Having regard to the constitution that has been given to animals and plants, it is absolutely necessary that heat and light should be meted out to them at intervals sufficiently frequent to guard against extremes of temperature. Therefore it is ordained that the earth shall revolve once upon its axis in a period nearly amounting to twenty-four hours, — an arrangement by which twelve hours of alternate day and night, of warm sunlight and cool darkness, are secured to each hemisphere. By the aid of certain cosmical conditions, elsewhere noticed, modifications in the distribution of light and heat are produced, by which animals and plants might obtain that particular length of day and night which is best suited to their nature and habits.

The intervals of night and day are, moreover, in perfect harmony with that law of Nature by which all animals require seasons of rest to alternate with periods of activity. The demand for repose is universally felt and obeyed. Even plants may be said to have their days and nights, in the sense of intervals for activity and rest; but the hours for labor are struck by the seasons — by orbital and not by axial rotation. In spring, summer, and autumn the sap circulates briskly, the manufacture of wood proceeds without intermission, and the various special products, as gum, starch, sugar, and other matters, are elaborated. But on the approach of winter — or toward the evening of their long day of work — plants turn weary, and, by a poetical yet truthful figure, we habitually speak of them as "falling asleep." So necessary is this period of repose that, in the tropics where there is no winter's cold to chill them into rest, Nature wraps them in salutary torpor by means of the sun's fierce rays. And how gladdening the dawn after the long night when plants awake from their sleep, and burst forth once more to resume their day of work!

Night mercifully beckons the world to rest. The busy sounds of day cease to distract the ear, and Nature gently points toward repose. How sad when the silent hours of darkness refuse to steep in sweet oblivion the senses of the careworn, or to dull the racked nerves of him who languishes upon a bed of sickness. Sleep is best wooed by labor — it is the reward with which Nature blesses exertion. How grateful sleep is to the busy workers of the world; to the drones only is it apt to be, like their life, a listless, scarcely enjoyed vacuity. Night, too, calls us to meditation. When darkness drops its curtain over the things of earth, the mind is prompted to look inward. The brief but salutary retrospect of the day should then be made, and the account closed. In prayer the soul finds peace, and sleep steals softly on amid thoughts that recall the Divine protection.

My trust is in the tender mercy of God for ever and ever. — Ps. lii.

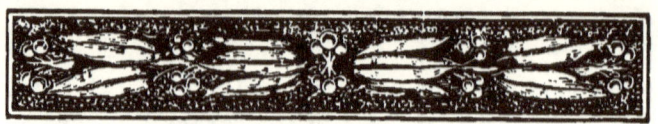

LIGHT AND DARKNESS.

O ye Light and Darkness, bless ye the Lord: praise Him, and magnify Him for ever.

AMONG those works of the Lord to which this hymn appeals there is not one more full of blessings to mankind than Light, or one which more praises and magnifies the Creator. But, though many of the laws by which Light is governed are now well known, its essential nature is still a mystery. Some philosophers suppose it to be an "emanation" from luminous bodies of inconceivably minute atoms which act on the retina of the eye like odorous particles on the nerves of smell. Others refer its phenomena to "undulations" excited in a subtle ether pervading space, and traveling onward to the eye by a movement resembling waves in the ocean. This theory, therefore, points to an analogy with the sense of hearing.

How wonderful is the construction of that little instrument by which light is made to minister to vision! There is truly nothing in the whole range of Nature which more convincingly demonstrates design than the mutual adaptations of eye and light. This organ, equally perfect in contrivance and in finish, exhibits the most wonderful combination of organic power with a mechanical apparatus formed on the regular principles of optics. We see objects by reflected light; in other words, the object must first be illuminated, and then it must reflect a certain amount of this light into our eyes. But as the entrance of too many or too bright rays would have dazzled vision, while too few would have left it obscure and indistinct, an ever-vigilant sentinel — the iris, on which the color depends — was posted in front across the interior of the eye, to regulate, by the expansion or contraction of the pupil, the exact number of rays that ought to be admitted. It was also necessary that the rays, after entering the eye, should be made to converge so as to depict a distinct image on the retina, or nerve of vision, spread out at the back of the organ. For this purpose a lens, as clear as crystal, has been fixed up immediately behind the pupil, to "refract" or bend the rays into the proper focus. Not less careful has the Creator been in regard to the safety of so delicate an apparatus. To preserve the eye from injury, it has been sunk as deeply in the face as was consistent with the free range of vision; it is defended all round by strong ridges of bone, and made to move softly on an adipose cushion. Eyebrows, moreover, have been placed above, and fringing eyelashes in front, to guard against excessive light; while, by the rapid movement of the eyelids, the tears are diffused over the surface of the eye exposed to the air so as to keep it moist and glistening. Such are a few only of the beautiful contrivances exhibited by this organ.

Light, though colorless and invisible, is in reality made up of seven different tints, which again may be reduced to three — red, yellow, and blue — out of which the others are formed. The whole series is finely displayed in that separation of light into its constituent parts which takes place in a prism of glass or in the water-drops of the rainbow. Objects which absorb nearly all the rays are black; those which reflect them all are white; and we owe the charm of color to the circumstance that most bodies, while decomposing the rays of light that fall on them, absorb some of the constituent tints and reflect the others. By the endless combination of these last every variety of color is produced. In many ways colors are convenient and useful, nor will any one deny that the face of Nature would have lost its highest charm had not this property been bestowed on light.

The sun is the great fountain of Light; but, without the coöperation of the atmosphere to diffuse it over objects, the illumination of this earth would have been most imperfect, and light could never have become the universal blessing which it now is. Objects on which the direct rays of the sun fell would, of course, have reflected light and been visible; but objects which were in shade, and which, therefore, did not receive any direct solar rays, would have been invisible. Let any one attempt to realize the confusion into which the world would thus have been thrown. Even in the brightest sunshine we should have seen things only in broken fragments. The varied beauty of scenery would have vanished, and every landscape would have been disfigured with seams and patches of inky blackness. The rays of the sun in passing through a window would have brightened the surfaces they touched, but all around would have been left in almost midnight darkness. In conversing with a friend, the side which was turned toward the sun would alone have been visible; and, if our own face had happened to be opposite to his and in shade, he could not have seen it. If a cloud had passed over the sun both of us would have vanished into darkness, as if from a sudden eclipse. The azure tints of the firmament would have disappeared, and the stars would have shone at midday from a vault of utter blackness. To improve the illumination it was, therefore, essential that something should distribute the light, so as to supply objects that were in shade with a certain amount of rays, by the reflection of which they might be seen. This task was given by the Creator to the atmosphere. Many of the sun's rays fall directly on the earth, but the rest are caught up by the air, and are reflected and re-reflected from one particle to another, and are scattered and diffused in every direction, until all objects within their influence are bathed in light. In this manner bodies in shade are illumined and become visible by reflecting into our eyes more or less of the light they have received at second-hand.

The service which the atmosphere renders to the sun, in diffusing its light equally over objects, is amply repaid by the sun in coöperating with plants to purify the atmosphere. A healthy condition of the latter is of primary necessity to our welfare; and, as the air is continually being vitiated in a variety of ways, some active agency is needed to check deterioration and preserve it in a state of purity. The essential constituent of the air is oxygen, which is diluted with nitrogen to a certain degree; and with this mixture is invariably associated a small proportion of carbonic acid gas. The latter is poisonous; but, under ordinary circumstances, the quantity existing in the air — only about one 2000th part of its volume — is too small to be attended with any inconvenience. There are, however, many causes in operation continually tending to destroy this balance, and to produce a noxious excess. In the first place, we manufacture the poison within ourselves to an extent which, though small in the individual, is enormous in the aggregate. With every inspiration we draw into the lungs a certain amount of oxygen, which, after combining with a certain amount of carbon or charcoal, is expired in the shape of carbonic acid gas. Now, although a small proportion of this acid was inspired as a constituent of the air, the quantity evolved exceeds by sixty times the quantity taken in; so that the whole amount of carbon thus daily carried off from the lungs of a healthy adult is not less than from nine to twelve ounces. When we multiply this unit by the population of the world, and add to it the product of respiration in the lower animals, we may imagine the extent to which the atmosphere is vitiated from this cause.

A quantity of carbonic acid gas still more enormous is produced by combustion, the decomposition of animal and vegetable matter, and by fermentation. Every candle and every lamp sends forth its little rill of poison into the air, while from fireplaces and furnaces it issues in streams. In all these cases the chemical action is the same; — the carbon of the fuel is changed into carbonic acid by its union with oxygen gas.

Notwithstanding these sources of vitiation it is found experimentally that the relative proportions of the constituents of the atmosphere vary very little, and that the amount of carbonic acid diffused through it never exceeds its due quantity. It is obvious, therefore, that the Creator must have set some potent machinery in motion to correct and purify. Rain and surface water carry off more or less of the gas, and some mineral springs sparkle with it; but the work is chiefly done through the agency of Light upon the leaves of plants. When it is said that we "vitiate" the air in breathing, the expression refers only to its salubrity as regards ourselves and other animals; but we should greatly err if we supposed that this apparent spoiling subserved no good purpose. That which vitiates the air to us only prepares and perfects it for the use of plants; and the carbonic acid which would be poison to us is food to them. Thus the leaves, while bathed in air, extract from it the chief bulk of the carbon which is to build up the woody substance of the tree to which they belong. It is to be observed, however, that they can only perform this function so long as they are stimulated by Light. In darkness, plants, instead of purifying the air, tend to vitiate it still further by a slight evolution of the very gas which it is their special function to remove. But in the day-time, the leaf seizes upon the particles of carbonic acid gas that come in contact with it; and, while it "fixes" the carbon in its substance, it liberates into the air the oxygen which is to restore its purity. It might be

Light and Darkness.

thought that, as there are no leaves in winter to purify, the atmosphere would then become poisonous. But by the cosmical conditions of our globe it has been wisely ordained that it never is winter all over the world at the same time. The work, therefore, is always going on, though the scene of the laboratory is shifted. But besides this, the period of a single winter, with its dispersing winds and currents, would be too short to allow any injurious accumulation to take place. Thus to vast causes of vitiation are opposed vast agencies that purify, whereby the balance which works for the good of all organized Nature is preserved.

At midday the unprotected eye cannot face the sun. But at sunset he ceases to dazzle, because his rays, from their greater obliquity, lose much of their fierceness while passing through the less clear and more vaporous layers of the atmosphere immediately investing the earth. The light is not only weakened, but it is altered in its character. In their passage toward our eyes many rays are absorbed and lost altogether, and many others are decomposed and only partially transmitted. Of the ray-fragments which thus survive and eventually reach our retina the red predominate; and hence the glowing hues of sunset.

When looking at the sun just as he begins to set, it is curious to reflect that he is not really where he appears to be, but actually below the horizon. We are, in fact, looking at his image or picture. There is a rim of the horizon interposed between us; he is in the position of the hull of a ship when, as sailors express it, the ship is "hull-down." Hence, were it possible that a cannon-ball could be projected in a straight line right through the bright disk before us, it would not strike the sun, but would pass clean over it. This "lifting up" of the image of the sun is due to "refraction"—that property which has already been noticed as enabling the lens of the eye to bend the rays of light, and bring them to a focus on the retina. Refraction is familiar to every boy who has thrust a stick into clear water, and noticed the broken or bent appearance it presents at the point of immersion; and a spoon placed in a teacup into which a little water has been poured will exhibit it equally well. For our present purpose, however, this will be better illustrated by another very simple experiment. Let a shilling be laid at the bottom of a basin placed on the table, and let the observer then move slowly backward, keeping his eye fixed on the piece of money, until the rim of the basin just intercepts his view. If water be now poured into the basin without displacing the coin, the latter will be as it were lifted up out of its real position, and will become visible. At first the shilling was seen in its true place. When the rays proceeding from it to the eye were intercepted by the rim of the basin, it became invisible. But when the water was added some of the rays from the coin in passing from the water into the air were "refracted," and bent downward toward the eye so as to fall within the range of vision. Now as in refraction objects are not seen in the direction in which the rays originally left them, but in the direction in which the rays ultimately enter the eye, it follows that the coin is visible in its "lifted up" position. In applying this experiment to the phenomena of sunset, we may consider the shilling as the sun, and the intercepting rim of the basin as the horizon behind which the sun has really sunk. The media of water and air represent the dense, vaporous, impure lower strata of the atmosphere, which gradually "refract," or bend down toward our eye, the rays that come to us from the sun, and thus lift up its image above its real position.

To the "reflecting" power of the atmosphere we owe that interval of half-light which in the morning we call the dawn, and in the evening the twilight. Were it not for this property, we should pass at once from darkness to light and from light to darkness. When the sun sinks below the horizon, and when his direct rays have bid adieu to the dwellers on the plains, they still continue to tint the tops of the hills; and when, from the further dipping of the sun, these also have passed into shade, the slanting rays still enter freely into the higher regions of the atmosphere. Most of these rays continue their course into space and are lost to us entirely; but others are caught up by the particles of air and vapor, as by mirrors of inconceivable minuteness, and are turned back and reflected from layer to layer downward until at length they reach the earth. The same operation is repeated as the sun approaches from the east in the morning. The soft, mild light of twilight is especially grateful in summer to eyes that seek repose after the hot glare of the sun. It is linked in most minds with pleasant associations. This is the time for leisure strolls on land or gliding movements on the water. It brings us into acquaintance with many animals which select it as their favorite period of activity. Soon as the swallows have ceased their twit-twit, the bats issuing from their retreat begin to occupy the vacant hunting ground, in which they display an activity on the wing scarcely less astonishing.

The length of twilight varies according to the latitude and the season of the year. It is shortest within the tropics, whose inhabitants may be said to plunge almost at once from light into darkness; and it lengthens as we proceed toward the poles. In the latitude of London, from the 22d May to the 21st July, so much light lingers behind between sunset and sunrise that, speaking astronomically, there is no night at all. At the north pole night lasts from November 12th to January 29th; it is preceded by one long twilight continuing uninterruptedly from the autumnal equinox; and it is followed by a dawn reaching to the vernal equinox. During the whole of this period of six months the sun is below the horizon. Those who enjoy the blessing of alternate day and night every 24 hours, can hardly realize the intense thankfulness with which the dawn and the sun are welcomed by men who have just passed through the depressing influences of the dreary polar night. We can sympathize with Doctor Kane in his brig among the Greenland ice, as he records his eager watchings for the sun, and the calculations which, by revealing its daily progress toward him, permitted him to anticipate with certainty the day of its reappearance. We understand the thankfulness with which he must have watched the dawn growing brighter and brighter, and the delight with which at length he scrambled up a neighboring height to catch a glimpse of the orb still hidden at the level of the deck. " I saw him once more, and from a projecting crag nestled in the sunshine. It was like bathing in perfumed water."

When wintering in the far north, Captain Sherard Osborn thus describes the return of the sun after an absence of 66 days. On February 7th " the stentorian lungs of the *Resolute's* boatswain hailed to say the sun was in sight from the mast-head ; and in all the vessels the rigging was soon manned to get the first glimpse of the returning god of day. Slowly it rose ; and loud and hearty cheers greeted the return of an orb which those without the frozen zone do not half appreciate because he is always with them. For a whole hour we feasted ourselves admiring the sphere of fire."

Light is one of the best and cheapest of Nature's tonics, and, unless it be habitually absorbed, neither animal nor vegetable can permanently prosper. Except in a comparatively narrow belt round the poles, this needful medicament is poured out at short intervals profusely over the world, and streams into every dwelling where it is not repelled by ignorance or folly. In man the habitual absence of sufficient light proclaims itself in the wan cheek and bloodless lip ; and in plants, by the general want of green coloring matter. The blood that has been long shut off from the renovating influence of sunlight-air may circulate through the various organs, but it lacks the power to impart to them a healthy vigor. In the night-time less carbon is expired from the lungs, and the purification of the blood, therefore, goes on less actively than during the day. The inhabitants of towns, where light is more or less excluded by lofty streets, are pale and feeble when compared with country cottages, although their food may be both better and more abundant. Those who pass their days in dark alleys, or in the basement dens of crowded cities, seldom enjoy perfect health; and this is due not less, perhaps, to the want of light than to the want of air. Where light is defective elasticity forsakes both mind and body, and the spirits of few are so buoyant as to be altogether insensible to the difference between a bright and a dull day. In the weary polar night there is always a struggle against the depressing influence of darkness. When Kane, wintering in Smith's Sound, saw his crew drooping and dying round him, he probably did not err in attributing the calamity less to the want of good provisions than to the want of light. His dogs, too, perished one after the other with strange, anomalous symptoms which he attributed to the same cause, and he looked forward with confidence to the return of sunlight as the charm that was to stay the pestilence.

It would even appear that some plants, acted on by light, give off that mysterious kind of modified oxygen, termed ozone, which is believed to contribute so peculiarly to the healthy condition of the atmosphere. Nor is the pervading influence of light unfelt even in the inorganic world. To light we owe the beauties of photography; and many other chemical actions can go on only under its stimulus.

"And God said, Let there be Light." Who can adequately appreciate the evidences of Power, Wisdom, and

Beneficence crowded into this glorious creation, and how little do they comprehend its full value who see nothing in it beyond its convenience or its beauty! Light is an essential condition of animated nature — the pivot on which life turns. All that lives upon the earth lives by light. Without it plants could not grow, or assimilate their food, or breathe, or purify the air; and, without plants, animals must perish. From the mineral kingdom alone the food-supplies of the whole world are ultimately renewed, and plants are the appointed channels through which those supplies must pass. The vegetable organism rakes them together, gathers them up, and hands them over to animals in a state fit for food. "If," says Professor Draper, "we expose some clear spring water to the sunshine, though it may have been clear and transparent at first, it presently begins to assume a greenish tint, and after a while flocks of greenish matter collect on the sides of the vessel in which it is contained." This first addition to organized life is won by the power of Light out of the inorganic atoms round the germ; it is, as it were, the minute, base-material out of which the fabric of life is woven. "If the observation be made in a stream of water, the current of which runs slowly, it will be discovered that the green matter serves as food for thousands of aquatic insects which make their habitation in it." Next come fishes to snap up the insects, birds may seize upon the fishes, and both serve as food to man. In endless variety, and often through a much longer chain, some such general "succession of nutrition" is always going on. The whole movement was started by a beam of light!

Light is truly one of the great "Powers of the Lord." It summons the whole plantal world to labor in the purification of the air, and it regulates the hours of work. The wages it gives to plants for their willing service is their daily food of carbon. Hardly had the green matter in the stream begun to form under the influence of sunlight than it commenced the manufacture of pure air for the use of man, and in token of its activity it was gemmed all over with bells of vital oxygen. Land plants are no less busy in the same task, although their labor is necessarily invisible. Thus by the aid of Light no plant is idle, nor is it useless in Nature's economy, though it may be unseen. Every scattered leaf and blade of grass has its appointed task, and every ray of light that falls upon them helps on the life of the world.

This is the Lord's doing, and it is marvelous in our eyes. — Ps. cxviii.

WATERS ABOVE THE FIRMAMENT.

O ye waters that be above the Firmament, bless ye the Lord: praise Him, and magnify Him for ever.

THE word Firmament is obviously used here in the same sense in which it is employed in the 1st chapter of Genesis. It is that space which immediately invests the earth, and which interposes between the waters which are below and those which are above it, or between seas and clouds. The Scriptures abound with imagery derived from this source. Clouds shut out the bright sun — they were therefore emblems of gloom and sorrow; at other times they sheltered plant and beast from his scorching rays, and they were then the symbols of tender care and protection. Of old, too, as now, poets turned toward the clouds for some of their grandest metaphors. The Psalmist says, " The Lord maketh the clouds his chariot;" and when the inspired writer of the Revelation exclaims, " Behold He cometh with clouds," the expression symbolizes both grandeur and majesty.

Clouds are among the first of the objects invoked in the hymn; and they are twice mentioned; once by themselves, as the "Waters above the Firmament," and again in another verse in connection with lightning. The prominence thus given to them accords with their importance in countries like Judea and Mesopotamia, where droughts are sometimes severely felt. Clouds, therefore, were watched for eagerly and anxiously, as signs that the parched earth was about to be blessed with refreshing rain. Unhappy the regions where "the waters" never collect "above the firmament." There "the clouds drop no fatness," and the land loosens into sterile sand.

In our own country, and still more in hot climates, clouds often interpose as a friendly shield between sun and earth, to check excessive evaporation from the one, and to ward off the too scorching rays of the other. Without this protection the surface of the soil would dry up, roots would find no moisture, plants would languish or wither, and cattle might perish for want of water.

The vapor issuing from the spout of a tea-kettle supplies a favorite illustration of the theory of clouds, or they may be studied on a larger and very beautiful scale as they are developed from the funnel of a locomotive. With every puff of the engine a quantity of steam is driven into the air. It will be noticed that this steam is invisible at the moment of its escape, and when it has as yet scarcely cleared the funnel; then it is quickly condensed into a white cloud; and, lastly, this cloud itself disappears. A moment's attention to these three points will unfold to us much that is interesting in cloud-philosophy. It is well known that, when water is heated to a temperature of $212°$ Fahrenheit, it rapidly passes into invisible steam. The steam produced by the engine boiler was, therefore, as transparent as air on escaping into the funnel. But when steam is cooled below the temperature of $212°$ Fahrenheit it is condensed into vapor; hence the white cloud which the invisible steam of the locomotive formed on coming into contact with the colder air around it. Finally, we observed that as this cloud was diffused more widely through the air it dissolved and vanished.

This last fact proves that the atmosphere has the property of absorbing or dissolving moisture, which it retains in an invisible state. Air, indeed, always contains an admixture of moisture, though the quantity is continually varying. The warmer the air, the greater is its capacity to take up water in this invisible state; on the other hand, the colder the air, the less moisture it can hold. It follows that the atmosphere of the tropics is much more loaded with vapor than that of temperate regions; while this latter, in its turn, contains more moisture than the air of higher latitudes. We speak of "a dry air," but the expression is only relatively correct. There is always enough of water even in the dryest air to moisten saline substances that are deliquescent; and every body has observed the streams condensed from unseen vapor which soon begin to trickle down the sides of a bottle of iced water brought into a room. Few people, however, would have expected to find that a cube of air measuring twenty yards each way and at a temperature of 68° Fahrenheit, is capable of taking up no less than 252 lbs. of water before it reaches the point of saturation. From this it may be imagined how enormous the quantity of water must be which is suspended invisibly in the entire atmosphere of the world.

It is out of this invisible steam pervading the atmosphere that visible vapors or clouds are manufactured. When one current of air meets another current colder than itself, they intermingle; and, if the resulting mixture be not of a temperature sufficiently high to retain in a state of invisibility the moisture that is diffused through both, the excess is necessarily condensed into cloud. The cloud itself is composed of particles or drops of water so extremely minute that they float in air. But if the condensation be pushed further, the minute drops coalesce into larger drops, and rain falls to the earth. On the other hand, if warm or dry currents of air happen to set in through the cloud, it will be again more or less completely dissolved, as was observed in the case of the vapor puffed out of the engine-funnel. Hence the continual changes going on in clouds — their thinning, thickening, enlargement, diminution, and the other alterations of form.

Waters above the Firmament.

The atmosphere owes its moisture to the evaporation going on at all temperatures both from land and water, and more especially from the great equatorial oceans of the globe. In temperate climates, like that of Europe, with a mean temperature of $52\frac{1}{4}°$, the annual evaporation is equal to a layer of water 37 inches thick; but within the tropics it is much greater, varying from 80 to 100 inches. The great stimulator of evaporation is the sun, and clouds check evaporation by intercepting his rays. A calm is less favorable to it than a breeze; in the former, the air resting on the water soon gets saturated, and ceases to absorb; but a breeze sweeping over the sea is continually presenting to it new and thirsty portions of air, so that the process goes on with great activity. The water thus sucked up is carried off into the atmosphere as invisible vapor or steam, which is ultimately condensed into clouds. These may be considered as huge aërial tanks or reservoirs filled with water handed up by the ever-busy air for the service of the earth. When clouds are not condensed in one place, the loaded air passes on with its burden to another; but sooner or later it is relieved either by the vanishing of the vapor through reabsorption, or by the formation of rain. Clouds may, in some degree, be regarded as regulators of atmospheric moisture, withdrawing it when in excess, and yielding it back when moisture is needed.

Besides supplying all the rain and filling all the rivers of the earth, the invisible moisture of the air is essential to the well-being both of animal and vegetable life. Were the thirsty air not abundantly fed with water from sea and land, it would in its eager search for drink suck out the moisture from every living thing, and in spite of all precautions we should soon pass into the condition of dried-up mummies. Our safety lies in the free admixture of water with the air, by which its keenness is tempered. Nevertheless it is astonishing to mark what care Nature has taken to protect the juices of plants and animals from this desiccating action, by investing them with coverings which are more or less impermeable.

In respiration the lungs cannot support an air which is too dry. When the supply of invisible vapor in a room is deficient, unpleasant sensations arise which are relieved by softening the air with steam from hot water. While wintering beyond Smith's Sound, Doctor Kane observed that his crew suffered from the excessive dryness of the air which, in breathing, was sensibly pungent and acrid. Nor is the invisible atmospheric vapor less necessary to the vegetable kingdom. Plants have the power of absorbing moisture not only by the roots but also through their leaves; and, in a fairly humid air, the evaporation going on from their surface is thus more or less checked or compensated. But in a too dry air this balance is upset, and the leaves droop or wither. The few plants that grow in the sandy desert are mainly dependent on the invisible moisture of the atmosphere for their supply of water, and the same may be said of those plants which live and grow when suspended in the air of a hot-house.

From the remarks just made it will be readily understood that clouds or wind coming from the north do not usually portend rain. The air, in passing southward, has its temperature gradually elevated; and, consequently, its power to hold vapor in an invisible state is being constantly augmented. Hence, not only is there no rain, but the clouds themselves are often seized upon by the dry air and dissolved. But a south wind, on the contrary, comes loaded with the vapor which it sucked up when its temperature was comparatively high, and its capacity for carrying invisible moisture great. In travelling northward it gradually cools, and the excess of moisture which it can no longer hold is condensed into clouds and rain.

Clouds are habitually less noticed than they deserve to be, and the pleasure which their contemplation is so well calculated to afford is too often lost from neglect. On fitting occasions cloud-gazing is no unworthy distraction wherewith to occupy a few of the fragments of time; and it belongs to those enjoyments which are all the more valuable because they so often lie within our reach. There is solid pleasure in letting our eyes lead fancy away among the mazes of cloudland. What endless variety of form! The cirrhoid groups — how light, feathery, placid, gentle, and cheery! The bulky cumulus — stately, sombre, threatening! What is there grand in Nature or in imagination which is not to be found among them? There are mountains and rocks, peaks and precipices, of which the aiguilles and domes of the Alps are but pigmy models, castles and cities, torrents and waterfalls! Imagination itself is beggared. Beautiful shapes float before our eyes for which we strive in vain to find a name. Under our gaze they melt, and change, and recombine, as if to show the limitless fancy of exuberant Nature. What colors! — the softest, the gravest, the richest, the brightest — hues of lead, copper, silver, and gold — all on a scale which mocks the rest of Nature's painting. What masses and magnitudes! Mounds of vapor, built up out of specky fragments, and rolled up the vault of the firmament by the power of the sun. In repose clouds are the emblem of majesty, but, driven before the gale, they are the symbol of force that is irresistible. "His strength is in the clouds!" When the vapory masses are burnished by the rays of the setting sun, we feel that the Psalmist, in calling them the "chariot of the Lord," has chosen for his metaphor the most gorgeous object that was to be found within the wide limits of the universe.

Thy mercy, O Lord, reacheth unto the Heavens, — and Thy faithfulness unto the Clouds. — Ps. xxxvi.

LIGHTNING AND CLOUDS.

O ye Lightnings and Clouds, bless ye the Lord: praise Him, and magnify Him for ever.

LIKE other natural forces, lightning might with propriety have been considered among the "Powers of the Lord;" but, from its being specially invoked, in conjunction with clouds, in a separate verse, we are reminded of the great part it plays in warm climates, and of the beneficent office it performs. Lightning, or Electricity, is believed to be a form of heat; but, whether it be essentially convertible into and identical with other great powers of motion, such as chemical force and life, we need not here discuss. The prevailing theory respecting its nature — one which at least harmonizes well with most of the phenomena it presents — is that electricity is of two kinds, positive and negative; and that these fluids always attract each other in order to establish an equilibrium. On the other hand, when bodies are charged with the same kind of electricity — whether this be positive or negative — they repel each other. When a certain amount of the one kind of fluid passes toward the other, it is attended with a flash of light which is termed the electric spark.

We have yet much to learn respecting the work done by electricity in the economy of Nature; but, both from its universal diffusion and from the provision made for its production, we may safely assume that the part it plays is most important to the welfare of the world. It certainly exercises great influence in meteorological phenomena —

as in the condensation of clouds and rain, the production of currents and storms and the aurora borealis — as well as in regard to the general sanitary condition of the atmosphere. We know how much our health and the comfort of our feelings are affected, even in this country, by the electrical state of the atmosphere; but we can form only a faint idea of the intensity of the inconvenience caused in hot climates where lightning is more common. The thunder-storm, notwithstanding the danger occasionally attending it, is there welcomed as a blessing sent to clear and purify the air, and restore it to its wonted salubrity.

The earth is the great reservoir of electricity, and its surface may be considered as a vast electrical apparatus on which the fluid is being constantly developed. When we desire by artificial means to exhibit the presence of electricity, we usually rub glass or sealing-wax with a silk handkerchief, or we cause a plate of glass to revolve rapidly and rub itself against a piece of silk, as in the common electrical machine. So, likewise, in the grand machine of Nature, the air is constantly generating electricity as it sweeps or rubs over the earth's surface, and the fluid thus evolved passes back into the earth or into the atmosphere.

The fluid passing into the air may accumulate unduly; and the balance between the atmosphere and the earth being upset, Nature steps in and takes means to restore the equilibrium. With this intent, copious rains charged with electricity sometimes draw off the excess to the great reservoir; but when the case is beyond this mode of relief, the firmament is filled with thunder-clouds from which dart the sparks that flash toward the earth. The same kind of action happens when neighboring clouds are differently charged, and the balance is restored by the passage of electricity from one to the other, as shown in the vivid sheet-lightning.

There are some substances — such as metals and water

— that are called "good conductors," because electricity passes easily through them; and there are other substances — such as glass or dry air — that are called "bad conductors," because electricity passes through them with difficulty. In running off through the former the fluid seems gentle and manageable; but in forcing a passage through the latter it tears and destroys. Thus the wire which conducts into the earth the discharge of an electric machine may be held safely in the hand. The fluid will pursue its easy course through the wire to the ground, and will not turn aside to enter the hand and give a shock to the body by forcing its way through so bad a conductor. On this simple fact depends the principle of the lightning-rod. In its flight toward the earth the lightning will avoid a bad conductor, and select a good one, if it is to be had; and thus it will spare the house or the tower so long as there is a sufficient iron rod attached through which it may descend to the earth. In this way the electric discharge, which would have shattered the "bad conducting" tower, glides easily, gently, and safely past it into the ground. Formerly people dreaded to enter a smith's forge during a thunder-storm; but now, being better informed, they wisely direct their steps toward it, well knowing that they cannot be in a safer position than when surrounded by masses of iron, that is, with good conductors in contact with the ground.

As there are comparatively few places which can be artificially protected by lightning-rods, Providence, ever wise and kind, has made various natural arrangements to diminish the danger by which we should otherwise be surrounded during every thunder-storm. Thus it so happens that water, whether in the form of liquid or of vapor, promotes the conducting qualities of bodies. How fitly, therefore, in this hymn has lightning been associated with clouds! Out of the clouds comes the danger, — out of the clouds, too, comes the water which helps to avert it from us. Dry air is a bad conductor, and favors undue electrical accumulations; but moist air is a good conductor, and drains the fluid harmlessly from the atmosphere. Each big, round drop of rain, as it falls, becomes freighted with some of the superabundant electricity, and carries it off in safety to the earth. The falling torrent, moreover, soaks house and tower, tree and shrub, coats and other vestments, and thus adds to the facility with which they conduct the fluid harmlessly from the air. If caught, therefore, in a thunder-storm and drenched to the skin, let us console ourselves with the thought that we are thus much safer than we were a few minutes before when our clothes were dry.

These means of safety apply chiefly to the thunder-storm itself — to the time when, an undue accumulation having occurred, the balance must be redressed even at the cost of danger. But Providence has not forgotten to take precautions by which undue accumulation, though not absolutely prevented, is at least rendered infinitely more rare than it otherwise would be had no such arrangement existed. The world is, in point of fact, studded all over with safeguards against disturbance in the electric equilibrium between the atmosphere and the earth. On this subject a recent writer has well observed that "God has made a harmless conductor in every pointed leaf, every twig, every blade of grass. It is said that a common blade of grass, pointed with Nature's workmanship, is three times as effectual as the finest cambric needle, and a single twig is far more efficient than the metallic points of the best constructed rod. What then must be the agency of a single forest in disarming the forces of the storms of their terrors? — while the same Almighty hand has made rain-drops and snow-flakes to be conductors, bridges for the lightning in the clouds, alike, it seems, proclaiming the mercy and the majesty of the Almighty hand."

The Three Children knew well the gladness with which,

toward the end of September, the lightning was welcomed in their beloved Judea. "He maketh lightning for rain," exactly expressed the message which it brought from the sky. It indicated that the rule of the scorching sun was drawing to an end, and that the "early rains" were about to fall and refresh the earth, and prepare it for the seed. The practically small danger that might attend the flash was forgotten in the paramount blessing of which it was the harbinger. Yet it must be confessed that, notwithstanding the conviction of its utility, feelings allied to dread attend the explosions of the lightning-cloud; and nothing else in Nature brings so home to our minds the conviction that we live in the midst of peril. After every precaution for safety has been taken, what can preserve us from the fatal flash but the ever-vigilant hand of God? Lightning seems to be the very type of those messengers of "sudden death" from which we pray the Good Lord to deliver us. The close air that precedes the storm stifles and depresses. Dumb creatures stand anxiously about, utter their cries of fear, and seem to recognize instinctively that the forces of Nature are in conflict. The clouds advance, roll up together, and thicken into lurid masses. The sun is walled out from the earth, and something less dark but more oppressive than the night lies heavily upon us. The dart we see cleaving through the blackness is winged with destruction; its course is wild and uncertain, its stroke is sudden, the death it deals is instantaneous. The sounding of the thunder is awful. From its lowest mutterings, scarcely breaking on the ear from afar, up to its loudest crash it is ever portentous, and no human heart can listen to it without emotion. The voice speaks to all, and it brings a double message: — it tells us that death is in the air; but it also recalls to us the thought that our lives are in God's keeping, without whose will the lightning cannot hurt us.

> Nevertheless, though I am sometimes afraid, yet put I my trust in Thee. — Ps. lvi.

SHOWERS AND DEW.

O ye Showers, and Dew, bless ye the Lord: praise Him, and magnify Him for ever.

THE prominence given in this hymn to water in all its forms is very remarkable, but is easily understood when we recollect that the Three Hebrews were chiefly familiar with "seasonal" countries. Such districts are strikingly and visibly dependent on the timely supply of Dew, Rain, and River water, to preserve them from the effects of the excessive droughts which usually set in at certain periods of the year. We read in Scripture of the "early" and the "latter" rain. The early or, as it was sometimes called, the "former" rain began to be abundant in October, and continued to fall more or less until Christmas. It then either ceased altogether, or became very moderate until spring, when it once more poured down copiously as the "latter" rain. The husbandman profited by the first of these periods to sow the seed which was to germinate and stand the winter; while the time that followed the "latter" rain was equally favorable to the rapid growth and ripening of the harvest. If few showers fell at those seasons, the hopes of the husbandman for a good crop were sure to be disappointed, for then, as now, little or no rain was to be expected during the summer.

There are few natural objects more frequently used as symbols in Scripture than rain and dew, and they invariably represent what is good and beneficent. The most blessed of all events — the coming of the Saviour, is thus foreshadowed by the Psalmist,—"He shall come down like rain upon the mown grass; as showers that water the earth." On various occasions rain represents the Creator's benignity toward man; while the force of the expression in Deuteronomy, chap. 32, "My doctrine shall drop as the rain," is derived from its enriching and life-giving virtue.

Besides bestowing fertility on the soil, rain cleanses and purifies both the land and the atmosphere. From the latter it often safely conducts the electricity which is accumulating unduly, and by thus restoring the equilibrium between the air and the earth renders the thunder-storm unnecessary. Rain also relieves the air of some of its superfluous carbonic acid, which it hands down to the rootlets of the plants; and, by means of its admixture with this acid, the surface water is enabled to take up a certain quantity of lime, which it transports down rill and river into the sea to furnish myriads of creatures with materials out of which to build their shells. Rain sweeps down into the plains the weather-worn particles of rock which are to form new soil; and, while it washes the surface of mountain and valley, street and house, it increases the general salubrity by clearing off the minute rubbish of the world.

When we consider the enormous volume of water which every year is rolled down into the sea by the rivers and rivulets of the earth, it is not to be wondered at that the annual rainfall which feeds them should be computed to have a bulk equal to 186,240 cubic imperial miles. If spread equally over the land of the globe — 50 million square miles — this rain would cover it with water to a depth of three feet. All this huge mass of water comes originally from the ocean, whence it is lifted up into the atmosphere by the agency of evaporation; and as the southern hemisphere has a water-surface of 75 millions of miles, while that of the northern is only 25 millions, it follows that there is a much greater quantity sucked up on

Showers and Dew.

the south than on the north side of the Equator. As it is chiefly for the sake of the land that rain may be said to fall, and as the land so greatly predominates in the northern hemisphere, it might at first sight appear that Nature had for once committed a blunder in thus making the greatest provision for rain in that hemisphere where, from the comparative scarcity of land, the smallest supply is needed. But on looking more closely we shall see that every thing is harmonized through one of those marvelous adjustments by which the whole economy of the universe is characterized.

A supply of water greater than what is locally required being thus drawn up into the atmosphere lying over the Southern Ocean, the problem is how to convey it into the northern hemisphere, where the chief masses of land lie, and where more rain is needed than can be obtained by evaporation? The machinery used in this gigantic task is found in the great atmospheric currents, which, though subject to occasional disturbance, do yet in the main act with perfect regularity. The chief evaporation from the Southern Ocean takes place when the sun is to the south of the Equator, and therefore when winter reigns in the northern hemisphere. At this season, the cold in high northern latitudes is most intense, and the heavy air has naturally its greatest tendency to pass toward the Equator. The air thus displaced over the Southern Ocean rises, charged with heat and moisture, into the upper regions of the atmosphere, and there forms a current whose general direction is northward, or contrary to the polar current beneath it. By this circulation of currents not only is the equilibrium of the air itself maintained, but a most necessary distribution of water and heat is likewise effected. One part of the globe which has an abundance is made to give to another part the supplies that are naturally wanted. Thus we can fancy the atmosphere to be a mighty ship indefatigably carrying on the beneficent commerce of Nature. Setting out from the bleak north, she sweeps round the earth to the regions of the south, refreshing them with cool, dry air; and then, having laid in her cargo of heat and moisture, she starts without delay upon her return voyage, dispensing as she goes the blessings of warmth and rain.

The cause of this regular precipitation may be readily understood by what has been said in regard to clouds. The tropical air, as it travels north, becomes colder and colder, and therefore its capacity to hold moisture becomes less and less. Hence it is forced at every stage to let go, in the shape of clouds and rain, the excess of moisture which it can no longer hold in solution; and as every drop of rain, on being condensed from invisible vapor or steam, gives out as much latent heat as would raise by one degree Fahrenheit the temperature of 1030 drops of water, a powerful influence in moderating the rigor of northern climates is exerted. The last remnants of moisture are squeezed from the air by the hard grip of the polar regions, where, as snow or ice, it adds to the desolation of those high latitudes. To any one contemplating the great arctic glaciers it must be curious to think, that much of the water there piled up in ice has been sucked up amid the warmth and sunshine of the distant Southern Ocean. The quantity of water thus carried and of heat thus diffused by the agency of the atmosphere almost exceeds belief, and ranks the operation among the greatest of those physical contrivances by which the welfare of the world is maintained. Wonderful Power of the air — working day and night, noiselessly, invisibly — mighty link in the water-circulation of the globe — "dropping fatness" over the earth, and with unerring instinct giving to it from year to year the exact supply that is needful.

In tropical countries, where a hot temperature prevails, a proportionately large allowance of rain is needed for vegetation. Notwithstanding the liberal supplies sent off toward north and south, enough is provided through the great capacity possessed by warm air for holding invisible vapor in suspension; and, when rain does occur, the quantity of water condensed is larger and the downpour heavier than in climates lying beyond. From this cause the annual rainfall also is usually much greater. By way of comparison it may be stated, that while the average rainfall of Great Britain is nearly 28 inches, that of the Equator, according to Humboldt, is 96 inches. In some parts of South America and elsewhere this amount is greatly exceeded. At Maranhao, in Brazil, the rainfall has been estimated at $280\frac{3}{4}$ inches. At Cherraponjie, in India, the enormous quantity of $605\frac{1}{4}$ inches have been known to fall during the southwest monsoon, which gives to this place the distinction of probably having one of the wettest climates in the world.

Within the tropics the year is divided into the dry and the rainy seasons. The dry corresponds to the winter of higher latitudes, during which plants take their annual rest. In the rainy season showers and sunshine alternate, and vegetable life is stimulated into its most luxuriant growth. The vegetation of warm countries, being habituated to abundant moisture, feels with corresponding severity any material diminution in the supply. Thus, at Bombay, the annual average rainfall may be taken at 80 inches; but in 1824 not more than 34 inches fell — an amount not differing much from our own yearly supply — and the consequences were direful famine and pestilence.

He whose lot has been cast in a temperate climate, where showers and sunshine chase each other throughout the year, can hardly realize the eagerness with which the return of the rain is longed for in seasonal regions. Listen to "old Indians" describing the anxiety with which they have watched for the coming of the monsoon, and the ecstacy with which they have hailed its arrival. Some friends may be gathered together within doors — languid, drooping, and spiritless. The drought of the preceding dry months has almost desiccated them. Every exertion is a trouble and thinking a fatigue; every thing around pants and fades. Suddenly — not the sound, but — the smell of the coming flood is sniffed in the air. Eyes brighten, muscles begin to be braced, the brain resumes its energy, and in a few minutes afterward — splash and patter — the rain is once more dashing to the ground. Tanks, buckets, jugs — any thing that will hold it — are spread out to be filled with the precious element. Not many hours elapse before the parched earth responds, as if by magic, to the blessing, and with renewed vigor clothes itself in green.

Some of the districts inhabited by our cousins in Australia are liable to suffer from extreme drought, when the river-courses dry up and the herds run the risk of perishing. In many places it would seem as if Providence had designedly mitigated this climatic evil by means of the deep hollows or wells which occur so frequently in the course of the streams. Thus the general bed may be dry, but these natural tanks continue to hold a supply of water; and, as if still more plainly to indicate their beneficent design, the surface of the reservoir itself often becomes covered with a thick coating of vegetation, which, by interposing a screen between the water and the sun, tends to prevent loss by evaporation.

Rain is so linked with fertility as almost to be synonymous with it, and where none falls there the desert must be. The exceptions to this rule are rare, and even these are seeming rather than real. Thus Egypt may be described as a rainless country; but the inundation of the Nile stands in the place of rain, and, in covering the land with its rich waters, deposits a soil of surpassing fertility Egypt could no more be fertile without water than other countries, and of this the proof lies close at hand, for immediately beyond the line of inundation the desert begins. The rains which enrich Egypt actually fall in Abyssinia, whence they are conveyed by the Nile as if by a channel of irrigation. The great deserts of the world are emphatically the rainless districts, and they stretch in an almost continuous belt across the centre of the old world. Beginning to the south of Morocco, not far from the Atlantic, they traverse wide regions lying beyond Algiers and Tunis; they next cross Egypt into Arabia; and thence passing onward through Asia by the great deserts of Tartary, Thibet, and Mongolia, they cease not until they have almost touched the shores of the Pacific. The moisture originally existing in the winds which blew from the sea toward these deserts has either been expended before the winds reached them; or, if a portion of the moisture still remain in the atmosphere, it is from local heat and dryness carried across their surface without precipitation. Let us take the desert lying to the north of the Himalayas as an illustration. During the winter half of the year the prevailing wind blows from the north and east. Being cold, it has little "capacity" for moisture; in other words, it is a dry wind; and as it travels south and gets warmer, its tendency is rather to absorb moisture from the sand than to let it fall. During the summer half of the year, on the other hand, the prevailing wind is from the southwest. Loaded with vapor gathered from the Indian Ocean, it sweeps over Hindostan, dropping rain abundantly in its course; and then, in crossing over the snowy ridges of the Himalayas, most of the remaining water is condensed out of it; — the monsoon sponge has been squeezed nearly dry. In this state it descends upon the plains of the desert; where the sand, heated as in an oven by the summer's sun, is not in a condition to draw down the remnants of moisture still existing in the air, and so they pass onward to the north. Thus no "fatness" is dropped upon those sands, which are surely doomed to barrenness so long as the present cosmical arrangements continue.

How many there are who thoughtlessly cry out against the climate of this favored land, and forget to weigh its many advantages against its few drawbacks. In regard to heat and moisture, it may be said with truth, that we are equally removed from extremes. We neither bake in the sun nearly all the year round, like the children of the desert; nor are we drenched in ever-falling rain, like the Indians of western Patagonia; neither are we dried up for one half of the year, and soaked in rain during the other, like the people of many tropical countries. With us, on the whole, rain and sunshine are well balanced; while the frequent changes enhance our perception of the beauty and the services of both. To our frequent, but seldom persistent, rains we owe it that nowhere is verdure finer, and that in few places is it less exposed to the destructive influences of extreme drought. Even in gloomy winter, when rain sometimes falls more abundantly than is consistent with comfort, there is consolation in the thought that the rain which descends at that season of the year, escaping the devouring rays of the sun, will sink deeply into the soil and fill the ample reservoirs of the earth with water. Thence, in the coming days of the hot summer, it will issue bright and sparkling to feed the springs and rivulets that glisten over the land and delight us with their freshness.

Dew may be considered as a kind of supplemental rain, depending on the same cause, namely, a condensation of moisture from the atmosphere. There is, however, this difference between them, that, while rain is formed at a greater or less height in the air, dew is formed on the surface of the ground.

We need scarcely remind the reader that air — even the dryest — always contains invisible vapor. During the day the earth and the air correspond sufficiently in temperature to prevent precipitation. But as the sun begins to set, the earth, losing its heat by radiation, suddenly cools, and condenses out of the air in contact with it a portion of its invisible vapor. Hence the night dew. After dawn the returning sun, by again warming the air, enables it to take up moisture; and then the land, having still the coldness of night upon it, immediately condenses this vapor into water. Hence the morning dew.

Whatever favors the rapid cooling of the earth's surface promotes the formation of dew. In cloudy weather heat is radiated as usual from the earth after sunset, but it is intercepted by the clouds, and radiated back toward the earth. The temperature of the latter, therefore, does not fall so much, and little dew is formed. But in clear weather the earth rapidly radiates its heat into space, and there are no clouds interposed to radiate it back. Hence the earth cools quickly and much dew falls.

When gardeners cover up their plants on bright evenings they act in accordance with scientific principles. The matting prevents radiation from the earth; or, rather, the matting takes the place of clouds, and gives back to the earth much of the heat it receives. In this manner the atmosphere round the plants retains an equable temperature.

Dew is twice specially introduced into the Benedicite, from which we may infer the extreme importance attached to it in the countries with which the Three Children were familiar. In most parts of western Asia little rain falls from April to September, and during this long period of drought the earth is dependent upon dew for the scanty supply of moisture it receives. How providential that, by the ordination of the All-wise Creator, dew should be most abundant precisely at that season of the year when the supply of moisture from other sources is most apt to fail. Scripture abounds in allusions to dew which, like rain, is always associated with what is good and beneficent. The "dews of Hermon" blessed the land where they fell, and the prosperity they brought passed into a proverb. When a patriarch wished to bestow his blessing, he prayed that "God might give of the dews of heaven;" on the other hand, there could be no more withering curse than what was implied in their withdrawal. "Ye mountains of Gilboa, let there be no dew, neither let there be rain upon you."

Although the quantity of water which is annually deposited as dew in this country is small in comparison to the rainfall, still it is by no means inconsiderable. Dr. Dalton has estimated it at five inches, or more than 22 billions of tons of water. In our moist climate it is naturally of less importance than in Syria or Mesopotamia; nevertheless it is extremely serviceable, and in autumn, more especially, the grass would often wither were it not for its daily steeping in dew.

From what has been said it will be perceived that, though we commonly speak of dew "drops," dew does not really "drop" from the sky, but forms upon the surfaces where it is found. Yet which of us would consent to surrender an expression that has been endeared to us by familiar associations since childhood? Dew "drops" create for us the most perfect diamond-gardens in the world. Well may they challenge not a lenient but a rigorous comparison with their rivals. No diamonds could be brighter, more sparkling, or play more fancifully with the rainbow colors of light. How incomparably finer, too, the setting! The rare and costly mineral is mostly to be seen in the worn atmosphere of crowded rooms, and, like an artificial beauty, requires the skillful hand for its display. Its brightness pales before the light of day, and needs the garish lamp to stimulate its sparkling. But the diamonds of the garden or the meadow are perfect from Nature's hand. They are set with boundless profusion on a ground of choicest green, and no art can improve their new-born loveliness. They are to be seen only in the fresh air of the morn, and the light that suits them best is the pure light of heaven.

Thou, O God sentest a gracious rain upon thine inheritance, and refreshedst it when it was weary. — Ps. lxviii.

WELLS.

O ye Wells, bless ye the Lord: praise Him, and magnify Him for ever.

IN a song of thankfulness and praise uttered by children of the East to the Giver of blessings, it was to be expected that the " springing wells " of the earth would not be forgotten. Almost always the comfort, and sometimes even the existence of whole communities are there dependent on them. In many districts of southwestern Asia rain is scarcely seen from April to September. The " latter rains " which fell in spring have run off, or been absorbed, or evaporated, and the land, thirsty and parched, gathers only its precarious supply of dew. The smaller streams and rivulets are dry also, and the people must then depend on such supplies as wells can afford for all the purposes of the household. Hence the prevalence of wells and fountains in the East. In the towns most of the fountains are public; other wells are private property, from which considerable profit is derived by the sale of water in dry seasons.

He who dwells amid the civilization of the West can scarcely realize the thankfulness with which wells inspire the mind of the Oriental. In the sandy deserts they are of the first necessity, forming as it were the stepping-stones by which travellers direct their route. Districts are named from their wells. Their geological history is often mysterious, but nothing can be more obvious than that they are providentially placed for the purpose of making those wastes passable. The overflow of the well sinks into the sand around, and illustrates in a very remarkable manner the fertilizing power of water. The *débris* of successive vegetations at length creates an oasis of richest soil — an island of verdant beauty in the midst of a sea of sand. The surface is softly carpeted with grass, while date-trees and other kinds of palms beckon the traveler toward it from afar, and shade him from the sun. What can be more natural than that the pious Arab should approach those wells with emotions of thankfulness, or that while quenching his thirst he should seldom omit to offer a prayer both for him who originally dug the well, and for the generous owner who permits it to be so freely used? It is said that, for the sake of the blessings thus daily poured upon his head, the proprietor of a well can seldom bring his mind to sell it, unless driven by dire necessity to make the sacrifice. To prevent loss by excessive evaporation, as well as choking up by drifting sand, wells in the East are usually kept covered, and so precious is the water that in many instances they are locked also. To poison a well is an act which is considered to be justified only by the extremity of warfare, while its complete destruction is thought to be little less than sacrilege. The well is universally held to be a special gift of God intended for all his thirsty creatures.

Holy Scripture abounds in allusions to wells, and nothing better illustrates the importance attached to them in the East from the earliest times than the narrative recorded in the 26th chapter of Genesis. Isaac, forced by famine to leave his country, dwelt in Gerar, and there "waxed great: for he had possession of flocks, and possession of herds, and great store of servants: and the Philistines envied him." Then Abimelech the king said unto Isaac, "Go from us; for thou art much mightier than we. And Isaac departed thence, and pitched his tent in the valley of Gerar, and dwelt there. And Isaac digged again the wells of water, which they had digged in the days of Abraham his father; for the Philistines had stopped them after the death of Abraham: and he called their names after the names by which his father had called them. And Isaac's servants digged in the valley, and found there a well of springing water. And the herdmen of Gerar did strive with Isaac's herdmen, saying, The water is ours: and he called the name of the well Esek; because they strove with him. And they digged another well, and strove for that also: and he called the name of it Sitnah," for it was associated with hatred. "And he removed from thence and digged another well; and for that they strove not." It was a contest between those who dug the well and the herdsmen who possessed the territorial right to the water. The possession of a well was the necessary complement to the other means of living, and so long as one could not be obtained the tribe was obliged to move onward.

The wells that form in the coral islands of the Pacific seem even more strikingly providential than those of the desert. Scarcely has the bare rock risen above the waves before it begins to possess its well of water. The salt ocean is without, and the salt ocean fills the lagoon usually included within, yet, on the mere rim of coral rock that lies between, fresh water is to be obtained when a hole is bored. So generally is this understood by sailors that they are in the habit of touching at these solitary spots to fill their tanks. Thus, in the creation of what is soon to be another island added to the fertile area of the world, wells of fresh water are the first provision for the higher forms of life which Nature produces. Whence comes this water? The general opinion is, that it freshens itself in filtering through from the ocean; but Darwin, after much attention to the subject, considers it to be the mere surface drainage of the island. In any case, the fact remains as a striking example of providential forethought in thus creating wells for the sake, not only of the traders who casually touch there, but also for the settlers who in process of time come to occupy the island.

Of the rain that drops from the clouds much is at once returned into the air by evaporation to keep up the supply of atmospheric moisture, while much also passes off as surface drainage, battling its way into the nearest brook. But after these demands have been satisfied, there still remains a third portion which sinks down into the porous earth, and commences by subterraneous routes its return homeward to the sea. Imagination longs to be able to follow the course of those mysterious wanderings, and to fill up the gap in the history of the spring which is seen bubbling up in the plain from the time when its constituent drops fell among the distant mountains. Through what curious scenery the source of the future river may have been creeping — among what rocks and caverns and windings in the secret paths of the earth — what miniature rapids it may form in regions too deep for human ken — now gliding gently along over rocky plateaus, now lingering among sands, or in the narrow slits of the strata! And thus the rill may journey on until, wearied with subterranean gloom, it regains the light of day as the useful well or gushing spring, nourishing the earth as it flows, and refreshing both man and beast with a constancy of supply which often contrasts with the fitful rainfall.

When it is desired to supply our towns with water we do not rest satisfied with converging upon them the contents of numerous rills by means of an ample conduit. During the hot summer days these sources might dry up, and the people might thus be left in want. So the danger is warded off by storing up water abundantly during the rainy season in a reservoir, from which supplies may be drawn for the town in times of drought. In this manner a liberal allowance of water is securely maintained independently of the vicissitudes of weather. Now in this arrangement we are only imitating the wise example of

Providence. The town which Nature has to supply is the whole earth. For this purpose the rainfall is undoubtedly her "main," and does the chief part of the work; but rain, though wonderfully regular on the whole, is sometimes capricious in single seasons, and oftener still in the different periods of a season. Something supplementary was, therefore, needed to husband and equalize the supply, and to provide for its regularity independently of the varying rainfall. So Nature formed reservoirs of water in the earth, which, taken on the whole, are subject to very little change. The superficial layers of the crust of the earth are in fact one vast storehouse of water, for moisture pervades them through and through. We habitually speak of "the dry rock;" but even the dryest rock contains water lodged in it as in a sponge, of which nothing less potent than the furnace can deprive it. "Some granites," says Professor Ansted, "in their ordinary state contain a pint and a half in every cubic foot." Limestone and marble find room for considerably more. Chalk is also highly absorbent, many of its strata being able to take up half their bulk of water without even appearing to be moist. Ordinary sandstones hold nearly a gallon in a cubic foot; and "in the best building-stones belonging to the sandstone group, from four to five pints of water are contained in each cubic foot of the stone." "The quantity of water capable of being held by common loose sea-sand amounts to at least two gallons in a cubic foot." But the great tanks of the earth are formed more especially by layers of sand, which everywhere alternate with the harder rocks. Into these the water is constantly soaking and accumulating for the supply of wells and springs all over the world. While rainy seasons fill these reservoirs, the dryest season does not exhaust them; and hence the springs in connection with them appear, like the conduits of a well-supplied town, to be independent both of rain and drought.

Wells.

Though limestone rocks absorb less than sandstone, they carry the water better; for they are more fissured, and their substance is more easily rubbed away or dissolved by the passing current. By this means, chiefly, have the famous caverns in the limestone rocks of Adelsberg, Derbyshire, and elsewhere been formed. Hence the subterranean rivers found in Styria and in various other parts of the world. No one who has visited the caves at Adelsberg can have forgotten how the Poik, there larger and swifter than the Mole where it joins the Thames, plunges amid the gloom into the tunneled mountain and is lost. Its course no one knows, but bits of wood and other pilot substances borne along in its mysterious wandering proclaim its identity with the Unz, which emerges as a full-formed river at Planina, ten miles beyond, on the other side of the mountain. At Cong in Ireland, famous for its Cross, there is another remarkable example of the same kind, where the river joining Loch Corrib and Loch Mask rushes through a subterranean channel in the limestone rocks. To this tendency in the limestone strata to fissure and separate into ledges which form underground passages we owe what are termed "swallows" in streams. Of these we have an example near London in the Mole, which partially "hides her diving flood" in traversing the picturesque vale of Mickleham; but a much more perfect instance occurs in the wolds of Yorkshire, not far from Malton.

In this moist climate of England a hole dug in the ground usually produces, at no great distance from the surface, a moderate supply of water from the superficial drainage; but such wells are, of course, much influenced by the season, and in periods of drought are apt to dry up altogether. By digging deeper, water-bearing strata are reached which are more abundantly supplied, as they represent the drainage of larger districts of country. If these districts lie no higher than the place where the well is sunk, the water will not rise so as to fill the shaft; but, on the other hand, if the water has flowed down from higher districts, it will, under certain circumstances, rise in the well to the surface, or even above it, to a height in proportion to the level where it originally fell. It is believed that the Egyptians and Chinese were practically acquainted with this fact at a very remote period, and the excavations that can still be traced attest how extensively they turned it to account. Of late years this mode of obtaining water has been largely adopted in Europe, and the name Artesian has been generally applied to these wells on account of the success which attended the earliest efforts made at Artois. Of all the wells of this kind the most famous is that of Grenelle, near Paris.

Geologically considered, Paris occupies a site very similar to that of London. The shaft at Grenelle, therefore, first pierced through layers of clay, gravels, and sands such as we are familiar with round our own metropolis, and then through the chalk, until it reached the underlying Green Sand. In the spongy strata of this formation vast quantities of water had accumulated by constantly draining down into it, as into a cistern, from extensive higher-lying districts beyond the chalk. The lateral pressure upon the water in this immense tank was therefore enormous. Its floor was formed of impervious clays or rocks, while it was shut in above by a thick lid of chalk. The moment the lid was tapped by the borer, up rushed the water as if through the pipe of a water-work, reaching not only to the surface but spouting into the air to the height of 120 feet. The supply was at the rate of a million gallons a day. There are many Artesian wells in London; but the water is obtained from the more superficial strata lying above the chalk; and as the water, therefore, does not in most cases rise nearly to the surface, it has to be aided or lifted up by supplemental pumps. Artesian wells are also common in Liverpool, in the new red sandstone;

at Cambridge, where the water-bearing strata lie under the gault; and in many other places.

Now and then it happens that Nature taps these high-pressure water-boxes for herself, and the stream rushes up through a "bore" of her own making with a force that projects it into the air. In the case of the famous Geysers in Iceland the projecting force, as pointed out by Sir C. Lyell, is due to the pressure of steam acting at intervals, somewhat in the same way in which the steam that accumulates under the lid of a kettle forces the boiling water with violence through the spout. Occasionally the force may be of a somewhat mixed kind, as in the case of the Sprudel at Carlsbad. Although the height to which that fountain spouts is not great, the gush of water is large; while the accessories of scenery are such as to produce one of the most beautiful and interesting sights to be found in Europe.

The water that sinks into the earth on higher levels, after collecting into tricklings, and wandering through chinks and over ledges, is ultimately turned by some impenetrable obstacle toward the surface, where it breaks forth as a sparkling fountain. In no fairer shape does Nature spread out her water-treasures before us. How refreshing the draught thus obtained at first hand! How cool in summer, how temperate in winter, for it comes from those deep regions of the earth which are equally shielded from sun and frost. What a difference there is between the tame water of the "main," and the living crystal of "the source." Such a spot is well worthy of a pilgrimage, and adds a fresh pleasure to the summer day's ramble. It is like repairing to a garden to eat fruit newly plucked by one's own hand from the tree. What sight more tempting when the sun is high. How pleasant to play with the clear water, and how difficult to pass before a gushing spring without lingering for a moment to listen and to look!

Springs sometimes partially tell the history of their own

wanderings when they assume the character of "mineral waters." The rain that has fallen often becomes charged with carbonic acid gas from the air, or from the vegetable soil through which it percolates, and, having thus acquired the power of dissolving the limestone or the chalk through which it has filtered, emerges into day as "hard" or calcareous water. Occasionally its route has lain among iron-freighted rocks, sands, or clays, and the ordinary strength-giving chalybeate of carbonated iron is prepared ready to our hands. Sometimes the water visits the secret laboratories of the earth, where chemical forces are at work on decomposing pyrites, from which it brings to us iron in a less common form, or in union with sulphuric acid. Or it may absorb the gases formed during these decompositions, and appear to us as the unsavory but useful sulphur well. Again, its course may lie among the salt-bearing strata of the earth, where the varying kinds of "saline mineral waters" are mixed by Nature herself to benefit mankind. Sometimes the subterranean streamlet may wander into those heated depths where chemical action is forging the materials of the earth into new shapes, or where the internal furnace of the globe imparts to the water a portion of its own warmth; and then the streamlet, turned in an opposite direction, may be urged toward the surface by pressure from below, until it bursts into the world as a "hot spring."

The water of springs and wells is never met with in a state of absolute purity, but the slight admixture of foreign substances usually present, while it does not impair general usefulness, is attended with certain special advantages. By distillation pure water can always be readily obtained, and it is then in its most active state. But this very condition, so essential to the chemist and the manufacturer, would diminish the utility of water for drinking and other domestic purposes. Water would then have been prone to dissolve many deleterious substances — such as lead — from contact with which it is difficult to guard it at all times, but on which, in its naturally impure state it cannot act. Another valuable "impurity" found in water is air, either fixed or common, by which it is rendered pleasant and sparkling as a beverage, while at the same time it acquires the important property of boiling without danger. When water has been carefully deprived of air, it may be heated up to 240° Fahrenheit before it begins to boil, but it is then apt to pass off suddenly into vapor with explosive violence. Let any one try to realize the inconvenience which so unmanageable a property would have introduced into the kitchen and the manufactory. We may here mark with admiration how different qualities, even to the most minute details, have been impressed on substances by the great Creator, with evident forethought for the comfort and happiness of His creatures.

In considering the fountains of the earth as blessings for which praise and thankfulness are specially due, we must not pass from the subject without more particularly alluding to those healing virtues with which some of them have been endowed. Mineral waters are of the most varied character; and there are, perhaps, few chronic forms of disease against which they may not be usefully employed at one stage or another. Providence, too, ever bountiful as kind, has scattered them profusely over most parts of the world, and thousands upon thousands annually owe to them the blessing of restored health. They are gifts from a source that lies beyond our ken, and modern science with all its progress cannot supersede them. We know to a nicety the constituents of the most famous springs; they have been analyzed and imitated most perfectly; but there is a point of difference between the real and the artificial which no art can seize. Nature is a cunning worker, and in her laboratory she compounds the "mineral water" under conditions of which we are ignorant, but from which, nevertheless, are derived special virtues which similar ingredients mixed artificially never acquire. Even in so simple a matter as the manufacture of hot water there is a difference; as all may have experienced who have contrasted the comparative pungency of a bath of artificially heated water with the softness of another that has been warmed in Nature's own boilers. It is a most singular circumstance that the ingredient to which many celebrated wells are believed to owe their chief efficacy is the virulent poison arsenic. Wiesbaden, Spa, and Kissingen contain that substance in union with iron, and it is also widely diffused in the waters of our own country. Thus may it be seen how skillfully Nature can administer the most active poisons for our advantage. The special virtue lies no doubt partially in the smallness of the dose and the accuracy of the compounding; but much may be due to those unknown conditions under which the mixture is prepared. It might have been expected that mineral waters, in passing among the beds whence they extract their components, would have varied materially by being sometimes strong and at another time weak. But although it is not to be denied that variations do occasionally occur, still it is found that substantially the same spring flows on with wonderfully little change from generation to generation. From this cause arises one chief reason of the safety of their administration and the uniformity of the results obtained from them.

In our own country* we have reason to be thankful for many famous wells, which, in a general way, may be considered efficacious for all purposes to which mineral waters are usually applied. Thus there are potent chalybeates at Tonbridge, Harrogate, and elsewhere. There are "salines" at Leamington, Cheltenham, Bridge of Allan, and in many other places. We have sulphur wells at Harrogate and Moffat, and hot springs at Bath, Clifton,

---

* England. The same may be said of the mineral springs of Saratoga and in Virginia.   E. J.

Matlock, and Buxton. In the olden time, when medicine was in its infancy, when no more skillful physician was to be found than the neighboring monk, and no better drugs than the simples that grew in the Abbey garden, our ancestors placed unbounded faith in wells, and there was not a county in the realm which could not boast of its famous spring. According to the custom of the time, every well was dedicated to the honor of some patron saint, and it may be affirmed that more than one name would perhaps have slipped out of the Calendar had it not been preserved in association with those springs. Pilgrimages of a mixed sanitary and religious character used to be made to wells of note, and it is curious to observe to how late a period the custom was kept up. Pennant tells us, that in his time pilgrimages to St. Winifred's Well, at Holywell in Flintshire, had not been entirely discontinued. "In summer," he says, "a few are still to be seen in the water in deep devotion, up to their chins for hours, sending up their prayers." How different the feelings with which gay spas, especially on the Continent, are visited in these days! Customs no doubt change. There is a time and a place for every thing, and the pump-room and the bath seem scarcely suited to religious meditation. Still it must be admitted that in principle, at least, our forefathers were in the right; and that their fervent thankfulness, even though shown under circumstances that might provoke a smile, was infinitely preferable to our frivolity. Surely the place where an invalid day by day is conscious of the blessing of returning health, ought above all others to be the place where the Giver of health should not be forgotten.

Like as the hart desireth the water-brooks; so longeth my soul after Thee, O God. — Ps. xlii.

SEAS AND FLOODS.

O ye Seas and Floods, bless ye the Lord: praise Him, and magnify Him for ever.

WHO is there that does not love to wander by the sea-shore? Its varying aspects have suggested to poets some of their finest thoughts; and, when they fail to inspire, they often lead on even ordinary minds to a point not far removed from the line where poetry begins. There are some subjects, indeed, which do a great deal for themselves, and from their own attractiveness are not easily spoiled even though handled clumsily. Thus the commonplace flights of fellow-strollers afford on such occasions a pleasure which their intrinsic merit does not explain; but sympathy is a powerful varnish which hides defects and stifles criticism. Poetical ideas, moreover, may lighten up the mind with their own beauty and be thoroughly felt and enjoyed, although, in struggling for outward expression, they cannot bring together the right words and often deviate into very common prose.

In strolling along the shore we find ourselves surrounded on all sides by objects to interest and admire. The cliff and the sands, the boulder rock and the pebbly beach — each has its charm. The ocean enhances beauty where beauty already exists; and it often creates beauty where, but for the charm which it bestows, there would be nothing to admire. On the open shore the air takes hold of us more bracingly than elsewhere; we realize more thoroughly the healthful consciousness of its presence; the drooping nerves are strung again into vigor, as if watered with its freshness. Here, as in other scenes, Nature has her characteristic sounds with which she regales the listener. The cry of the wildfowl is music to him especially whose path of life lies in the crowded city; and the murmur of the crisp ripple or the booming of the wave falls pleasingly on the ear. There is a world of plantal and animal life spread out before us, and we have only to look and to handle in order to be interested. How precious now are the scraps and fragments of Natural History which we can bring to bear. Nowhere is knowledge more enjoyment-bringing, for nowhere are the arrangements which God has made for the welfare of his humble creatures more conspicuous. How swiftly the time flies as we probe and peer into the clear lakelets that gather round the boulders on the sands or in the hollows of the rocks. The eye wanders delightedly among the many-colored tufts of algæ that clothe their coasts and depths. These miniature forests teem with varied life, and many a little creature finds in their recesses a secure retreat from cruel foes. Stealthily we draw near to those pools, seeking not to destroy but to admire, and feel well rewarded if we obtain but a glimpse of their inhabitants.

Not less pleasant is it to retreat step by step before the returning tide, to lose the dreary sands as they are again covered up in their mantle of water, and to watch the thousand eager streams rushing in from the sea among the rocks, and once more joining on to the boundless ocean the pools we have been surveying. What a change suddenly passes over the black and yellow seaweed! A moment before it lay dingy and motionless upon the rocks, but now, revived as it were into new life by the return of the sea, it begins to float and wave its pennons. The mussels and periwinkles, the limpets and the sea-acorns which, an instant before, were glued to the rocks as faded and dead-like as the stones themselves, now hear the rushing sound and welcome the returning water. In another minute these trusting waiters upon Providence will be opening their mouths to the currents which bring them their "daily bread," rasping their food from the tough seaweed with their file-like tongues, or raking in supplies with their handy tentacles. The ever-bountiful Sea will surely bring nourishment to them all — not one will be forgotten by Our Father.

> The eyes of all wait upon Thee, O Lord; and Thou givest them their meat in due season. — Ps. cxlv.

The lower depths of ocean are still a mystery, although of late years the diving-bell, the dredge, and the plummet have added much to our knowledge both of its bed and its inhabitants. In a general way its bed resembles the land — now rising into mountains, now sinking into valleys, or spreading out into table-lands. The deepest recesses below the level of the sea-surface are believed to be about equal to the height of the highest hills above it; but so inconsiderable is this depth in relation to the diameter of the earth, that a mere film of water laid upon a sixteen-inch globe with a camel's-hair pencil would adequately represent it. It is difficult to say at what depth life becomes extinct; but just as in ascending into the air on lofty mountains there is a limit beyond which nothing living can maintain itself, so in descending into the depths of ocean a stratum is reached below which life cannot exist. The life which we know has a frontier downward as well as upward. The floor of the Atlantic appears in some places to be a vast sepulchre, for at Telegraph-ridge it was found at a depth of two miles to be completely covered with calcareous and siliceous remains of microscopic animalcules. There the deposit may go on increasing and thickening, until, under the vast pressure of the overlying mass, the limestone strata of new continents have been founded. It need scarcely be said that modern observation has completely overturned the gloomy picture of the bottom of the ocean which fancy suggested to Shakespeare, but which, in the absence of all practical data, has stood its ground popularly almost up to the present time. Schleiden says that "we dive into the liquid crystal of the Indian Ocean, and it opens out to us the most wondrous enchantments of the fairy tales of our childhood's dreams." The Professor's description is too long for quotation here, but it introduces us to sub-marine scenery where " strangely branching thickets bear living flowers. The coloring surpasses every thing: vivid green alternates with brown or yellow: rich tints of purple, from pale red-brown to deepest blue." "There are Gorgonias with their yellow and lilac fans, perforated like trellis-work: leafy Flustras adhering to the coral branches like mosses and lichens: yellow, green, and purple-striped limpets resembling monstrous cochineal insects upon their trunks." " Like gigantic cactus-blossoms sparkling in the most ardent colors, the sea-anemones expand their crowns of tentacles upon the broken rocks, or more modestly embellish the flat bottom, looking as if they were beds of variegated Ranunculuses. Around the blossoms of the coral shrubs play the " humming-birds " of the ocean, little fish sparkling with red or blue metallic glitter, or gleaming in golden green, or with the brightest silvery lustre." The many-tinted phosphorescent lights of the ocean crown this gorgeous painting, and "complete the wonders of the enchanted night." "The most luxuriant vegetation of a tropical landscape," continues the Professor, " cannot unfold as great wealth of form, while in variety and splendor of color it would stand far behind this garden landscape, which is strangely composed exclusively of animals, and not of plants. Whatever is beautiful, wondrous, or uncommon in the great classes of fish and Echinoderms, jelly-fishes and polypes, and mollusks of all kinds, is crowded into the warm and crystal waters of the tropical ocean."

The abundance of animal life in the ocean greatly exceeds that on land. The sea affords a home for the largest of known animals as well as for the most minute: life teems everywhere. Scoresby once sailed through a patch of the Greenland Sea — 20,000 square miles in extent — covered with a species of medusa on which the whale feeds, and he calculated that every square mile contained 23 quadrillions 888 trillions of independent living creatures! He did his best, moreover, — we shall not pronounce with what success, — to bring the number contained in one of these miles within the range of our conception by saying, that "to count them would require 80,000 persons, and a period equal to the interval between the present and the creation." Yet it must be recollected that this was only the aggregate of life in one of the 20,000 square miles, and that the whole scene was but a mere fragment of the ocean. Such numbers are incomprehensible; but even viewing the statement as metaphorical it conveys a lofty idea of the profusion of marine life. In the coral polyp we have another example of a creature whose numbers equally baffle our conception. In many parts of the ocean, islands and reefs are now being constructed by countless myriads of these animals. Off the east coast of Australia there is a single coral reef a thousand miles long, and vast tracts of the Pacific are studded with islands of coral formation. Placed side by side with the productions of these pigmy laborers, our pyramids and breakwaters, and the most stupendous works reared by man, sink into utter insignificance.

It is noteworthy that amidst this richness of life the sea, like the land, has its deserts — "desolate regions," as they are termed by mariners — in which few signs of life in air or water are to be seen. In many maps such a region will be found laid down in the South Pacific, between Patagonia and New Zealand. Birds that have followed a ship for weeks together seem to recognize this blighted ocean-desert, and fall away as soon as they enter it.

The blue color of the sea is one of its chief attractions, and, as the intensity is greatest where the saline matters are most abundant, there would appear to be a close connection between the two conditions. Thus the water of the Gulf Stream, south of Newfoundland, is bluer than the fresher water beside which it flows, and the line of demarcation between them is so sharp as to be easily distinguished. "Off the coast of the Carolinas," says Maury, "you can see the bows of the vessel, as she enters the Gulf Stream, dashing the spray from those warm and blue waters, while the stern is still in the sea-green water of the Bank of Newfoundland." The "blue Mediterranean" has become a proverb, and the fact is explained by the circumstance that the sun, by causing enormous evaporation, strengthens the brine of its confined waters as in a salt-pan. On the other hand, seas that contain comparatively little salt, such as the German and Arctic Oceans, are of a green rather than a blue color. By this easy test it is said that manufacturers of salt sometimes judge of the richness of the water.

Navigators tell us of other colors which the sea exceptionally assumes. Thus there is a Yellow Sea, called so from the color of the sand, or mud; a White Sea, from the weakness of the saline solution; and a Red Sea, from slimy fuci cast up from the bottom of its bed. Near Terra del Fuego Darwin observed patches of a brown-red color, produced by prawn-like crustaceans floating in it. The sailors called them whale-food; and in truth, they appeared to be just the sort of banquet on which a whale would feast. Near the Galapagos Darwin also remarked that a film of floating spawn gave a dark yellowish or mud-like color to the sea; on another occasion the ocean was covered for miles with a coating that displayed iridescent colors. The sailors, who are often shrewd observers, attributed it "to the carcass of some whale floating at no great distance." A patch of white water, twenty-three miles in extent, was observed in the Indian Ocean. "In appearance," says Darwin, "it was like a plain of snow." "The scene was one of awful grandeur; the sea being turned to phosphorus, the heavens being hung in blackness, and the stars going out."

Phosphorescence is one of the most beautiful appearances presented by the sea. We sometimes fancy it to be very vivid upon our own coasts, but sailors nevertheless assure us that the light is pale in comparison to the brightness with which it shines in tropical regions. There are two forms in which it appears. In one, bright isolated specks are seen from the shining of star-fishes, annelids, medusæ, and various kinds of crustacea and mollusca. In the other, there is a diffused luminosity, often flashing into coruscations, which is produced by a profusion of microscopic animalcules. The phosphorescence of the Noctilucæ is sometimes beautifully seen while steaming along our coasts at night, as the water is dashed from the bows; but it is also very conspicuous when a glass vessel, filled with water containing them, is placed in the dark.

These creatures occupy one of the humblest positions in the animal scale. Yet, though they look like mere specks of animated jelly, they are by no means insensible to rough treatment, under which they shine with increasing light.

If all the salt in the sea were collected together it would cover the entire surface of Europe with a layer one mile in thickness. Whence comes this saltness of the sea, and what is its use? The first point is doubtful. The earth, it is true, contains vast stores of salt hidden away among its strata, and in the convulsions through which it has passed the salt might easily have been washed out into the sea. But on the other hand, the beds of salt found in the earth show unmistakably that they themselves have been deposited from water. Not improbably the sea was created salt, just as we now find it; and, from its almost unvarying constitution preserved amid causes tending to disturb the balance, it seems to retain by special ordinance the exact amount of saltness best adapted to the uses it has to fulfill. At first sight it might appear as if this saltness would detract from its utility, for there are few purposes to which it can be applied in comparison with those for which fresh water is suitable. But a little reflection will show us that, while there has been no stinting in our supplies of fresh water, the additional gift of salt water has added largely to our resources by properties peculiar to itself. It is thus fitted to be the habitation of countless tribes of fishes and other creatures which afford us most abundant and welcome supplies of food, and brings to every shore the means of obtaining salt, which is an essential element of healthy nourishment.

The ocean is "ever restless." There are interstitial movements between the drops themselves of which it is composed, and there is a grand circulation in the whole mass of water to which the term current is usually restricted.

The necessity for this circulation may be inferred from the care which Providence has taken to insure its efficient performance. Within the tropics the fierce sun is constantly skimming the surface of the sea, and creating a void that has to be filled up by the surrounding water. Among the most powerful agents of circulation is the moon, by whose attraction is raised the wave of the tide, which, setting out from one extremity of the ocean, traverses it unto the other. The willing atmosphere, seldom standing idly by when any of the grand operations of Nature are going forward, takes its share of the work, and by its trade-winds, monsoons, and other breezes helps on the good cause. Sometimes the wind churns the waves, as in the storm; at other times it drives them before it, and piles them up in confined bays, such as the Mexican Gulf, whence they fall down as a current across the neighboring sea, and thus restore the equilibrium. But the mainspring of the machinery is to be found in the ocean itself, which, by means of differences in its weight, or specific gravity, establishes the principal currents. In equatorial regions evaporation thickens the brine, and makes it dense and heavy. In the Polar Sea evaporation is checked by the cold, while melting snows and glaciers pour into it immense quantities of water during the summer, by which it is made fresh and light. There is thus at one end of the mobile mass a dense fluid, and at the other end a light one; and the necessary result is a circulation from the equator to the poles to displace the fresh water, and a counter-current from the poles to the equator to fill up the void which the dense water leaves behind it. Distance counts for nothing in such a chain, and when one link is moved all the other links must move also. By this means a thorough circulation is effected. On the one hand, the ocean is being continually poured into the polar seas; on the other, it is in an equal ratio emptied back into the regions of the tropics.

The proofs of this "greater circulation" are to be found in many places, but they are less conspicuous in the southern than in the northern hemisphere, on account of there being comparatively so little land between the tropics and the antarctic regions. The polar and equatorial streams are consequently more diffused than in the northern hemisphere, and their force, with few exceptions, is not so great. Toward the north, on the contrary, the channels of communication between the equatorial and polar seas are narrower, and the currents, therefore, are more distinctly marked. It is just the difference between a river whose strength is wasted by the width of its bed, and one whose waters being confined within a narrow channel rush impetuously along.

The surface of the ocean is thus mapped out into currents by the constancy of which the navigator profits. But besides these stronger streams there are others whose force is so gentle and diffused that their existence cannot be detected by the reckoning, and is only made known by the thermometer. In pursuing an eastward or westward course across the ocean, an alteration in the temperature tells where the water comes from. Thus, if the temperature increase, it may be inferred that there is a flow from the south; and if the water get colder, a northern origin is equally indicated.

The Gulf Stream is the most famous of all the currents that flow toward the north, and is in itself one of the most wonderful physical phenomena in the world. Its great historian, Maury, thus eloquently describes it:— "There is a river in the ocean. In the severest droughts it never fails, and in the mightiest floods it never overflows. Its banks and its bottom are of cold water, while its current is of warm. The Gulf of Mexico is its fountain, while its mouth is in the arctic seas. It is the Gulf Stream. There is in the world no other such majestic flow of waters. Its current is more rapid than the Mississippi or Amazon, and its volume more than a thousand times greater." Rushing past the point of Florida, it starts on its path across the Atlantic as a compact river sixty miles broad and three thousand feet deep, and at a pace of four or five miles an hour. Onward it streams in a northeasterly direction, spreading out its waters like a fan, until it approaches the Cornwall coast, the west of Ireland, and the Hebrides of Scotland. The great bulk of the still warm waters flows onward between the Shetlands and Iceland; and then, after laving the northern shores of Norway, the current is gradually lost in the Spitzbergen seas. Whether the waters of the Gulf Stream, still recognizable by their temperature, are destined to be rediscovered as an open, comparatively mild sea under the pole, surrounded by arctic deserts that lie outside the influence of this offshoot from the Sunny South, is a problem which the next few years will probably resolve.

Side by side with this warm northward-moving flood there is a great polar stream bearing down in an opposite direction, which appears to be more especially its compensatory current. It rises in the distant recesses of Baffin's Bay and the Greenland Sea, and then, studded with icebergs, sweeps along the Coast of Labrador, encircling the island of Newfoundland in its chill embrace. To the south of the Bank it encounters the Gulf Stream running northeastward; — the paths of the two giants cross each other, and they struggle for the right of way. Their hostile waters refuse to mingle, and each continues to retain its color and its temperature. But, though neither is vanquished, each leaves its mark upon the other. From the force of the shock the Gulf Stream for a moment falters in its course, and is deflected toward the south; while the polar current, unable to break through the concentrated mass by which it is opposed, dives under the bed of the mighty stream, and hastens on toward the tropics.

The higher latitudes of the Southern Ocean are even more numerously studded with drifting icebergs than the northern, from which, were other proofs wanting, we might safely infer the existence of currents analogous to those just described. The superficial polar currents are sometimes very baffling to navigators desirous of penetrating into high latitudes. One of them was carried — ship and all — a distance of 1200 miles upon the ice, as it drifted down the centre of Baffin's Bay. Captain Parry, too, found all his efforts to penetrate toward the pole counteracted by the circumstance that the distance traveled in sledges during the day was only equal to the southern drift of the whole mass of the ice during the night. Under this superficial polar current there is in some places, perhaps in all, a deeper current running in the opposite direction. Thus it has occasionally happened in Baffin's Bay, that while ships in calm weather have been drifting to the south on the superficial stream, large icebergs, whose bases must have sunk deep into the lower current, have been observed to move in the opposite direction.

These currents of the sea aid commerce, distribute seeds over widely distant regions, and sometimes afford abundant supplies of timber to countries destitute of forests. In this way the Icelanders are furnished from the woods bordering the rivers in Siberia. In high latitudes it is obviously important that the sea should remain free from ice as long as possible, both for the sake of commerce and because the Esquimaux find in it their chief stores of food. The saltness of the ocean helps to keep it open; for while fresh water freezes at 32 degrees, salt water remains fluid down to a temperature of about 28 degrees. But the polar seas, from the rains and melting of the ice, combined with the small evaporation going on in them, tend to become less salt; while, at the tropics, from the great loss of water by evaporation, the saltness tends to increase. The equatorial current, therefore, assists in keeping the Arctic Sea open by bringing to it supplies of stronger brine from the South.

By means of the great currents of the ocean another extremely important function is performed. One of the chief cosmical problems which Nature had to solve was how, on the one hand, to warm the North, and on the other to cool the South, to the degree best adapted for the development of life. For the regulation of the heat account between them Nature has employed the most powerful machinery that exists on the earth. We have already seen how heat, packed up in the vapor arising from southern seas, is borne along by the atmosphere to regions where it is wanted; and we now perceive that this machinery — vast as it is — requires to be supplemented by the heat conveyed toward the poles in the currents of the ocean. The means are marvelously great, yet not out of proportion to the magnitude of the work to be done. Pouillet and Herschel have estimated the daily amount of heat received by the earth from the sun as sufficient to raise the temperature of 7513 cubic miles of water from the freezing up to the boiling point, and of this heat equatorial regions receive a proportion which would be incompatible with life did not some contrivance exist for carrying off the excess. Owing to the preponderance of sea between the tropics, the ocean of course receives the largest share of this heat. It has a mean temperature of about 80°; while in the Caribbean Sea and in some other places the temperature rises nearly to blood-heat. Were the water not renewed in the Mexican Gulf, it would soon become destructive to life. To prevent this, Nature establishes currents by which some of the hot water is continually drawn off from the caldron, and an equal portion of cold water is continually let in. The operation may be compared to a kitchen boiler fed with cold water through one pipe, and from which a proportionate quantity of hot water escapes through another. The "main" that issues from this tap is the Gulf Stream, and, in order to form some idea of the service it renders, let us consider the amount of heat it carries along. As it leaves the caldron there is a mass of water, 60 miles broad by 3000 feet deep, with a maximum temperature of 86°; and before it is lost in the Polar Sea its temperature has fallen to nearly 32°. All the heat implied in this difference has been distributed by the way, and has been spent in improving the climate of the regions through which it passed. Maury calculates that the heat discharged over the Atlantic by the waters of the Gulf Stream in a winter's day would be sufficient to raise the whole atmosphere covering France and the British Islands from the freezing point up to summer heat; and in another place he says that it would be sufficient to keep in flow a molten stream of iron greater in volume than the Mississippi. There is "a Providence" even in the refusal of the giant streams to unite together off the coast of Newfoundland. By this designed separation "the heat and the cold" are carried better and further, and the object of the distribution is more perfectly attained. It is indeed remarkable how well heat and cold are thus conveyed. The cold polar current which we lost to the south of the Bank of Newfoundland, where it dipped under the bed of the Gulf Stream, could still be reached by deep soundings, and recognized by its temperature of 35°, while the "river" flowing above it was 80°. And by the same means it is again to be recognized among the West India Islands, with the cold label of its origin still attached to it. In those seas the temperature of the surface water may be 85°, while that of the deep water is 43°, or only 11° above the freezing point. There is another evidence of design about this wonderful stream which must not be passed over. Maury says, "Its banks and its bottom are of cold water;" and, indeed, this was essential, in order to make it a good hot-water pipe. Earth and rocks are better conductors of heat; and, consequently, if the banks and bottom had been constructed, as they usually are, of these materials, the Gulf Stream would have held its heat with a less tenacious grasp, and could not have carried it, as it now does, 3000 miles across the ocean to improve the climate of cold latitudes. At Newfoundland in winter-time the thermometer is often at zero, while within a good day's sail to the south may be enjoyed the genial climate of the Gulf Stream. Its influence in warming the winters of the British islands is shown by a comparison between their thermometric register and that of places situated on the same parallel of latitude on the other side of the Atlantic. When it reaches Hammerfest, near the northern extremity of Norway, and considerably within the arctic circle, its influence suffices to keep the harbor open in the severest seasons. It is even asserted that, in the ocean near Spitzbergen, water is occasionally to be met with in the track of the Gulf Stream which is only one degree colder than it is in the depths of the Caribbean Sea.

From this general outline some idea may be formed of the way in which God has made the ocean currents co-operate with other causes in equalizing temperature over the globe. By their means the heat which would otherwise accumulate at the tropics is carried toward the poles; while the cold which would oppress the polar regions is, if we may so express it, carried toward the equator. By this beautiful provision the climates of the world are improved; the bleak North is made less bleak than it otherwise would be, and the temperature of the over-heated South is kept within due bounds. In these islands, more especially, we have reason to bless God for the beneficence of an arrangement which softens the rigor of our climate, and gives to some parts of the kingdom a winter season which in temperature may compete with many in the south of Europe. Nor can any one who considers the vastness of these operations fail to perceive how much the Creator is praised and magnified both by the simplicity of the means employed, and the perfection with which the end is accomplished.

The great currents we have been considering form the main arteries and veins of the ocean; but there is also a constant interstitial movement and mixing going on among the particles themselves, which might by comparison be termed its capillary circulation. The dynamic force is derived from local changes in temperature or in the degree of saltness. Every beam of sunshine that falls upon the sea, by altering the specific gravity of the portion on which it falls, sets a current in motion to reëstablish the equilibrium. In like manner every kind of fish, and more especially every kind of shell-building creature that lives there, as soon as it has absorbed a particle of lime, silica, or other matter, alters the specific gravity of the atom of water whence the matter was extracted, and creates a minute current of denser water to restore the equilibrium. Plants which, like corallines, absorb lime act in the same way. The amount of each operation is infinitesimal, but the grand result is that a capillary circulation of minute currents is everywhere going on, by which the salubrity of the general mass of the ocean is maintained. How wonderful the simplicity of the means by which all this is accomplished. A grain more or a grain less of common salt contributes its share in keeping the ocean in healthy movement! Nor is it to be forgotten that the inhabitants of the sea, by withdrawing lime and silica, prevent these substances from unduly accumulating in its waters. For as all the rivers that fall into the sea are continually bringing saline matters into it, these would soon exist in hurtful excess if no arrangement had been made for their removal.

There are some inland seas of the highest value to mankind, which would ere this have degenerated by evaporation into pestilential swamps, had not the Great Architect insured their safety by establishing permanent currents of supply which flow into them from the ocean. The Mediterranean — one of the greatest water-highways of the world — may be cited as the most remarkable example. It is computed that the evaporation going on from its surface skims off no less than three times as much water as it receives from all its tributaries taken together, and it would, therefore, be inevitably dried up were it not fed with a corresponding equivalent of water from the Atlantic. Yet even this arrangement would not of itself suffice to obviate the threatened danger. It is evident that excessive evaporation, besides lowering the level of the surface, would also have the effect of concentrating the brine; and this would go on until, the point of saturation having been reached, layer after layer of salt would be precipitated to the bottom so as ultimately to fill up the entire bed. The purpose of the current from the Atlantic is to provide for the waste by evaporation, but being itself salt it does not tend materially to dilute the brine that remains. A sure remedy, however, is found in that law which governs the universe —

gravitation — and thus the saltness which caused the danger, brings also with it the means of safety. For as the deep water in the Mediterranean increases in saltness, it becomes heavier than the less salt water of the adjoining Atlantic, and consequently acquires a tendency to fall in upon and displace it, just as a portion of heavy air displaces a contiguous portion that is light. In this way a counter-current is established at the Straits of Gibraltar. The superficial current runs in from the Atlantic to maintain the level of the sea that has been lowered by excessive evaporation; and the deep current runs out from the Mediterranean to carry off that excess of salt which, if retained, would in the end convert its bed into an unhealthy swamp.

The Red Sea would have been even in a worse plight but for a similar arrangement. The sun beats so hotly upon it that its waters are often raised to a temperature of 90°; consequently, the evaporation is excessive. On the other hand, throughout its whole length of about 1200 miles not a single stream that can be called a river falls into it. But all is adjusted, and safety is secured by the existence of a double current at the Straits of Bab-el-Mandeb. That which is superficial brings an abundant supply of water from the Indian Ocean; that which is deep carries off the excess of salt from the Red Sea.

Another well-known sea — the Baltic — is in danger of losing its healthy amount of saltness from causes the reverse of those just mentioned; for while many rivers bring to it supplies of fresh water, it lies so far to the north that comparatively little is dissipated by evaporation. The brine is thus in danger of being over-diluted. The remedy, however, is found in a double current. By the superficial current, some of the brackish water is decanted off into the North Sea; by the deep, a supply of salt is brought from the North Sea into the Baltic.

The tidal floods which add so much to the interest of our sea-side strolls are also of the highest utility. Though little else than mere undulations without movement in the open sea — like those we admire in fields of "wavy corn" when agitated by the wind — tides are strong currents in the narrow seas and the rivers where they ebb and flow. Tides, therefore, facilitate commerce; and from their undeviating regularity enter as a certain element into the sailor's calculations. The wave of water thus sent up a river deepens its channel, and gives to many an inland town the advantages of a sea position. But for the tide, the miles of wharves which border the Thames at London would never have existed; and it is not too much to say that to its tide the metropolis owes its rank as the foremost commercial city in the world. At high water the channel at London Bridge is deepened to about 18 feet; while Bristol and Glasgow are even more dependent upon the tide than London. The Avon, at St. Vincent's Rocks, when the tide is at the lowest, would hardly swim a boat; but after it has received its forty feet flood it could float a man-of-war. At Glasgow there are persons living who recollect when the river could be waded across at low water. The height of tides varies extremely. Where there is nothing to confine them, as in the open ocean, they seldom rise above two or three feet; and the same effect happens if the direction of an inland sea lies out of the course of their flow, as in the Mediterranean. On the other hand, where a gradual contracting estuary, like the Bristol Channel, opens fairly to the flood, it sweeps in from the ocean with full volume, and being hemmed in more and more between converging shores it mounts higher and higher as it advances. Thus at Chepstow the tide occasionally attains an elevation of 50 feet. Still more extraordinary is the tide in the Bay of Fundy, on the east coast of New Brunswick, where a wave one hundred feet high is sometimes piled up by the flowing flood. This wall of water advances at such a pace that it often overtakes deer, swine, and other beasts feeding or rambling about the shore, and swallows them up. The swine, as they feed on the mussels at low water, are said to smell, or perhaps to hear, the "bore" while it is yet distant, and sometimes dash off at the top of their speed to the cliffs to avoid the coming danger.

There is something mysteriously melancholy in the first glance which the voyager unaccustomed to ocean life takes from the deck of his ship when it has borne him fairly "out of sight of land." With nothing visible around but sea and sky, he sees his ship a mere speck upon a trackless waste. Yet there is no hesitation among those who guide the noble bark which forges onward to its destined port. The "pathless" ocean is in fact a mere figure of speech, for its highways and by-ways have been surveyed and accurately mapped. On deck is to be seen the trusty compass, pointing out the course, like an attendant monitor, with a finger that never tires. Above, there are the sun, the moon, or the stars — beacons fixed high in the heavens — sign-posts that never deceive the mariner who has skill to read their writing. The accuracy of modern navigation is truly miraculous. Ships start on a voyage of 15,000 miles, say, from New York to California, during which they may not once see land, yet they strike the sought-for harbor as if the goal had been always before their eyes. The late Captain Basil Hall once sailed from San Blas, on the Mexican coast, round Cape Horn to Rio Janeiro. He was at sea three months, during which he saw neither land nor sail, yet he struck the harbor's mouth so exactly that he scarcely required to alter his course by a single point in order to enter it. Had God not provided for accurate navigation by means of astronomical signs, and had He not designedly endowed man with special faculties capable of understanding their import, commerce as it is now developed could never have existed; and there is not a nation on the earth which would not thereby have lost many of the comforts and blessings now brought to it. Through His beneficence the "pathless ocean" has become the world's greatest highway; and, instead of separating nations, it joins them together. It is easier now to reach the remotest corner of the globe by sea, than it is to penetrate into Siberia or Arabia, though these countries lie comparatively close at hand.

The sea is slightingly called the "unstable element," but in the permanence of its condition it is much more stable than *terra firma*. The land is in some places being heaved upward, in others it is sinking downward; but the level of the ocean never changes. Sometimes the sea is hastily identified with "treachery," but its currents are more trustworthy than the winds on land. True it is that, in obedience to the law of gravity, a ship sometimes sinks and a gallant crew perishes. But upon the upholding of this very law of gravity every other life in the world depends, and its suspension even for an instant would involve universal destruction. The sea sometimes bursts its bounds and desolates the dry land, or sweeps the useful pier into the deep, or destroys the light-house; but God has given us faculties and provided us with means to grapple with all these evils, and control even the ocean itself. Man's industry and skill again shut out the sea with stronger dykes, he builds a better pier, rears another light-house round which winds and waves dash in vain, and he plants the solid breakwater athwart the deep to create the safe harbor within. Thus some of man's greatest victories are won in his battles with the sea. Modern skill in building and in navigating ships has reduced the dangers of the sea at least to a level with those of the land, and has in most cases made ocean disaster synonymous with ignorance or want of care.

The great rivers of the earth are preëminently its Floods, and the harmony with which rivers and ocean are regulated in relation to each other is another marvel of creative adjustment. "All the rivers run into the sea," saith the

Preacher, "yet the sea is not full." Great as are the volumes of water poured into it by rivers like the Mississippi, the Amazon, the Nile, the Ganges, the Yang-tse-Kiang, as well as by every stream and rivulet throughout the world, the ocean knows no change, but preserves its level with a constancy which geologically distinguishes it from the land. The supplies of water poured into it from every source have been measured by the Creator with a nicety which satisfies all wants but leaves no surplus. With the same exactness the rivers throughout the world are fed with a uniform supply. In certain years, or at certain seasons of the year, the level of their channels may vary; but, notwithstanding climatic disturbances, the freaks of the rainfall, the dry and wet years, the irregular melting of the snows, and other causes, the great rivers show no sign of change in the amount of their annual tribute to the ocean. The streams that feed them may change; they may dry up at one season or be swollen into torrents at another; but ultimately an average balance is struck, and thus the mightiest rivers, like the Amazon, take little note of such disturbances. The Nile at first sight seems an exception to this rule, but the exception is apparent rather than real; for the Nile, when the mean between its lowest and highest state is taken into account, probably varies as little in its yearly average as other rivers. Thus may it be seen how that most gigantic and wonderful of all hydraulic machines — the atmosphere — does its work to perfection. By evaporation it yearly lifts up from the ocean the quantity of water that is needed by the land; and it pours into the channels of the rivers a supply which from year to year scarcely knows variation.

The great inland seas of the globe present to us features which illustrate even more strikingly the power and wisdom of God. Look at the Caspian, and the Sea of Aral in Central Asia, or at the Great Salt Lake of North America. Each of them receives the drainage of a large district, and yet there is no outgoing stream to carry off the water. If we were to continue pouring water into a basin we know what would happen;—the basin would be filled to the brim, and would then overflow. And in like manner the water in these inland seas would overflow and devastate the country had not a safety-valve been provided in evaporation. But again, the evaporation might have been too little or too much. It might not have been sufficient to correct this tendency to overflow; or it might have been excessive, so as ultimately to have sucked the sea dry, and left its bed an arid, salt-encrusted desert. But no such blunders are to be found in Nature's operations. The waste on the one hand, and the supply on the other, are so exactly adjusted as to equalize each other, and thus the level of those inland seas is for the most part preserved. In some districts of Asia, however, are to be seen what may be called the ruins of ancient seas, which, in the all-wise plans of Providence, were not intended to endure. In them the moisture was in the course of years dissipated by evaporation; the brackish water thickened into brine, and the brine solidified into salt-encrustations which mark the site of the old bed.

Another evidence of providential design is seen in those lakes which so frequently spread themselves out near the chief sources of rivers. In the language of physiology they might justly be called "diverticula," since they are reservoirs in which water that is in excess is stored up until it is wanted. If there were no provision of this kind inundations from the rapid rise of torrents during heavy rains would occur more frequently, but by the aid of these natural reservoirs the storm passes over in safety. A great portion of the rain, instead of running off at once in violent floods, accumulates in the lake, whence it is given out gradually and profitably, and thus often suffices to keep up a flow of water when drought might otherwise have left the river dry.

Rains, rills, and rivers alike rasp off the surface of the globe as they pass over it or through it. The rubbings of the rocks go to increase the store of fertile soil. As earth or mud they are washed along by the current, and deposited over the slopes and plains. Sometimes, from peculiar causes, inundations periodically occur, as with the Nile in Egypt, whereby, after subsidence, a rich coating of fertile soil is found deposited over the surface of the land. Most great rivers transport to the sea enormous quantities of earthy matters and gravel, which in the course of ages form round their mouths a "delta," or projecting tongue of rich alluvial soil. Besides these more bulky matters, rivers bring down into the sea supplies both of lime and silica, which they have dissolved out of the soil or the rock. With such materials of ocean architecture myriads of fishes, mollusks, polyps, and other creatures obtain all they require for the growth of their skeletons, the building of their houses, and the construction of those mighty reefs of coral which are slowly rising like new continents from the deep.

In Holy Scripture we are not less struck with the beauty than with the exactness of expression in which some of the leading points connected with the water-system of the globe have been described. In Ecclesiastes the sea is recognized both as the beginning and the ending of all the rivers of the earth, — "Unto the place from whence the rivers come, thither they return again." Nothing could more truly express the fact. The ocean-vapor which has been the sport of winds and currents in the atmosphere knows its true home; for no sooner does it touch the earth as rain than, with a seeming instinct and a movement that knows no rest, it hurries down the mountain side and across the plain, or trickles through the mysterious by-paths of the rocks until, collected into brook or river, it plunges once more into its parent ocean.

With the exception of the rain that has fallen directly

into the sea, every drop of returning water has gone a long round since it issued from the deep, and by God's goodness it has scattered blessings all the way. Water truly is a blessing to us in every form of its existence. It is a blessing in the ocean, where it diffuses life and the means of living to myriads; as vapor, cooling and refreshing the air at one time, warming and moderating the rigors of climate at another; as cloud, shielding the earth from sun, checking excessive radiation, and tempering electric influences; as rain, clearing the air from impurity and reviving the thirsty soil; as surface moisture, bringing nourishment to plants and animals; as streams, irrigating and fertilizing the land; as springs, infusing health into many a shattered frame; and lastly as rivers, bearing along on their deep currents the commerce that multiplies the comforts of life. Such are a few among the most obvious of its services, but to complete the list would be found an impossibility. In every form and stage God has chosen water as His servant to scatter good gifts among His creatures.

Ocean, clouds, rain, and rivers are the elements of a gigantic circulation on which the life of the world depends. The ocean is the mighty heart — the clouds and vapors driven by the wind are the conducting arteries — the minute rain-streamlets are the capillaries vivifying and nourishing every corner of the earth; while the tiny rills, soon swelling into brooks and then into rivers, are the returning veins which empty the water back into the mighty heart. Water is the blood of the earth: where it falls, the surface is living and fruitful; where it is denied, the ground withers into sand. Without the ocean there would be no rain; without rain, no fertile land; without fertile land, no plants; and without plants, no animals.

He gathereth the waters of the sea together, as it were upon a heap; and layeth up the deep as in a treasure-house. — Ps. xxxiii.

THE WINDS OF GOD.

O ye winds of God, bless ye the Lord: praise Him, and magnify Him for ever.

ONE cannot bestow a thought on the machinery by which the various operations of Nature are carried on without perceiving how much is accomplished by means of air and water. In one shape or another these ever-busy agents meet us at every turn;—sometimes acting singly, sometimes in combination, but always playing into each other's hands with a perfection which might almost be called intelligence, and which nothing short of infinite wisdom could have devised. Animated by solar heat they form the mightiest engines in Nature's workshop—laboring with unerring instinct, fetching and carrying, fertilizing, vivifying, and supporting life. They form, as it were, the right hand of Providence, and their appointed task is to distribute blessings over the world.

As in water, so in air a continual circulation among the particles is going on; which is not less necessary to maintain the atmosphere itself in a state of purity, than it is to insure the performance of the various purposes it has to fulfill. These movements constitute currents and winds, and they all originate in a difference in the density of one portion as compared with another. This difference in density may be caused by the presence of vapor, or by the agency of heat, to which may be added the influence of electricity, as is exhibited in the gusts that often suddenly arise in the still, close air which precedes the thunderstorm.

Winds range through an atmosphere encircling our globe to a height of forty-five or fifty miles, and the thickness of this belt in relation to the diameter of the earth has been compared by Maury to the down upon a peach. As air is a fluid, we may consider the atmosphere in its totality as a gaseous ocean, at the bottom of which we living creatures exist and move about. The upper surface of this ocean obeys the law of gravitation, by which all fluids are compelled to maintain their level; and hence, when accumulations of air arise upon its surface from internal disturbance, they must, like the waves of the sea, flow down upon the lower levels around, until the equilibrium is restored. The air varies in its density at different heights, according to the pressure of the mass above it. It is greatest, therefore, in low situations, as at the level of the sea, where it weighs fifteen pounds to the square inch, or nearly one ton to the square foot. In ascending, the weight of the aërial column diminishes in a nearly fixed ratio, so that by ascertaining the amount by means of a barometer, the altitude of any given spot may be pretty accurately determined. So rapidly does the weight diminish that, at the top of Mont Blanc, for example, no less than one half of the total mass of the atmosphere is found to have been left below.

One chief cause of the varying weight of the atmosphere at the same level is the greater or less abundance of aqueous vapor present in it. Dry air is 60 per cent. heavier than vapor, and consequently when vapor takes the place of a portion of air the weight of the atmospheric column is diminished. This may be illustrated by filling a teacup to the brim with water to represent a column of atmosphere. Our position as mortals upon earth is, of course, at the bottom of the cup where the tea-grounds usually lie; but for the moment we may suppose ourselves looking down upon the top of the atmosphere represented by the surface of the full cup. If we now displace a portion of the water by pouring in some lighter fluid, as spirits of wine or ether, the weight of the column will be necessarily diminished; for the teacup, instead of being completely filled as before with the denser fluid, will be partly filled with the lighter fluid also. In exactly the same ratio the weight upon the bottom of the cup, representing the surface of the earth, will be lightened. There can be no permanent accumulation on the top, for the excess of aëriform fluid, in obedience to the law of gravitation, runs down upon the surrounding lower levels, like a sea wave, by which means the same atmospheric height is always maintained. The instrument with which we measure the varying weight of the air is the well-known barometer. A low state of the barometer, therefore, indicates a light or vaporous condition of the atmosphere and a disturbance in the aërial equilibrium; hence, in a general way, rain and wind are to be expected. But in interpreting its announcements many other points have to be taken into account, more especially with regard to the direction of the wind, and the rapidity with which changes are taking place in the height of the mercurial column.

How many there are who habitually pass by the little instrument as it hangs in its corner in the hall without a thought of gratitude or of admiration at the wonderful series of adjustments on which its signals are founded. How different it is at sea! There the mariner consults it often and anxiously, as he would a truthful friend who can point out to him betimes when danger threatens. Every movement is analyzed, its slightest hints are carefully pondered. Never does a day pass by on which lives are not saved by the warning throbs of this atmospheric pulse. Of late years the barometer has been conspicuously placed in almost every fishing village on the coast, and its signals are explained by the best code of instruction which science can supply.

To be "as fickle as the wind" is one of those proverbial reproaches which are sometimes with scant justice made at Nature's expense. In reality, however, the laws of the winds are as fixed as other physical laws, although, from the difficulty of tracing their action in the aërial regions where they rule, we are as yet in the infancy of our knowledge respecting them. That little, however, is of immense service to mankind, and from the attention now given to this department of meteorology we may soon expect to derive from it still greater advantages.

In Ecclesiastes we read, — "The wind goeth toward the south, and turneth about unto the north; it whirleth about continually, and the wind returneth again according to his circuits." This is one of those profound expressions in physical science often met with in the sacred volume, which, though greatly in advance of the knowledge prevailing at the time when they were written, have been confirmed with literal exactness by modern investigation. It contains, indeed, the pith of all we know in regard to atmospheric circulation, and it could hardly be more clearly or beautifully stated. The grand circuit of the wind is from the poles to the equator and back again in unceasing rounds; at one time sweeping broadly across the surface of the earth; at another passing in vast volumes in the contrary direction in the upper regions of the atmosphere. It is true these great streams of wind are so often deflected from the straight course to form the most varying local currents, that it might at first sight appear as if all were confusion in the atmosphere. But those local currents, though they retard and complicate, do not ultimately prevent the final result by which the "wind returneth again according to his circuits." The "circuits" are the great wind-channels of Nature, and in them we see established in the atmosphere a system very analogous to those polar-equinoctial streams forever flowing in the ocean.

The power which sets these currents in motion is Nature's mainspring — the sun. An enormous body of air lying over the surface in equatorial regions, being heated and rarefied by the sun, is forced to ascend by the pressure of the adjacent heavier air brought from the north and the south by means of the Trade-winds, and this loss is supplied by air from higher and higher latitudes, until at last the poles themselves are reached. But no sooner has this tendency toward a vacuum been produced at the poles, by the current flowing from it, than an equivalent current begins to be drawn from circumpolar regions to supply the void, and this suction force, acting backward through lower and lower latitudes, at length arrives at the original fountain, which was the heated air rising up from equatorial regions.

Such, in general language, is the circuit of the wind upon the globe, although locally the greatest variety in the direction of the currents is observed. Aëronauts experience different currents at different heights; and the thunder-cloud may sometimes be seen advancing, under the influence of an upper current, apparently in the teeth of the wind that prevails below. On the Peak of Teneriffe Humboldt found himself exposed to a west wind so violent as almost to prevent him from standing upright, while the people on the plain below were under the mild influence of the northeast Trade.

It has been proved by many interesting observations that currents rising from the earth in warm regions sometimes take long courses through the air in a direction contrary to the wind prevailing below. Thus, in various parts of Europe bordering on the Mediterranean, red sand, called sirocco-dust, is occasionally deposited by the south wind. According to popular belief this dust comes from the interior deserts of Africa; but science, aided by the microscope, has proved that sometimes at least it has travelled from regions much more remote. A little of this red substance being submitted to Ehrenberg, he found that it clearly told its own history, being, as it were, labelled with the *débris* of infusorial animalcules, whose home he knew was in the mud of the Amazon. It appears that in seasons of great drought the river-mud, charged with these minute remains, is first thoroughly desiccated, and then reduced to so fine a powder that it is taken up by the heated air into the higher regions of the atmosphere. The current there joins company with winds bound for the northeast, and carries its freight some thousands of miles across the Atlantic. It next sweeps over the northwest quarter of Africa, and after traversing the Mediterranean deposits its load upon the adjacent lands. In this long journey its route has lain through the upper regions of the atmosphere, passing for a considerable part of the way over the Trade-wind which was blowing in exactly the contrary direction.

Let us here briefly notice a few of the principal winds that prevail in different parts of the earth. In tropical countries lying near the ocean, the inhabitants would languish under the stifling air were they not regularly refreshed by the "sea and land breezes." In the West India Islands, more especially, these fannings of Nature are described as delicious. Soon after the morning sun begins to glow upon the land, the air, heated as in a furnace, ascends in volumes, and its place is immediately supplied by the cool air that has been resting all the night upon the neighboring ocean. Hence the "sea-breeze." In the night-time, on the contrary, the temperature of the land falls in its turn, from radiation, below the temperature of the sea, and the direction of the current is reversed. It is now the air over the ocean which is displaced, and the air on the land which rushes off seaward to supply the void. Hence the "land-breeze." In latitudes far beyond the tropics, as on our own coasts, a sea-breeze is often felt in hot weather toward the middle of the day.

The path across the ocean is long and tedious. More

than 4000 miles of water lie between the Cape de Verde Islands and Mexico; more than 8000 miles intervene between South America and Australia. Unfortunate would it have been for commerce had there been no steadiness in the breezes of those regions — if there had been nothing for the sailor to reckon upon, and if every ship in traversing them had necessarily to become the sport of ever-changing winds. Ocean voyages, instead of being performed with a regularity that astonishes, would have been in the highest degree uncertain. The Ruler of the winds has happily ordered it otherwise. Under the Equator there is a narrow belt of calms, broken by fitful storms of rain and thunder. But on both sides beyond there is a broad region reaching to about the 28th degree of latitude where the wind blows regularly all the year round. North of the Line, it comes from the northeast; south of the Line, from the southeast; and thus a favorable breeze is secured for ships sailing across the Atlantic or Pacific in a westerly direction. These are the famous winds called The Trades, in token of the benefits they bring to commerce; and so steadily do they blow, that the sails of a ship may sometimes be set when off the Cape de Verde Islands, without requiring to be shifted until the opposite shore of America is sighted. In the Indian Ocean the Trades likewise prevail, but owing to the influence of the great Asian deserts elsewhere considered, the northern Trade is seasonally interrupted and changed into the Monsoon.

As the Trades help ships across the ocean in one direction only, the question naturally occurs, — How do they get back again? Immediately beyond the Trades there is providentially another region of ocean where the winds, though far less regular, have yet a prevailing direction exactly the reverse of that which governs the Trades: in the northern hemisphere, the set is from the southwest; in the southern, it is from the northwest. Practically, therefore, in whichever direction a ship may be crossing the ocean, the skillful mariner knows that there are tracks in which propitious winds will for the most part be found.

The cause of the Trade-winds has been thus explained. As the earth spins round in diurnal rotation, it is obvious that the land near the equator, being farthest from the axis of movement, must go faster than places situated either to the north or to the south. The former lies, as it were, on the rim of the wheel, while the latter are nearer the axle in proportion as they approach the poles. Hence, at the equator, the surface rotates with a velocity equal to 16 miles per minute; while in latitude 45°, say at Bordeaux or Venice, the velocity does not exceed 11 miles. Accordingly, as the aërial polar current, with the slower rotatory speed of higher latitudes impressed upon it, approaches the tropics, it is unable to keep pace with the increased rotatory movement of the surface, and it lags behind, or is "deflected" in a direction which must necessarily be the opposite to that in which the earth is moving. Now the earth moves from west to east. The north polar current, therefore, gradually becomes converted into a northeast Trade, while the south polar current gradually changes into a southeast Trade. If all parts of the earth moved with the same speed, or if there were no rotatory movement at all, the polar currents would be due north and south, or at right angles to the equator; but the eastern impulse which they gradually acquire causes them to move in the diagonal between.

The westerly winds prevailing beyond the Trades are due to causes just the reverse of those now mentioned, being produced by currents of air returning from the equator toward the poles. In commencing its journey the current had acquired, like the surface on which it rested, a velocity of 16 miles per minute in an easterly direction; which merely means that its movement was in equilibrium with that of the earth itself. But when it reached a latitude, say as high as 45°, it found itself in a part of the globe where, from the contraction of the circle, the rotatory pace had been reduced to 11 miles per minute. Instead, therefore, of lagging behind, as in the case of the Trades, the tendency of the momentum it has acquired is to push it on toward the east more rapidly than the surface over which it passes. The result is a prevailing southwesterly wind.

In thinking of the benefits derived from these useful winds, it is impossible not to admire the combination of wonderful adjustments by which they are brought about. The very same cosmical conditions which give us the Trades, are made likewise by the All-wise Creator to produce the winds which blow in the opposite direction. The constitution of the atmosphere, the shape of the earth, the rapidity of its axial rotation, the effect of the sun's rays, are all regulated and fitted into each other in such a way as to secure for commerce the advantage of these regional winds.

Although the Trades blow with regularity nearly across the entire Atlantic, there is a strip extending about eighty miles off the coast of Africa where the influence of the northeast Trade is scarcely perceived, forming a remarkable example of the effect of deserts in turning the winds out of what may be considered their natural course. At no great distance in the interior the scorched sands of Sahara are continually sending up vast streams of air into the higher regions of the atmosphere, and hence the cooler air off the coast, instead of being left free to the influences which rule the Trades, is sucked away in the opposite direction — rushing to the east, and not to the west — in order to supply the void in the atmosphere of the desert. It is, in reality, a perpetual sea-breeze on a large scale, neutralizing and vanquishing the influences which create the Trade. It was, probably, this very breeze which prevented the Portuguese from exploring in a westerly direction, and retarded the discovery of America; for, in pushing toward the south, they hugged the coast of Africa, within safe reach of this wind, and therefore never got within range of the Trade. On the other hand, had there been no Trade, Columbus would never have discovered America. That daring explorer, instead of creeping along the coast kept well out to sea, and soon, therefore, fell in with the Trade. It blew so steadily and carried him so far and so swiftly to the westward that his crew began to fear it was a wind that would never change. The ceaseless breeze seemed hurrying them hopelessly on and on into that mysterious sea which tradition had crowded with superstitious terrors. Fear, as usual, was fast loosening the bands of discipline, and mutiny was on the point of breaking out, when the sight of the eagerly desired land rescued Columbus from his difficulty, and placed a new world in the hitherto unknown void.

The same conditions which produce the Trade-winds on the ocean exist, of course, on land also, but the disturbing influences of hills and other circumstances generally prevent them from being so well marked, or even distinguishable at all. In tropical plains of great extent, however, they are sensibly perceived. Thus in South America there is a variable Trade-wind which, sweeping up the level Valley of the Amazon, enables vessels to sail against the course of the stream.

The Monsoons of the Indian Ocean are likewise great aids to commerce, and both on this account and for other important reasons are charged with blessings to man. They may be described generally as blowing six months in one direction and six months in another, but there is a longer or shorter interval of variable winds and storms interposed between them. From April to October the southwest Monsoon prevails, and ships sailing northward from the Cape find, about the latitude of 12 deg. south, a wind which wafts them toward the southern shores of Asia. From October to April the northeast Monsoon has its turn, and speeds the homeward-bound merchantmen across the Indian Ocean on their way to England. The southwest Monsoon is due to the same cause which has been pointed out as interrupting the continuity of the Trades off the coast of Africa — the influence of the desert. In the present instance, the work of the Sahara is done by the deserts lying in Central Asia, beyond the Himalayas; and the wind, while being drawn in toward them, showers down in profusion over the parched plains of Hindostan the refreshing water it has gathered up in the Indian Ocean. Some additional observations on these winds will be found in the chapter which treats of "Showers and Dew."

The hot sand of the Asian desert during the summer half-year attracts the southwest Monsoon, but it has no corresponding action in causing the northeast Monsoon. In winter the sand of the desert partakes of the surrounding comparatively cold temperature, and exerts no special influence on the direction of the wind. The northeast Monsoon in the Indian Ocean is, therefore, merely the resumption by the air of that course which it would have taken in summer also but for the disturbing attraction of the desert. It is in reality the northeast Trade, similar to that which prevails in the Atlantic and Pacific. But there are no extensive deserts situated in the southern division of the Indian Ocean, and consequently the southeast Trade blows there with comparative regularity all the year round.

It is interesting to remark that the sandy deserts, which one might have been inclined to consider as mere incumbrances on the earth, are thus of high importance in Nature's economy. They may, indeed, be often regarded as vast suction-pumps, providentially placed at certain stations on the earth, to create winds and help on the transport of moisture to lands that are in want of it. But for the Thibetian deserts there would have been no southwest

Monsoon; and without the Monsoon, the fertile plains of Hindostan would have been a waste of sand.

It is at first sight more difficult to understand the advantages of winds like the Khamsin and Harmattan, overpowering the traveler in the desert with their suffocating blasts; or the Sirocco of Italy and Greece, prostrating mind and body under its hot, moist, relaxing breath; or the Typhoon of the China seas; or the hurricane of the West Indies; or the Cyclone which revolves across the ocean. The evil they inflict is obvious, while the good they do is obscure. But that they harmonize with all God's other laws, and that their operation is ultimately beneficial to the world, we may confidently believe. The currents and admixture they promote in the air are of importance to the general welfare, and without doubt outweigh the local inconvenience they produce. It is often observed that great storms are followed by a sensible improvement in the air and by a feeling of increased comfort; hence it may justly be inferred that they are sent to cure something that is going wrong in Nature's household. We know that the storm sometimes checks the pestilence which human skill fails to subdue. On the banks of the La Plata, in South America, there is a prevailing wind which comes, charged with the germs of intermittent fever, from the marshes lying to the north. The wretched inhabitants droop and sicken and shiver into their graves. Suddenly a hurricane sweeps over the pampas from the cold summits of the Andes in the southwest, and in a few days the seeds of the disease are roughly yet effectually expelled. It has, moreover, been remarked that cholera epidemics in this country have usually been attended with great stillness in the atmosphere, by which the operation of causes tending to concentrate the disease was no doubt favored. Therefore, when we hear the stormy wind howling round our houses, and sweeping through our courts and closes, let us think of it as one of Nature's most efficient sanitary agents, by which she renovates the air that was tainted through stagnation, and scatters the seeds of the pestilence that were growing up for our destruction.

He bringeth the wind out of His treasures. — Ps. cxxxv.

FIRE AND HEAT.

O ye Fire and Heat, bless ye the Lord : praise Him, and magnify Him for ever.

IRE and Heat enter so essentially into the grand operations of Nature that there are few of them which might not fitly be considered in this place. Heat is truly an almost universal "Power of the Lord;" it is the force of forces, the mainspring of movement, and nothing is either too great or too small to be beyond its action. How busily it is ever at work among the natural features invoked in the hymn! It streams from the sun and the stars; it rules among the planets. Winter and Summer, Climate, Winds, Showers and Dew, Ice and Snow, Cloud and Seas, exist only through its operation; the Green Things upon the earth, Cattle, the Fowls of the air, and all that move in the waters, depend on it for life. Under its agency the earth itself has been compounded and shaped. Heat is the great antagonist of the attraction exercised between the particles of matter, which, were they not forced by it into expansion and openness, would condense into one solid mass.

In the affairs of daily life Fire and Heat are absolutely necessary to our welfare. Without them the thousand needful processes of home would be brought to a standstill. Of Fire steam is born — a power which we have subdued and trained to do our work, which fetches and carries, which lifts and lowers for us with more than a giant's strength, which feeds and clothes us, and which wafts us for business or pleasure over land and sea. Fire wins our metals from the ore, and fashions them into a thousand shapes for our convenience. Heat is the strongest of that band of Nature's servants which work without ceasing and which know neither fatigue nor slumber.

The great fountain of Fire and Heat is the sun. "There is nothing hid" from it. Its rays, however, are very unequally distributed over the earth, and without some corrective agency there would be an excess of heat at the tropics, and a degree of cold in high latitudes incompatible with life. Now the great equalizers of heat are, as we have seen, air and water, and, to a less extent, the crust of the earth itself, whose superficial layers are continually transmitting a wave of warmth from the tropics toward the poles.

When we say that, in the ordinary business of life, the source of heat is the combustion of fuel, we may probably be only indicating another shape in which the sun's rays minister to our welfare. It may truly be, as is suggested in the beautiful theory of Professor Tyndall, that the heat given out by bodies in combustion is only the yielding up of those rays of the sun which had for ages been imprisoned within them, and that a piece of coal is only a store of condensed sun-heat, absorbed during the time when it was being formed.

The fuel which offers itself most obviously to the notice of man is wood; and, as it exists abundantly in most countries, it has invariably happened that the fagot preceded the use of the mineral. That the employment of wood should have continued so long in England is easy to understand when we consider the extent of her ancient forests. When Julius Cæsar landed on these coasts the whole country was a vast wood, and a British town meant little more than a patch inclosed and cleared, with a few huts for men and sheds for cattle. But before a thousand years had passed the character of the country had altogether changed; and the Conqueror, in carving out his

New Forest, so far from merely appropriating an unoccupied woody country, pulled down thirty villages and churches, and dispeopled a wide, cultivated district. It must be recollected, however, that this occurred near Winchester, the then capital of the kingdom, where the population was comparatively dense, and the proportion of arable land greatest. Elsewhere forests abounded, and for centuries continued to abound, all over England. Alas! where are her old forests now? Of the ninety that were flourishing in the last century barely half a dozen survive. Among these the Conqueror's forest, though shrunk from its old limits, still ranks first in extent, and affords some of the finest "rambling" ground in England. Nor let us be unmindful of Royal Windsor, where scenes of sylvan beauty occur that are unsurpassed on earth. Of the other forests some, we grieve to say, like glorious old Hainault and Epping, are being nibbled and pared out of existence before our eyes, and no voice is raised to save them from ruin. Soon they will exist only in song and story. The loss of others, such as Bere in Hampshire, is less to be regretted. They had served their time, and fell naturally before the plow in their old age, after centuries of usefulness. With forests like these we part reluctantly, but the demands of agriculture must be satisfied.

In the olden time, as now, abundance of fuel carried with it the principal manufactures, and, for obvious reasons, the smelting of iron more especially. This most useful of all metals, like nearly every thing else that is serviceable to man, has been distributed very widely over the earth. It is a constituent of nearly every soil and rock, it can often be traced in water and even in air, and it also exists in the tissues of most animals and vegetables. The great storehouse, however, from which we derive our supplies is iron-ore, in which the metal is usually combined with oxygen or with carbonic acid, and in no instance is iron found naturally in a pure state except when it exists in the meteoric form. In the various processes for reducing it to its metallic condition, Fire, aided by a certain amount of carbon, and with a portion of limestone as a flux, is the chief agent employed. Wherever, therefore, iron-ore and fuel are found near together there the manufacture establishes itself, and it is to this circumstance more especially that England owes her preëminence in the production of this metal.

Before the days of coal, iron was smelted with wood; and as Sussex and the forest of Dean not only contained the ore but were abundantly provided with timber, they became the first seats of the English iron manufacture. In process of time, as the forests were cut down, the works were transferred from Sussex to the iron fields of the north and west, where the furnaces would be heated and the ore smelted by coal found abundantly on the spot. And in proportion as, in these days, the use of iron has expanded and driven other competing substances almost out of the field, an ever-bountiful Providence has led man to new stores of the metal practically inexhaustible. The most recently discovered field in Yorkshire has an extent of several hundred square miles, and alone would be sufficient to meet the present enormous demand for many centuries to come. In the year 1863 considerably more than nine millions of tons of iron were produced in the United Kingdom, at the cost of a consumption of coals equal to two millions of tons. Most of the other valuable metals obtained in this country are also won by the agency of Fire and Heat, from which may be estimated the services performed by them in a single department only. If we add to the operations of metallurgy the labors of the coal-pit, we have a branch of industry in the prosecution of which immense numbers of our population obtain the means of daily support.

Coal is the most valuable fuel in existence. It is, however, a singular illustration of the slowness with which useful discoveries are made, even under favorable circumstances, that some thousands of years should have rolled over the world before the superiority of coal over wood as a heat-producer came to be generally recognized. The inferiority of wood is in great measure due to the quantity of water which it contains; as the water, in passing off in a state of vapor, absorbs much heat which would otherwise have become sensible. Hence, also, the advantage of keeping wood that is to be used for fuel until it becomes dry. Coal was unknown to the Greeks and Romans; and although cinders have been found in the excavations at Uriconium, it is doubtful if it began to be burnt as fuel in England until long after the Romans had left. It is probable, however, that the black lumps found here and there upon the surface, or in digging for wells, or in other accidental ways, were known to be combustible long before the increase of population and the dwindling away of the forests forced men, as it were, to the regular use of coal. Like many other valuable discoveries, it had for centuries to contend against the prejudices of numerous enemies, and many evil things were said about it. In the 13th and 14th centuries it was the fashion to petition against it as a nuisance, just as we now protest against noxious exhalations from chemical works. So prejudicial to health were coals considered, that they were not tolerated in London, or even in its vicinity, under the severest penalty, and a smith who used them in his forge instead of wood was in danger of being sent to prison. Not until toward the year 1400 did the use of coal become general in the metropolis, and, even after that, wood continued to be the fuel of the country until the time of Charles I.

Although we speak of coal as a mineral, it is nevertheless of vegetable origin. Every particle of it, except that earthy residuum which in good coal is very small in amount, once formed part of a living plant. There is a kind called Lignite, which often consists of little else than fossilized trees; but the more perfect varieties may be considered as having their origin in peat-producing plants — chiefly mosses — which have been in the course of time compressed and metamorphosed into coal. All traces of moss structure have for the most part been obliterated. But in the same way as fragments of wood have been abundantly preserved in our bogs, so in the coal strata — those bogs of ancient days — relics of the trees which once flourished beside the peat are frequently found, likewise converted into coal, and in them the original structure of the wood, even to its microscopic details, is often beautifully displayed.

The quantity of carbon anciently extracted from the air, fixed in the tissues of plants, and then gradually converted into coal, is enormous. The area of all the known coal-fields in the world is computed to be 220,000 square miles — more than the whole surface of France — which, allowing a moderate average thickness of 20 feet, would be equal to a solid cube nearly 10 miles in dimension. As Professor Rogers observes, it would form "a square plateau 100 miles wide at the base, and more than 500 feet in height." The proportion of our British lump of coal "would be a cube of a little more than three miles in diameter."

Within the last century the consumption of coals has increased to an extent never dreamt of by our forefathers. In round numbers we are using up about 100 millions of tons annually. Who can enumerate or even conceive the sum of enjoyment which is daily extracted from this huge black heap? How many millions of hearths are made cheery by its glow, how many palaces and cottages are filled by it with comfort-bringing heat. What countless numbers of things of use or beauty are manufactured by its aid for our enjoyment. For how many mouths does it not prepare daily food. What great work is there which it does not help on? From its dull-looking fragments is distilled the gas which brightens up our houses and our streets. To coals we owe steam, and what is there in these days which we do not owe to steam? Steam gives us muscles stronger than iron, and yet finer in action than the most delicate hand. With the tools which man's ingenuity has provided, it labors incessantly without rest, and performs its task with a certainty and exactness with which nothing human can compete. Be the work rough or smooth, coarse or fine, steam adjusts itself to it with matchless skill. Steam wields the ponderous hammer as if it were no heavier than a feather, and can with equal ease crush an iron beam or crack a nutshell. The amount of labor saved and the physical strength thus gifted to man are enormous. Give a good steam-engine a bushel of coals, and it will lift a weight of 125 million lbs. one foot from the ground! Every three tons of coals are "the convertible equivalent of one man's life-long muscular activity." The 15 millions of tons annually consumed in this country in the production of mechanical force is equal to 20 millions of horses, or to a band of 100 millions of men! The power thus acquired is turned at will into an infinity of channels, all working in the service of man.

By the beneficent design of Providence coal-mines are widely distributed over the earth, and our own islands, more especially, have been blessed with an abundance that calls for thankfulness. The aggregate extent of our coal-fields amounts to no less than five thousand four hundred square miles. Yet when we consider our enormous consumption and reckless waste, we wonder not that thoughtful minds should look forward with anxiety to the possible advent of a day when our pits shall have become exhausted. That day may be distant; still it is confessedly not so very remote as to lie beyond the range of present interest. In a question of this nature, where the difficulty of obtaining exact data is so great, it is but natural that opinions should widely differ; but, on the whole, we may accept with some confidence the assurance that the stock of coal yet on hand will suffice for at least a thousand years to come.

Within the last few years the bounteous earth has yielded up to man another source of light and heat in Petroleum, which has already assumed commercially the highest importance. It was observed during the Burmese war that rock-oil was much used by the natives for ordinary illumination; and, when peace was concluded, it began to be imported into this country. It is now obtained in considerable quantities from other quarters also, especially from the districts on the Lower Danube. But all these sources are thrown into the shade by the oil-wells of North America. In 1863 the quantity raised from the Pennsylvanian springs alone was 40 millions of gallons, while that from Canada amounted to 250,000 gallons; and since then the produce has been steadily increasing. In this country, after purification, Petroleum is much used as oil for lamps; and paraffine, or mineral-wax candles, are also extensively manufactured from it. Large quantities of oil of an excellent quality are likewise obtained from the shale in contiguity with the coal measures, a substance which only a year or two ago was deemed refuse of no value. A single ton of the Torbanehill mineral is capable of producing 120 gallons of oil. Recent trials also indicate that Petroleum is well adapted as fuel for marine engines, as it produces a larger quantity of steam in proportion to its bulk than can be obtained from coal.

How much it seems to be a matter of course to see the fire burning brightly on a cold winter night. We enjoy the comfort it diffuses, and, perhaps, we congratulate ourselves that coals are so easy to be had. But how rarely do we carry our thoughts a step further, or reflect upon the extraordinary nature of the blessing. Countless ages ago our Father anticipated our wants and provided for their relief. The coal we burn is, so to speak, manufactured, and the manufacture was established thousands of years ago, when God caused to grow the mosses and other little plants which by slow accumulation became masses of peat. The raw material then went through other long processes. It was compressed and solidified and chemical changes were wrought in it. Then, lastly, the precious coal was stowed away carefully in the cellars of the earth on purpose that we might be made warm and happy by the "Fire and Heat," which from the beginning of its creation it was designed to supply.

In looking back at the history of fuel, the mind that loves to trace design in the ways of Providence cannot fail to be struck by the wise economy with which the treasures of the earth have been gradually unlocked, and one supply after another has been granted as the necessity for it seemed to arise. In the old time, when forests were everywhere and population was sparse, wood was the fuel invariably used. So long as manufactures were in their infancy the primeval forest answered all demands made on it. But in process of time population multiplied, and it was necessary to strip the land of trees on purpose that it might be sown with corn. Wood then became less abundant. New sources of heat were, therefore, absolutely needed; so God taught man the use of coal, which had previously been esteemed mere rubbish. Again, as oil from the old supplies became more scarce, and the demand for street and house lighting increased, the gas imprisoned in the coal was discovered, and our power of illumination was thereby almost indefinitely augmented. To economize Nature's resources vegetable wax and various vegetable oils have also recently been much employed. Lastly Petroleum was discovered, and the oil fountains of the earth were made to flow for our use. There is still the probability that some of the metals may be made available for illumination, and that before many years are over our means may be still further economized by a more frequent application of the electric light. Have we now arrived, it may be asked, at the end of the long list of Nature's resources, and are we to believe that when the last coal-pit has been worked out, and the last oil-spring emptied, we shall be left to perish with cold, or at least to live miserably, deprived of the comforts which for so many ages have been placed within our reach? With the firmest conviction we repel such a thought. It is utterly repugnant to our knowledge of the merciful ways of Providence. Our Father enriches but never impoverishes the earth, and the intelligence of His creatures is ever made the means by which new gifts are discovered. The essential constituents of fuel are only two — carbon and hydrogen. To them wood, coal, and every other kind of fuel owe their heating virtue. Now the world is literally packed with carbon and hydrogen, and it is not in the power of man to dissipate these elements of supply. Carbon is the staple out of which animals and vegetables are built up; it is a constituent of many rocks and of every soil, and it pervades the air. Hydrogen is even more abundant. It forms one ninth part by weight of every drop of water on the globe, and therefore it may be said that rivers and lakes and the ocean itself are vast reservoirs of latent fire. Of the two constituents of water, one — oxygen — is an admirable promoter of combustion, and the other — hydrogen — burns under ordinary circumstances with more heat than coal, while by the skillful admixture of the two a temperature of the highest intensity is produced. We do not attempt in these conjectural hints to indicate the way in which such materials will be made available, and the want of coal supplied, but only to point out that sources of "Fire and Heat" exist everywhere around us, and that, when need comes, God will inspire His children with wisdom to turn them to account.

In looking into the future, therefore, let us dismiss anxiety from our minds, in the firm conviction that Nature's resources are boundless, and that, if the world be still existent in those far-off days, God will not forsake the race for whom His providence has done, and daily does so much.

O put your trust in Him alway. — Ps. lxii.

FROST AND COLD.—ICE AND SNOW.

O ye Frost and Cold, bless ye the Lord: praise Him, and magnify Him for ever.

O ye Ice and Snow, bless ye the Lord: praise Him, and magnify Him for ever.

FROST and snow are so often associated in the mind with physical suffering, or with bleak winter and inhospitable polar regions, that their services in Nature's economy are apt to be overlooked. That the Three Children understood their operation better is obvious from the circumstance that cold and its effects are dwelt upon in the hymn with a minuteness bordering on redundancy, as illustrations not only of Power but also of Goodness and Wisdom.

It seems unnecessary to remind any of my readers that cold has no existence as a separate or independent principle, and that it merely implies in a general way the lower ranges of temperature. The word, therefore, will frequently be found in the remarks that follow, both because it is a convenient term, familiarly used and well understood by all, and because it has been specially introduced into the hymn.

Snow has its well-known aspects of beauty. Where can the eye rest upon such an expanse of purest, dazzling white as the unbroken sheet it lays upon the fields in winter, and how picturesque the trees appear with the snow-flakes clinging to their twigs and branches. Bathed in the light of the sun the snow-wreath often sends back the color in pale but beautiful reflection. At sunrise and at sunset the snow-clad Alps glow in rose and gold. Sometimes the snow, especially of polar regions, is tinted red by myriads of minute algæ which a pass frugal life upon its sterile surface, and the famous crimson snow-cliffs of Baffin's Bay arrest the attention of the passing navigator at a distance of ten miles from the shore. The beauty of snow is of that true kind that bears a close inspection. A few grains taken from the heap that gathers upon the window-sill will exhibit the prettiest crystals when looked at in the microscope.

Ice is even more beautiful than snow. Who has not stopped to admire the sunbeams playing with the icicles and winning glowing tints from their cold surface, or the windows encrusted with their frosty featherings, or the trees decked stiffly in fleeting robes of crystal? Who has not peered curiously at the stones and plants lying under the clear sheet of glass in which ice wraps up the brook in winter. Sometimes it is prettily "belled" with air, as if the water had been suddenly struck motionless in the act of effervescence; sometimes the tiny air-globules are so crowded together as to make the ice look white like hardened snow. But it is in glaciers, more especially, that the most beautiful tints are to be seen. Transmitted light frequently imparts a greenish color to their masses; at other times, they assume the milky dimness of the opal. Sometimes their huge fragments have been compared to blocks of beryl; more rarely their blue has the fine tint of aquamarine. Not unfrequently the ice decks itself in all the colors of the rainbow. The play of the low, midnight sun on the glaciers of the coast of Greeland has been described as making " the ice around one great resplendency of gem-work, blazing carbuncle and rubies and molten gold."

Ice water is purer than that procured from snow. The latter, besides the air mixed with it, usually contains some animal matter and other impurities gathered from the atmosphere. In freezing, water has a strong tendency to free itself from the foreign matters it may contain; and advantage has been taken of this circumstance, in arctic regions, to procure, on the one hand, salt; and, on the other, drinkable water. McClintock found that in each successive freezing the ice became less salt; until, after the fourth time, ice was formed which on melting yielded fresh water. From the brine left behind salt was readily procured by evaporation.

The Three Children could not survey the river that washed the walls of Babylon without being reminded how much it owed to frost and snow. In the fierce Mesopotamian summer, when wells were drying up and many streams had ceased to flow, the Euphrates was still fed from the snowy reservoirs of the Armenian Mountains. And when the people, like Nature all around, drooped under the withering heat of the sun, the winds which braced their exhausted nerves gathered coolness from the same high sources.

As there are "sweet uses in adversity," so does the rigor of winter in northern climates enhance the enjoyment of summer. Thankful thoughts should rise when we call to mind the wood and coal and springs of oil given to us as means by which cold may be mitigated or subdued. These, no doubt, are commonplace subjects and reflections. Our life itself is spent among commonplace things; but, when we make them lead to thoughts that honor God, we elevate them above their commonness and invest them with the dignity of aiding devotion.

It is well known that water under ordinary circumstances freezes at 32° Fahr. In passing to the solid state it expands with a force sufficient to burst pipes of lead, or even of iron, as householders know to their cost. This force, which acts on a vast scale over the greater part of the world, may well be deemed one of the "Powers of the Lord." Thus it splits wood, rends the rock, and breaks up the weather-worn fragments into fertile soil.

Ice and Snow.

Under varying circumstances cold produces the different effects mentioned in the hymn. It converts water into ice, and atmospheric vapor into rain or snow or hail; and when the vapor is in contact with the ground, instead of being deposited as dew, it may be frozen into hoar-frost. Cold brings sleep to the vegetable world, and prepares it by a period of rest to burst forth with fresh vigor in the spring. Snow and frost are valuable servants to the husbandman. By expanding the moisture with which the hard clods are permeated, Frost crumbles them down and renders the stiff land friable, porous, and mellow. Frost, likewise, rids the soil of some of its insect or vermin life, which, but for this check, might increase to an extent that would seriously damage the crops. In winter it gives the soft, moist ground the necessary hardness to allow field operations to be carried on. Snow is even more useful. It covers up the tender plants as with a blanket, and preserves them against the effects of excessive cold. "He giveth snow like wool." The blanket thus softly laid on is "a bad conductor," neither allowing the heat which is in the earth to pass out, nor, if we may use the expression, the external cold to pass in. Observation shows that the inner surface of the snow seldom falls much below $32°$ Fahr., although the temperature of the air outside may be many degrees under the freezing point; and it is found that the crops can stand this amount of cold without injury, so long as their covering protects them from the raking influence of the wind. In climates where the winter's cold is longer and more intense than in our sea-girt island, the protecting influence of the snow is more conspicuously marked. In northern climates snow, in its own fashion, sometimes opens out routes which were impracticable in summer from their ruggedness, and prepares a path for the sledge, or for the "lumberer," over which the largest stems of the forest may be dragged with ease to the canal or river.

In polar regions snow supplies the ever-ready material out of which the Esquimaux construct their houses, and hardy explorers extemporize the huts in which they find shelter when absent from their ships on distant expeditions. Nor are the ships themselves considered "snug in winter-quarters" until their sides have been banked up in walls of snow, and the roof raised over the deck has been thickly covered with it. Experience has proved that a layer of frozen snow, four inches thick, forms an excellent thatch for houses and ships in those biting regions. Snow huts are warmer than might have been anticipated. If built on ice covering the sea, their temperature is sensibly affected by the heat of the unfrozen water below, which is said seldom to fall much under 40° Fahr. in any part of the ocean. Even where the external temperature has sunk to 20° or 30° below zero, sufficient warmth is produced in a snow hut by the huddling together of three or four persons within it. When Kane passed a cold arctic winter's night in the hut of "Mrs. Eiderduck," beyond Smith's Sound, the temperature produced by its complement of lodgers and two or three oil lamps reached 90° Fahr.; so that he was compelled by the heat to follow the example of the rest of the party and partially to divest himself of his clothing. In latitude 79° north, Kane marked a temperature of 75° below zero in the month of February. No fluid could resist it. Even chloric ether became solid, and the air was pungent and acrid in respiration.

How great soever may be the intensity of the cold which is naturally produced in high latitudes, it is moderate in comparison to that which can be obtained by artificial means. The principle of freezing-mixtures depends on the fact that heat is absorbed and becomes "latent" whenever a solid passes into a liquid state, or when a liquid passes into vapor; and that cold is, therefore, produced in the medium from which that heat is withdrawn. This is easily illustrated by the cold which is excited when a little

Eau de Cologne is placed on the forehead and allowed to evaporate. The intensity of the cold is in proportion to the rapidity with which the vaporization is accomplished. Snow melts in temperatures above 32°, and produces a certain amount of cold; but if we can, by mixing it with some solvent, make it melt faster, a greater degree of cold is the result. Thus a mixture of equal parts of snow and common salt brings down the temperature from 32° to zero, merely from the rapidity with which the salt causes snow to change from the solid to the liquid form. When, therefore, in winter the pathway is strewn with salt, the snow no doubt quickly disappears, but at the cost of an amount of cold which may be very dangerous to persons who have to wade through it.

The greatest artificial cold, however, is produced not by liquefaction but by evaporation. Alcohol, ether, and Eau de Cologne evaporate quickly and cause cold; but there are substances which by skillful management can be made to evaporate much more rapidly, and, therefore, to produce a much greater amount of cold. There are many substances, of which carbonic acid is an example, which in their natural state exist as gases, but which by a combination of pressure to eliminate, or, as it were, "squeeze out" their component heat, and of a surrounding cold mixture to absorb this heat the instant it is developed, may be made to assume a liquid, or even a solid state. Subsequently when these agencies are removed the solid evaporates, or resumes its natural condition of a gas with almost explosive rapidity, producing, by its inordinate absorption of heat, a most intense cold in things in contact with it. By employing a bath of solid carbonic acid and ether, Faraday produced a cold equal to 106° below zero in the open air, and 166° in vacuo. But even this intense temperature has been left far behind by Natterer, who, by employing in vacuo a mixture of protoxide of nitrogen and bisulphide of carbon, produced a cold equal to 220° below zero.

It is scarcely necessary to remind the reader that heat, as a rule, causes bodies to expand. The iron rod which, when cold, just passes easily through a ring, can no longer do so when it has been made hot, on account of the expansion it has undergone. It is to make allowance for this swelling during the summer's heat that the ends of the iron rails "on the line" are not placed in actual contact, but have a little space left between them; and it is from the contraction which the heated iron tire undergoes on cooling that it is made to clasp firmly round the wheel, when water is dashed upon it. In this manner the expansion or contraction of bodies under the application of heat or cold is turned to account in many operations. Sometimes, on the other hand, those qualities lead to inconveniences, which for the most part may be removed by the exercise of that ingenuity which man has received for the purpose. There is one substance — water — which has been made an exception to the general rule by the Creator, with a design so clearly merciful that none can fail to appreciate it with thankfulness. Let us first consider what would have happened if water had been subject, throughout all temperatures, to the regular law of contraction on the application of cold. We will suppose it is winter, and that sharp frost is at work upon lake and river. As each layer of water on the surface cooled, it would contract, and by thus becoming denser it would sink to the bottom. Another layer of water would necessarily take its place upon the top, and being cooled in its turn, would likewise sink. In this manner a continuous circulation of cold water to the bottom and warmer water to the surface would go on until all the water had been cooled down to $32°$ Fahrenheit, when the whole mass would suddenly set into ice. Consider the evils that would arise over a large part of the world from such a physical arrangement. Breaking through the ice would lead to no unfrozen reservoir below. The mills would stop. Spring, river, and lake would be equally involved when frost was intense and long continued. Animal and vegetable life existing within them would perish. The fishes would be caught in their swimming, and frozen as rigid as the prison walls of ice in which they were inclosed. From surface to bottom movement would cease, and the water would be changed into a solid block of crystal.

After the frost had yielded and the genial sun once more shone forth, his brightest rays would have encountered difficulty and delay in unsealing the solid mass of waters. A pool, no doubt, would speedily have formed upon the surface of the ice, but water is a "bad conductor," and would act as a screen partially to intercept the heat from passing more deeply. The temperature of the pool of water might even have been raised considerably without transmitting much heat to the mass of ice underneath. We all know that when heat is applied to water from below, as in a kettle, it is speedily "carried," not "conducted," to all parts by the currents immediately established. But if, on the other hand, the heat be applied at the top, no downward currents are formed, and it must be slowly propagated by "conduction," as in a solid body. To exhibit the bad conducting power of water, Count Rumford devised a very striking experiment, which can be easily repeated. Having fixed some ice at the bottom of a tall glass jar, he filled the jar with cold water, and then applied heat round it near the top. In a short time the fluid at the upper part of the jar was found to be boiling briskly, while the ice at the bottom remained almost unaffected. Now if we imagine the ice in this experiment to be the ice at the bottom of a lake, and the heat artificially applied above to be the warmth imparted to the water by the sun's rays and the adjacent air, we may form some idea of the difficulty with which the mass of ice accumulated at the bottom of the river or lake would be dissolved.

But the disorder in Nature's economy and the destruction of life which would arise under these circumstances have been foreseen and obviated by a very simple and perfect arrangement. Providence has willed that the densest point of water shall be about 40° Fahrenheit. In cooling down to the temperature of 40°, therefore, water follows the universal law, and contracts. But when cooled beyond this point, until it passes into ice, instead of contracting it expands and becomes lighter and lighter. Therefore, as each successive layer on the surface attains a temperature of 40°, it naturally sinks to the bottom, *where it remains, without rising to the surface again to undergo further cooling.* After the whole mass of the water has attained this temperature, subsequent cooling makes it lighter, so that *the coldest layer floats at the top* until it freezes. The result is a sheet of ice on the surface with a temperature not higher than 32° Fahrenheit; while there is a large, free body of water underneath with a temperature of about 40°. In this temperate region the fishes swim about, and with other creatures find a secure and genial refuge.

The absolute perfection of this arrangement is completed by another law which now comes into play. Ice, like water, is a bad conductor of heat, and therefore, of cold. Consequently, when a sheet of ice has once formed on the surface, it interposes a barrier which fences off the warm water below from the outside rigor of the air. It is as truly a blanket to the water in winter, as snow is a blanket to the ground, or as a great-coat is to us; and as its thickness slowly increases, its efficiency augments in proportion. It is for this reason that the sea, even in the most rigorous polar climates, never freezes beyond the thickness of a few feet. The temperature of the air outside may be 50° or more below zero, but the "slow conducting" power of the blanket of ice defends the sea underneath against the climatic rigor. It may be here

Ice and Snow. 191

remarked that sea-water does not follow the same law in cooling as fresh-water. Thus it freezes, according to Despretz, at a temperature of nearly $27\frac{1}{2}°$ Fahrenheit, while its density increases regularly up to that point.

We have seen that in falling below 40° fresh-water expands, but if in the act of solidifying it had contracted, much of the benefit of the arrangement just described would have been lost. The particles of ice as soon as formed would have sunk to the bottom, where they would have remained and been continually increased by new accumulations. Water being "a bad conductor," the heat of the winter sun would have reached the bottom with difficulty, while every new touch of frost during the cold winter nights would have precipitated more ice to add to the deposit below. The intervening mass of water would thus have been placed between two cold strata, by which its heat would soon have been exhausted, and the whole mass converted into ice. There is, perhaps, nothing within the range of physical science which more strikingly displays the forethought and mercy as well as the Power of the Great Designer than the relations which He has established between water and heat. So long as the result was good, water was made to follow the general rule; but the instant when the continuance of the law would have produced evil, He designedly reversed its operation, and thus restored harmony and safety to the world.

The work of "Frost and Cold" is seen in its grandest forms amid the mighty glaciers — those "silent cataracts" which return the waters that are above the firmament to those that are below the firmament in rivers of solid crystal. No picture or description can excite such emotions as stir the mind of him who, standing for the first time on the glacier's brink, thoughtfully surveys its rugged desolation, and in the midst of summer feels its icy breath creeping over him. The giant crystals of creation are before him — a strange, unearthly sea, with fantastic, foamy waves stiffened into stones, with domes and pinnacles and endless fanciful resemblances of common things, with chasms which the eye cannot search or fathom, with caverns out of whose darkness mysterious streams steal forth into the light. What power is here sealed up! Loosen but for a moment the fetters that hold this pile of waters together, and try to imagine the force with which the valley, with its green fields and smiling villages beyond, would be overwhelmed. What an emblem of desolation! Life hurries across, but neither lingers nor lives upon it. The sounds that break upon the ear are all its own: the trickle of dropping water so clear and distinct amid the stillness; the ringing click of the unseen atom of ice falling down from ledge to ledge in some neighboring *crevasse;* the sharp crack of some new fissure, drowned from time to time in the thunder of the distant avalanche. The silence that reigns between these sounds is so profound as to be almost oppressive.

Glaciers are formed in the highest valleys of the Alps out of the snow precipitated directly from the atmosphere and the avalanches which from time to time crash down the mountain's side. In summer the sun partially dissolves the surface, and the water in percolating through the mass fills up the interstices with ice. The enormous pressure to which the glacier is subsequently exposed as its bulk increases, has a still more powerful effect in condensing and welding it into compact, slightly plastic ice. No sooner is the glacier formed than it begins to glide downward through the valley, receiving many contributions by the way. The motion of glaciers was long a disputed point, but for some time past it has been established beyond all question. In 1836 a Chamounix guide fell into a *crevasse* in the glacier of Teléfré, a feeder of the Mer de Glace, but contrived to escape, leaving his knapsack behind him. In 1846 the identical knapsack was yielded up by the glacier 4300 feet below the place where it was lost.

In an expedition to the summit of Mont Blanc in 1820 three guides lost their lives by the fall of an avalanche, which buried them beyond recovery in the glacier below. Forty years passed by, and then some relics of their bodies came to light on the Glacier des Bossons, far below the point where the accident occurred. In the course of 1863 and 1864 various other fragments were recovered; and in 1864 — that is, 44 years after the accident — there was found, projecting from a large hummock of ice, "an entire leg from the knee downward, in a state of perfect preservation, with the nails on the toes as perfect as those of the living." From certain marks it was recognized as having belonged to one of the lost guides. Many other relics have since been recovered, and it would appear from a carefully kept register that only one leg and two hands are now missing. From the above and other evidence there can be no doubt as to the motion of those enormous masses of ice. The force that pushes them onward is chiefly the weight of the accumulation behind. The rate of traveling varies according to the steepness of the valley through which they slide, the shape of its bed, and the rocky obstacles that oppose their descent, but it is computed to be from a few inches to two or three feet daily. The rising and sinking, the rending and fissuring of the glacier give to the surface its tempest-tost appearance. Under favorable circumstances it is pushed onward into the cultivated valley or the plain, where its rugged, uncouth masses stand out in strange contrast to the bright corn-fields or meadows upon which it has intruded. At the point where the melting power of the sun balances the supply of ice coming from above, there the glacier ceases to advance. Round its termination is found the "moraine," or mound of rubbish formed of fragments of rocks, with sand and mud, which have either fallen upon the glacier or been scraped off from the sides of the valley in its downward progress. When the ice melts they are, of course, deposited on the ground. These moraines are very characteristic, and can be easily recognized even in places from which the glaciers themselves have long since disappeared. Glaciers often leave behind them other marks by which their former presence may be safely inferred. Thus, the enormous pressure of the ice sometimes scrapes the rocks which form their bed, until the surface is smoothly polished, or grooved and fluted. The markings are of course parallel to the direction in which the glacier moved, and they are of so peculiar a character that geologists can recognize them in many countries — as in England and Scotland — where glaciers no longer exist. The remains just mentioned reveal a period when the condition of Europe was much colder than at present. The Jura Mountains, for example, are labelled all over with moraines and markings. The glaciers are gone, but the "boulders," or fragments of rock they transported, are left behind; and when these are examined they are found to be strangers, having no affinity with the rocks around, but pointing to the distant Mont Blanc, or Monte Rosa, or the Alps of Schwytz, or the Oberland, as the home from which they originally came. Fractured roughly off from the parent mountain, many of them were carried tenderly across the intervening space by the old glacier, and were then so gently deposited in the moraine-bed that their edges remain sharp and fresh as if they had been laid there yesterday. Great though the size of those ancient glaciers must have been, they were small in comparison to the mighty Greenland glacier of the present day.

By the transporting power of ice the whole of the vast plain of Northern Germany, Poland, and Russia have been strewn with boulders brought from Scandinavian or other distant mountains. As a specimen we might refer to the magnificent tazza of granite, which has been carved out of one of them and placed in front of the Museum at Berlin. The mountains of Scotland, Cumberland, and

Wales abound with old glacier markings, and the plains of our island are strewn with fragments of foreign rocks which were probably ice-transported. It awakens curious thoughts to stand on the top of Snowdon, and in imagination look back to the time when it was a Welsh Mont Blanc, piercing through its Mer de Glace, and launching from its sides seven huge "cataracts of ice" to fill the neighboring valleys where Llanberis, Bettws Garmon, and Beddgelert now bloom in beauty. Nowhere in Great Britain, and scarcely in any other part of the world, can the traces of ancient glacier action be seen in greater perfection.

The icebergs of the ocean are means employed by Nature to provide fresh water to compensate for the evaporation going on in southern seas, and to temper the heat of southern latitudes. The "cold," if such an expression may be used, is locked up in them as they are formed in polar regions, and it is given out during the process of melting. Stated more correctly, melting produces cold by absorbing the heat around as the ice is passing into the state of water. In the district of the Gulf Stream the cold of the iceberg is sometimes perceived at a distance of 40 miles, and the temperature which a few miles off may be 60°, falls to 43° or even lower in the immediate vicinity. In the north Atlantic, icebergs are seldom seen below $40\frac{1}{2}$ degrees of latitude; but in the southern hemisphere, where they are much more numerous, they are sometimes seen about latitude 35°, off the Cape of Good Hope. Some idea of their size may be formed from the fact that they are occasionally two miles in circumference, with a height of 200 feet; and it must be borne in mind that only one seventh part of the whole mass appears above the water. Parry estimated that a single iceberg which he saw aground in 61 fathoms must have contained 1 billion 292 million tons' weight of water. Sometimes the ocean is studded with them. On one occasion Scoresby counted a fleet of 500 icebergs sailing majestically toward the south. Favored by wind and current their speed is equal to that of a well-manned boat. Fearful collisions sometimes occur between them, and pieces of wood have been ignited by the violent compression of the blow. Icebergs carry a freight of rocks and rubbish, estimated by Scoresby to be in many instances not less than 50,000 tons in weight, which is ultimately deposited over the bed of the Atlantic, to the south of Newfoundland.

Icebergs are born in the remote polar regions, being the offshoots of the huge glaciers which there cover up so much of the soil. The whole interior of Greenland is filled by a Mer de Glace, which in its enormous proportions dwarfs every other sea of ice that has as yet been discovered. It is estimated to have a length of 1200 miles, while some of the glacier-spurs proceeding from its flanks down the valleys into the sea have a breadth of 60 miles. This stupendous ice-mass is thus described by Kane:—
"Imagine the centre of this continent of Greenland occupied through nearly its whole extent by a deep unbroken sea of ice that gathers perennial increase from the watershed of vast snow-covered mountains, and all the precipitation of the atmosphere upon its own surface. Imagine this moving onward like a great glacial river, seeking outlets at every fiord and valley, rolling cataracts into the Atlantic and Greenland seas; and having at last reached the northern limit of the land that has borne it up, pouring out a mighty frozen torrent into unknown arctic space." In another place it is finely said that this mighty glacier "seems to remind one at once of time and of eternity: of time, since we see portions of it break off to drift and melt away; and of eternity, since no change is perceptible in its appearance from age to age."

Darwin describes icebergs crashing into the sea from the precipices of Terra del Fuego, and raising a wave high enough to swamp boats exposed to their influence.

But the icebergs of northern polar regions are seldom produced by the fall of ice-cliffs; on the contrary, they are launched or floated off from the glacier. The latter pushes onward into the sea, plowing up occasionally the bottom on which it rests, just as an Alpine glacier plows up the plain; and after it has advanced to a distance which is often sufficient to submerge a large mass under water, the huge fragment breaks off, rises out of the sea, and floats away as an iceberg. The great drift of the glaciers in our hemisphere is down both sides of Greenland. Luckily for us the strong current established on the west of Iceland then lays hold of them, and carries them toward the American side of the Atlantic. Had their course lain toward the British Isles, our climate and our comfort would have been materially affected.

For God is King of all the earth: sing ye praises with understanding. — Ps. xlvii.

POWERS OF THE LORD.

O all ye Powers of the Lord, bless ye the Lord: praise Him, and magnify Him for ever.

"WHITHER can we go from Thy presence," or in what direction can we cast our eyes without perceiving that we are hedged in on every side by the Powers of the Lord? Above, below, around — in the air, in the water, on the earth and under the earth they pervade creation. At every turn they reveal themselves in the mighty language of physical, chemical, and vital force, bringing home to our minds at every instant our dependence upon Him, and leading us on to thankful adoration.

The verses of the Benedicite may be considered as a summary of these Powers, and many of them, therefore, will be found noticed elsewhere in this book. In this place we shall confine our attention to a few of the more striking illustrations drawn from the familiar objects around us.

The Powers of the Lord shine forth in the heavens — in sun, moon, and stars — with a grandeur which we cannot fully comprehend, but which nevertheless elevates our nature in the mere effort to grasp it. In every meditation on those Powers we find ourselves instinctively turning again and again toward the sun, the great messenger of the Lord, which brings to our earth so much of the force and movement we see continually displayed upon it. Under Providence, the sun stands forth as the pivot of the solar system, sustaining and preserving by the power of gravity the planets that circle round it. On earth the operation of the same power is no less necessary and universal. By solar gravity all things are attracted toward the centre of the sun, while by terrestrial gravity every thing belonging to our globe is drawn toward the centre of the earth. Terrestrial gravity, therefore, counteracts the centrifugal tendency of objects, resulting from the earth's rotation, and keeps them fixed upon the surface with a force of which the amount is termed their weight. Let us reflect how universally useful this power is. It holds every thing in its place. It keeps one stone pressed down upon another, and thus makes building practicable. Bodies that have little gravity, or that are light, possess little stability and are readily tossed hither and thither. Our bones and muscles, and the strength of plants and all other materials, are adjusted to the strain which gravity makes upon them. In obedience to its laws the ship floats upon the water, and the balloon soars into the air. It is gravity which enables us to balance ourselves in walking, running, or riding. By the adjustment of their gravity to the medium in which they are placed birds fly and fishes swim. In short there is no limit to the conveniences and benefits we derive from this " Power of the Lord."

Another Power essential to our well-being is Friction, which, in conjunction with gravity, regulates physical motion. It is the force which opposes displacement, which keeps things steady, and finally brings them, if in motion, to a state of rest. With every kind of movement some frictional opposition will always be found at work tending to stop its continuance. It may be the rough surface of the ground, or the comparatively unresisting water, or the still softer air, but each with varying degrees of frictional energy ultimately subdues the moving force, and sets the body at rest. Many are the attempts ingenious man has made to overcome this difficulty, but his search after " perpetual motion " is ever baffled by omnipresent friction, and his greatest success is measured only by the gain implied in substituting a friction that is less for one that was more. Thus we oil axles and hinges, to diminish the rubbing opposition. Thus wheels were invented to escape in some degree from friction by rolling over the rough ground instead of scraping over it. Thus, also, by gradual improvement rude tracks were changed into smooth, macadamized roads, and these last in their turn are yielding to the even rail. Every new success has been merely the lessening of friction.

In these and in many other ways friction may be said only to create difficulties which man's ingenuity enables him to overcome with more or less success; but, as a set-off against these evils, let us for a moment try to realize what would have happened if there had been no such Power in existence. When a surface offers little friction we call it slippery; and ice, though offering resistance sufficient to bring a skater or a stone gradually to rest, is yet remarkable for the comparative absence of friction. What occurs? In venturing upon it most persons find their movements difficult even when the surface is level, but they find it impossible to stand when ice is upon the slope. Now if there were no such thing as friction, land would be no longer *terra firma*, but would be as slippery as ice. Without mechanical support it would have been impossible to ascend a hill. Horses could not have kept their feet against a strain; every thing we handled would have slipped through our fingers with eel-like glibness. Quiescence and steadiness would have been banished from the world, and objects once set in motion would have gone on without stopping until brought up by some equal opposing force. Thus it may be perceived that the friction of matter assists us in almost every act we perform; and, without its aid, the innumerable purposed movements of every-day life would have been impossible in the general confusion of the world. "Without this property," says Dr. Whewell, "apartments, if they kept their shape, would exhibit to us articles of furniture and of all other kinds sliding and creeping from side to side at every push and at every wind, like loose objects in a ship's cabin, when she is changing her course in a gale."

Seeing that the frictional power of the atmosphere is sufficient to bring all things exposed to it to rest, some may be inclined to ask why the heavenly bodies do not gradually move more slowly and ultimately stop? Long continued observation proves either that the orbital course of the heavenly bodies lies in a vacuum where friction does not exist, or that it takes place in a medium so attenuated that the frictional resistance practically amounts to nothing. All astronomers agree that the friction must in any case be extremely minute. "If," says Whewell, "Jupiter were to lose one millionth of his velocity in a million of years (which is far more than can be considered in any way probable), he would require seventy millions of years to lose 1-1000th of his velocity; and a period seven hundred times as long to reduce the velocity to one half."

In sauntering among the scenes of this solidly planted world, how few there are who ever bestow a thought upon the Powers enchained within it. Yet our daily life is spent over an abyss, and comparatively a mere shell is all that is interposed between us and destruction. As the crust of the earth is explored the temperature is found to increase about a hundred degrees for every mile of depth; and consequently, if this ratio be maintained, thirty or forty miles beneath our feet there is a temperature so intense that most substances with which we are acquainted must exist in a state of fusion. Great though this depth may at first sight appear, it is only a hundredth part of the space interposed between us and the earth's centre; and, if we were to imagine the globe represented by an egg, the shell would be comparatively much thicker than the thin layer which forms its crust. Far down in the mysterious caverns of this crust, the molten rocks, the incandescent vapors, and bursting gases, heated by the internal furnace, are ever battling together and struggling with inconceivable force to rend their prison walls. Sometimes we hear with awe the distant thunder of the conflict, and sometimes the foundations of the earth itself are shaken or torn asunder. Those are the regions where fierce chaos is mercifully held down by the weights which God has heaped upon it; but, be it remembered, the Power is there, and is ready, if the word be spoken, to burst forth and in an instant submerge this fair world in molten fire, and change it into a ruin. In this internal crucible were compounded in olden time the granites, the porphyries, and the basalts which subsequently forced their way roughly through overlying strata, and consolidated themselves, lava-like, into rocks and mountains. The convulsions of the early world must have been truly awful, for in every country the rocky layers bear testimony to the violence then sustained. Many of the strata have been started from the bed on which they had been gently and evenly deposited as a sediment, and have been cracked, splintered, or tilted over in all directions. Sometimes the fiery giant, unable to burst completely through, has lifted and strained the brittle strata over him until they rose into ridges, or, by causing partial upheavals and subsidences, has produced those dislocations or "faults" which are now so perplexing to the miner. Nor are the marks of heat less evident than those of the violence which attended it. Sometimes the soft sandstone touching the fiery stream has been fused into quartz, or indurated into a flinty hardness which shades off into the natural texture of the rock as it recedes from the point of contact. Occasionally the glowing stream baked the contiguous clay into coarse porcelain. The chalk and the limestone, instead of being changed into quick-lime, as would have happened had they been calcined in the open air, have been indurated and sometimes fused into crystalline marble, such as is quarried at Carrara, from their having been heated under the pressure of superjacent strata. Owing to the same cause shales are found occasionally converted into hard, porcellaneous jasper, while seams of coal are coked or charred to a varying distance around.

Although internal igneous action has happily been now restrained within moderate bounds, yet have we sure proof in the volcano and earthquake that subterranean fires do still possess much of their ancient fury. At never-distant intervals Vesuvius, Ætna, and Hecla heave up their molten lavas out of depths that lie beyond our power to explore; and during the spring of this year, 1866, a volcano has been cast up in the harbor of Santorin. The great centres of volcanic action, however, are now to be found in South and Central America, along the line of the Andes, and in the nearest islands of the Pacific. In one of the Sandwich Islands, for example, there is a crater nine miles in circumference, and 1200 feet deep, in which a broad sea of molten lava surges and splutters. The caldron, however, never boils over. Apparently the pressure occasionally forces an opening in its side through which the lava runs, as through a spout, down into the ocean, where it quickly consolidates and tends gradually to enlarge the area of the island.

Sometimes the internal force, instead of assuming the fitful violence of the volcano or earthquake, operates with regularity, as if through the expansion or contraction of large masses of heated matter, by which the surface-land is slowly upheaved in some places and lowered in others. It is remarkable that in all such cases, the only trustworthy standard of measurement is the sea, which, in regard to permanent level, is far more stable than the land. The more this subject is inquired into, the more common are such movements proved to be; and it is, perhaps, not too much to say that there are probably few regions in the world which are absolutely stationary. The southern shores of the Firth of Forth are rising at a rate which allows a sensible difference in their shape to be noted in the course of a single generation. Southern Sweden and Norway are sinking, while their northern end is rising. On the shores of the Bay of Baiæ the columns of the ruined temple of Jupiter Serapis are seen oddly planted in the sea. The base is covered with the water. They were originally built on dry ground; then they were gradually lowered so as to dip into the sea; after the volcanic turmoil of 1538, they were again elevated out of it. In 1819 the floor was six inches above the sea-level; in 1845 it was eighteen inches below it at low water. And it still continues to subside in consequence probably of the shrinking of the strata beneath from loss of heat.

The connection between volcanoes, earthquakes, and the upheaval or subsidence of tracts of land is most clearly exhibited in those countries where the evidence of the action of subterranean fire is displayed with greatest intensity. Along the line of the Andes, more particularly, these phenomena go hand in hand together. On the 20th February, 1835, an earthquake, which has been graphically described by Darwin, occurred at Concepcion. The city itself was shaken into ruins, together with 70 neighboring villages. One of the most singular and fearful evidences of the "Power" at work was the rising of a wave or mountain of water, 23 feet higher than spring-tides, which rolled in from the Pacific and broke with fury on the town, surging and swirling along its streets, and drowning many inhabitants and cattle. The adjoining country was strewn with the *débris* of what a few minutes before had been a noble town. A heavy gun, 4 tons in weight, was lifted 15 feet from its position. One ship was deposited high and dry 200 yards from the beach. Some ships riding in 36 feet water were for a few minutes aground; another ship was knocked about like a shuttlecock, having been twice lifted on to the shore and twice replaced again in deep water.

The connection between this earthquake and subterranean fire was made abundantly clear from attendant circumstances. On the same 20th February the island of Juan Fernandez, 360 miles northwest of Concepcion, was violently shaken by an earthquake, and "a volcano burst out under the water close to the shore." Moreover, in the Andes behind Chiloe, 340 miles south of Concepcion, two volcanoes suddenly broke at the same instant into violent action. Thus the subterranean struggle raged along a line of at least five hundred miles, at either end of which its violence culminated in volcanoes. Over large districts where the imprisoning walls of rock were not absolutely broken through, they were yet forced to yield to a certain extent before the expansive efforts of the subterranean fire, and were lifted up above their former level, as if upon the back of some mighty monster. The amount of elevation of the shore round the bay was three feet, and at the island of St. Maria, 30 miles off, Captain Fitzroy subsequently found beds of putrid mussel shells still adhering to the rocks at a height of 10 feet above high-water mark. "For these very shells," says Darwin, "the inhabitants had been previously in the habit of diving at low-water spring-tides." In many places the hills in that volcanic country are strewn with sea-shells to a height of a thousand feet, a circumstance probably due to the upheavals to which the coast has at various times been subject.

Even in our own quiet islands we are every now and then reminded that they by no means lie beyond the reach of these fearful "Powers of the Lord." On two occasions recently the shocks of earthquakes have been felt in England, and almost every year it happens that volcanic disturbance in the south of Europe causes responsive throbbings among the Perthshire Hills.

Chemical force is another "Power of the Lord" from

which this verse of the Benedicite receives some of its most striking illustrations. Many of the greatest workings of Nature are chemical processes. It is by virtue of this power that digestion and fermentation are accomplished, and that those preliminary steps are taken in the seed by which germination is promoted. To it we owe the tints of red and yellow which paint the leaves in autumn. By the aid of carbonic acid, abstracted from air or soil, water carries off into the sea the lime which, after having been built into shells for living animals, is ultimately to be laid down to form new strata. To the energy of chemical force we owe combustion, which, by producing "Fire and Heat," ministers in so many ways to our happiness. To man himself Providence has vouchsafed to impart a certain knowledge of this Power, which he wields to his infinite profit and advantage. But, in the vast domain of chemistry, when the known is contrasted with the unknown, man will for long ages to come continue to resemble the little child wandering on the sea-shore and "picking up now and then a pretty pebble, while the great ocean of truth lies undiscovered before it."

It has been finely observed that chemistry confers a kind of creative power upon man, by which he produces many substances which have no independent existence, and decrees at will unions and separations among the passive objects around him. There is scarcely a domestic operation or a manufacture in which the energies of chemistry are not turned to account. Nearly all the metals, for example, are presented to us by Nature in a crude state, and the power through whose intrumentality they are obtained in purity is chemical action. Many of the most serviceable substances we employ in daily life are the products of the same force — set in motion and guided by our skill. To chemistry we are indebted for the perfection of our sugars, soaps, candles, leathers, dyes, medicines, paper, and glass; and the list might be extended so as to include nearly every manufactured article in use.

Chemistry is the science of experimental surprises, and its transmutations, while they transcend imagination, afford evidence of the wonderful power of which they are the effects. Thus, the most inert substances often produce by combination a compound of the greatest energy. "Nitrogen and hydrogen," Brande and Taylor observe, "are two comparatively inert gases, while carbon is an innoxious solid. The combination of these three elements produces a highly poisonous liquid — Prussic acid. Hydrogen has no smell, and sulphur only a slight smell on friction; when combined these bodies produce a most offensively smelling gas — sulphide of hydrogen. Carbon, oxygen, hydrogen, and nitrogen are innoxious agents, and have no taste; but when combined in certain proportions they form strychnia, remarkable for its intensely bitter taste, and highly poisonous qualities." Sometimes the most worthless substances, under the magic touch of chemistry, cast off their commonness and become things of value and beauty. Who, for example, could have anticipated that matters so dull and common as sand and the ash of a wood fire should under certain circumstances unite to form bright, transparent glass? What feat can be conceived more wonderful than from a substance so dingy, dirty, and unpromising as coal-tar, to create the beautiful series of aniline colors which we admire as mauve, Magenta, Solferino, and Bleu de Paris. To such perfection, indeed, has chemistry now carried this branch of manufacture that there is hardly any tint which many not be obtained from coal-tar by skillful treatment. Chemistry is a wonderful economist of Nature's means, and never shows itself to more advantage than when it takes in hand and turns to account the fragments that would otherwise be lost. As the highest praise that could be offered, it may now almost literally be said that chemists have of late years expunged the word "rubbish" from the dictionary, as well as "waste" from the workshop.

The vegetable kingdom, although it consist of a great variety of forms, tissues, and products, is essentially built up out of a very few ultimate elements. Whole classes of products consist merely of carbon and hydrogen; and, as a general rule, only three principal constituents are found in plants — carbon, hydrogen, and oxygen — to which a small quantity of nitrogen is sometimes added. Thus there is often a remarkable similarity, and sometimes even an identity of composition, between substances in common use which differ widely in their properties. Sugar and gum, for instance, consist exactly of an equal number of atoms of the same elements — carbon, hydrogen, and oxygen; while starch and cellulose, the base of wood, are most closely allied. In the same manner whole classes of vegetable substances, presenting a similarity in their atomic composition, are, nevertheless, possessed of very different properties, of which oil of turpentine and oil of lemons may be adduced as examples. Differences in the properties of many vegetable substances, therefore, appear to depend not only on the nature of the ultimate atoms of which they are composed, but also on the peculiar way in which these atoms are arranged. The idea naturally suggests itself that this remarkable system of similarity in composition must be intended to subserve some useful purpose; and, perhaps, the opinion might be hazarded that it is not without relation to the eventual increase of the world's food-supplies by chemical means.

Seeing that many vegetable substances are identical, or nearly allied in composition, it scarcely appears surprising that chemistry should have already demonstrated the convertibility of some into others. Thus gum and starch are changed into sugar by the action of sulphuric acid. Much sugar is now manufactured in France from potato-starch and sago. Sugar acted on by nitric acid is changed into oxalic acid; so is sawdust when treated by potash. The common, woody fibre of plants, freed from impurity, is convertible by sulphuric acid, first, into a substance like starch, and then into gum and sugar. Thus the proposition, that in times of scarcity some ligneous matter in the shape of fine wood-powder should be added to bread to eke out the supply of flour, does not appear so very extravagant; and, indeed, in Sweden and Norway the inner bark of the pine is often used for the purpose. The stomach, in its own work of digestion, possesses ways and means of operation with which we are unacquainted. We know that the elephant in his native forests mashes up with its food a considerable quantity of woody fibre, and that it has been provided by Nature with powerful machinery for the purpose. Few branches of chemistry are making more rapid strides than the one we have been noticing, and, in the words of Brande and Taylor, " there is scarcely a limit to the power of transforming one organic substance into another."

Considering, then, on the one hand, the identity, or at least the similarity, of composition; and, on the other, the proved facility of transmutation in may cases; considering, too, that this includes the possibility of converting one vegetable substance that is abundant, but of comparatively little use, into another which might be eaten as nourishment, it is evident that there is here involved a principle which may yet prove to be of the highest importance to man. It seems no extravagance to believe that in the few facts just mentioned there are resources indicated which may yet be largely drawn upon before the world has run its course. Chemical power is merely beginning to be developed in this direction, it can be exerted over a very few substances only, and the processes hitherto discovered are often imperfect and costly; but the time may come when these will be cheaper, better understood, and applicable to a variety of common vegetable products. Thus, perhaps, we may humbly yet confidently believe that if, from the enormous increase of the world's population, the necessity for augmenting the old sources of food-supply should ever become urgent, God will inspire his children with the means of unlocking those latent stores, and of turning them to account; for chemical force is eminently a Power of the Lord, to whose conquests no limit can be assigned.

Having drawn some illustrations of the "Powers of the Lord" from the domain of physics and chemistry, we would now invite attention to some examples taken from that other field of Nature, in which vitality works with a force even more wonderful and mysterious.

It is no part of the object of this book to enter into any discussion of what is termed the correlation of the great natural forces, or to inquire how far these are in reality only different manifestations of the same Power. In time this question, like many others that have perplexed mankind, will be sifted until the truth becomes apparent; but, in the mean time, we cannot help thinking that the argument is pushed too far when the principle of life is reduced to nothing more than a mode of physical or chemical action, or a mere manifestation of motion or of heat. Analogies may exist which seem to level the barriers between them, but it seems to us that, notwithstanding all that has been hitherto alleged, the presumption is in favor of the opinion that life is something apart and essentially different from all other kinds of force. God has willed that we should, to a certain extent, fathom the depths both of physical and chemical force, and for reasons obviously connected with our welfare many of their secrets have been committed to our hands, so that we can wield and direct them. But the living principle is a power which, for the wisest purposes, He appears to have reserved solely to Himself. That is delegated to none. From Him alone are "the issues of life." Every effort to penetrate into the mysterious temple of life that we may lay bare its principle has utterly failed, and the greatest philosopher approaches no nearer than the crowd. We know not where to seize the principle of vitality, or what to look for; and we understand nothing more of its essence now than was known a thousand years ago. Under these circumstances we must believe that God does not intend we should comprehend or in any way become masters of that mystery; and, if this be the case, we may rest assured that, as He has meted out to us our faculties according to the work He intended them to accomplish, there is no likelihood of our ever being able to penetrate a secret over which He has thrown an impenetrable veil.

In reflecting on some of the grand operations of Nature one is surprised to find that they are often accomplished not only silently and invisibly, but by agents which at first sight seem strangely out of proportion to the magnitude of the task on hand. Thus at the very bottom of the animal kingdom there are workmen busily engaged day and night in the service of Providence, in numbers which, like the stars, baffle computation. No one even dreamt of their existence until about 200 years ago, when Leeuwenhoek, a Dutch philosopher, discovered them with his newly invented microscope, and exhibited them to an astonished and incredulous world. Yet in these animalcules — so minute as to be invisible to unaided vision — is to be recognized one of the "Powers of the Lord!" As we take our first glance at the little creatures careering over the field of the microscope, it seems as if a new world has been opened out to us; nor is the expression extravagant when we call to mind that this is a corner of Nature into which few ever turn their eyes, and that the forms of life seen here are altogether unlike those with which we were previously familiar. Our first emotion is astonishment; our next, curiosity; and we wonder what purpose in the economy of Nature can be served by creatures so small and insignificant.

But before noticing their operations more fully, it is right that we should become better acquainted with the workmen themselves. If we desire to find them, it is more difficult to say where they are not than where they are. They abound in sea and river, pond and puddle. Wherever an organized atom can swim — and the minutest drop of water is an ocean to thousands — there they are often to be found. If a few shreds of meat, or blades of grass, or stalks of a bouquet be placed in water in a glass, infusorial animalcules will be found to swarm in it after a few days. The population of this minute world varies much under different circumstances; but a great observer in this department, Ehrenberg, tells us that, in a single drop of an infusion he examined, there were probably no fewer than 500 millions of independent individuals! The spectacle of miniature bustle disclosed in one such drop surpasses imagination. The atoms dart forward and backward and sideways with most perfect movement; some shiver or shake; others spend their time in wheeling round and round like dancing dervises. Many show a graver temperament, and stalk across the "field" in a style which by comparison we must call majestic. Yet it will be observed that there is order in all these movements. Though "fidgeting about" in a way that realizes the idea of perfect restlessness, they seldom jostle each other; and they twist in and out, avoiding the rocks raised up by minute particles of dust with as much precision as if they always maintained the keenest "lookout." Occasionally one sees in their movements something that recalls the hunting of well-bred dogs in search of game.

Infusoria assume an endless variety of shapes. One of the simplest among them, the slow-moving Amoeba diffluens, may be compared to an atom of transparent jelly; but it is so often changing its outline by its contractions and protrusions that, except when it is shrunk together into a roundish dot, it can scarcely be described as having one special form more than another. There is neither mouth nor stomach; but when a particle of food touches its sensitive surface, it is soon included or overlapped by a fold of its "diffluent" body, and in the hollow thus made the food is digested and disappears just as if it were in a real stomach. Or the particle is thrust by the inverted fold into the yielding substance of the body, like a pea into a lump of paste, and it is made to move slowly through the body by means of forcible contractions until it is finally absorbed as nourishment. Another animalcule, Actinophrys sol, has flexible tentacles, like rootlets, streaming from its round body in a way which, as the name implies, reminds one of the rays of the sun in a picture. With these he seizes his prey and slowly thrusts it against some part of his surface, which, by first yielding and then closing over it, improvises a stomach for the occasion. After the nourishment is extracted the refuse is thrown out, and the little glutton again stretches out his arms in search of food. These infusorial animalcules are for the most part very voracious, and sometimes gorge themselves until from distortion they can scarcely be recognized. Who can set bounds to Nature's fertility in expedients? In the higher classes of animals we are accustomed to see certain parts of the body "specialized" into particular organs, whose functions are limited to one particular purpose; but on the lower steps of the ladder we see many purposes accomplished by one single means. Thus a little dot of living jelly moves without muscles, enjoys the light of the sun, and sees without eyes, feels without nerves, digests without a stomach, and circulates its nutriment without the vestige of a vessel!

We can merely touch upon this fascinating branch of Natural History, for it would take more space than can here be given to describe, even in the most cursory way, the various groups of animalcules associated together for the work we are now about to describe. Many of these are much higher in the scale of organization than the two mentioned: — thus the curiously beautiful wheel-animalcules belong to the Rotifera, and other nondescript looking creatures belong to the same natural group as our lobsters. But, in their general habits and functions they resemble the infusoria, with which many of them were formerly classified.

When we consider the magnitude and utility of the work performed by these animated atoms, the feeling suggested by their insignificance is exchanged for wonder at their aggregate power. They form, in fact, another of those mighty mechanisms by which Providence insures the salubrity both of land and water; and with this function is combined the equally important task of economizing the stock of organized matter already gained from the mineral kingdom, and preserving it in a state fit for animal food.

These objects are so important in Nature's household that their attainment, as is usual in such cases, is insured by being associated with the instincts and wants of the creatures themselves. Their voracity was necessary to accomplish Nature's design. But for their labors the atmosphere we breathe would become tainted with the exhalations of decaying animal and vegetable matter, and every drop of water in which putrefaction was going on would cast up into the air its germ of malaria and fever. Without their aid the surface of our pleasant earth and our bright seas would be covered with impurity. Think of the myriads of fishes dying at every instant in the ocean, and the quantity of putrescible matter which must thus be diffused through it! Were no provision made for its speedy removal, it would rot, fester, and corrupt both air and water. But these willing workers are always at hand when wanted, and, by voraciously feeding on the decaying atoms, preserve both air and sea in sweetness and salubrity.

With this general purification is combined, as has been said, another scheme of providential utility. Nature is the most admirable of housekeepers, and is full of thrifty contrivances even in the midst of her proverbial profusion. It has, therefore, been so arranged that dead animal matter, often got from the mineral kingdom at the cost of tedious, time-consuming processes, shall not in every case immediately revert back to it through decomposition, but shall be saved and preserved in its organic form so as to be at once again available as animal food. The decaying atoms thus saved, though but the rubbish and sweepings of the world, are yet so valuable that innumerable myriads of creatures specially adapted for the purpose have been stationed at the outlets of organization for the purpose of intercepting them; and, though they are singly minute enough for the digestion of microscopic animalcules, they nevertheless amount to an enormous aggregate by reason of their almost universal diffusion. Had the decaying animal matters been left to their fate without this intervention, they would have been quickly resolved into their ultimate mineral constituents, and, in the form of carbonic acid, hydrogen, oxygen, and nitrogen, would have been speedily dissipated by the winds in all directions. Who can tell how long these gases might have been blown about the world before they again became fixed in vegetable shape, or how long it might have been, even after that preliminary step had been accomplished, before the plants that fed upon them served in their turn as food for animals? Yet not until this cycle had been run would they again have been won back to the animal kingdom, and the loss that would have been thus sustained may be imagined from the amount of decay going on around us. To avoid this evil Providence has drawn as it were a cordon round the frontier of the animal kingdom, and has intrusted the guarding of it to uncountable numbers of Nature's "invisible police," with orders to seize upon escaping particles of food, and to turn them back again by a short route into the active stream of life. Hence, just as the fugitive atoms were on the point of decomposition, they were caught up and imprisoned for a time in the bodies of these animalcules, and then began the quick process of "consecutive nutrition." The infusory was devoured by some microscopic tyrant a little bigger than itself, which in its turn was snapped up by a hungry larva or some prowling insect; the latter afforded a tempting mouthful to a greedy fish or bird; and these again, secured by the rod, or the gun, helped to supply some hungry man's dinner.

We are accustomed, and with reason, to speak of the "lower or inferior" ranks of animal life; but we must recollect that the expression is one of relation only, for every thing about all God's creatures is perfect in respect to the place they inhabit and the functions they perform. In mere beauty and finish the structure of the highest classes of animals is equaled and often surpassed in creatures very near the bottom of the scale. To the Great Creator structural loveliness and perfection cost but the Word; and they are lavished without stint on all His living works. One cannot look at those curious, infusorial animalcules without being convinced that in their way they are perfection itself, and that what we might have been pleased to call higher development would only have impaired their efficiency for the work that was given them to perform. Every thing is in all-wise harmony. Their size and strength correspond to the minute atoms they have to deal with; their numbers, to the stupendous task before them; their simple organization, hardy constitution, and wonderful tenacity of life, to a geographical distribution stretching, so far as we know, from pole to pole. Wherever moisture is found and organized matter can decay, there they flourish in numbers to which the work to be done alone assigns the limit. When we look round and see how good every created thing is, how perfectly the system works, and how even these invisible atoms of life are provided with their daily food, we can throw ourselves with reliance on Our Father, and realize the full comfort of the thought that He careth for us also.

Emblems of science triumphant — telescope and microscope — twin hands of vision — with one we grasp the mighty orbs that were lost to us in space, with the other we bring into view the incomparable atoms of life that were before unseen. To what more noble work can science be consecrated than thus to win for us glimpses of the mightiest and minutest of His works, and, by enlarging the field over which we humbly follow the Creator's hand, to add to the intensity of that perception with which we adoringly recognize His Power?

The accidents fraught with suffering to mankind which now and then happen through the agency of the great Powers of Nature have always been a stumbling-block to short-sighted critics of the ways of Providence. It is not enough for them to know that in the dispensation of things here below there is no absolute good, or that the admixture of bad is often less essential than it seems, and is mainly due to blamable want of forethought. With dismay they read of conflagrations and earthquakes, the bursting of reservoirs and other accidents, and they are tempted secretly to question the wisdom of laws under which such disasters are entailed. The most cursory glance at the government of the world must convince every body that Providence legislates on the widest basis for the well-being of the whole, and we must ever weigh the ill occasionally sustained by a few through the operation of these Powers against the necessary services rendered by them to the universal world. It must be recollected, too, that God has given faculties to man for the very purpose of enabling him to avert or control the danger thus arising. Fire causes direful conflagrations, it is true, but how generally it is in man's power to prevent them by proper precaution. The means are placed within his reach. On the other hand, when we weigh this comparatively rare evil against the blessings showered upon man at every instant by "Fire and Heat," into what imperceptible dimensions does not the accidental evil shrink! The noble ship sinks under the waters and its crew perishes, or a Sheffield reservoir bursts its dam and submerges villages and plains, or laborers are crushed by a falling bridge or tower. Well — all this mischief results from the inexorable law of gravity; but would any one wish. that, in order to prevent these accidents, there had been no law of gravity in existence? In most cases these calamities might have been prevented. Were gravity an uncertain, capricious thing, then, indeed, there would be cause for fear and lamentation, and it would be impossible to cope with the evils attendant on its action. But care has been taken that a Power operating thus universally should be subject to the most rigid laws, and that man should be able not only to parry many of the dangers to which it may lead, but that he should also be able to turn it to account for his own purposes. Let us reflect that, in order to have absolutely prevented such accidents, the law of gravity itself must have been suspended; and were that law suspended but for an instant, the earth and the whole heavens would collapse into destruction. A law so essential to the existence of the world must be made peremptory and universal — it cannot be made to hold for some occasions and not for others; it is a chain of safety that must not be left to be slackened at discretion. If it extinguish life now and then, we must not forget that it alone makes life possible for all. In the same way the tempest, the lightning, and the stormy sea have their uses in Nature's economy, and these will be noticed in another place. The earthquake and the volcano appear to be agents employed in modifying the crust of the earth, and preparing it for future purposes in which we of the present generation have no part. But even in regard to these terrible displays of force we must not forget that they are the result of that same Power of the Lord which is almost universally working for our advantage. And when we are assailed with difficulties in regard to the material government of the world — when we see evils prevailing for which we cannot even imagine any equivalent advantage — let us fall back with confidence on our experience of God's ways. Surrounded as we are on every side with evidence of the care bestowed by our heavenly Father on all His creatures, we can well afford to wait with patience until these and other perplexing questions are solved, in the full conviction that, when the fitting time comes, they will be found to exhibit new proofs of God's Power and Goodness.

Great is our Lord, and great is His power; yea, and His wisdom is infinite.
Ps. cxlvii.

MOUNTAINS AND HILLS.

O ye Mountains and Hills, bless ye the Lord: praise Him, and magnify Him for ever.

IF it were required to name the grandest natural objects upon earth, it is probable that "mountains and hills" would rise to the lips of not a few. In sublimity they take rank with the ocean and the clouds. They were chosen by the Psalmist to typify God's power, — "And the strength of the hills is His also." On the one hand, their height, their mass, and the deep planting of their roots in the earth; and on the other, the beauty which rests upon their varied outlines, which clothes their sides and precipices, and lies among their wide valleys and deep glens, mark them out not only as the most conspicuous, but also as among the most attractive objects in the world. Nor is it without wise design that these grand features of the earth should twine themselves round the affections. The love of the Highlander for his hills is proverbial. Love for the spot where one was born — for the district where one has lived, secures for it the interest of friends who will look to its welfare. Memory lingers over the dim outline of a mountain long after other scenes grouped round its base have faded away; and one can easily understand that the eyes which day by day rest on the familiar hills must ultimately open up for them a way to the heart. Exiles from a country abounding in famous mountains, it was to be expected that the Three Children, in their survey of Nature, should invoke them as testimonies of the Mercy and Power of the Lord. Had not their beloved land been traversed with hills to bring down the fertilizing rain from the clouds, Judea might have been as arid as the neighboring desert. The dying Moses had, in blessing the tribes, spoken of "the precious things of the lasting hills." Many of the mountains which they might have seen in their childhood, and with whose names we, too, are familiar, were treasured in their thoughts as enduring monuments of the power of God in delivering His chosen people. The hill of Bashan marked for ever the spot where Moses gained the victory over Og, its king. Mount Carmel was identified with the deeds of the Prophet Elijah. It was here that the "fire of the Lord fell and consumed the burnt-sacrifice" which the servant of God prepared when he would confound the priests of Baal. From the top of Carmel, too, the Prophet discerned the "little cloud out of the sea, like a man's hand," which announced the welcome rain. They might have known Mount Tabor, conspicuous among all the hills of Lower Galilee, with its plain where Sisera "with his chariots and his multitude" was delivered into the hands of Barak, and where more recently their oppressor Nebuchadnezzar had striven with and vanquished the children of Israel; but they knew not that it was destined in after ages to become still more interesting to us as the traditional scene of the Transfiguration. From the rock in Horeb Moses miraculously drew forth the water to quench the thirst of the children of Israel. Nor from this list can Sinai, the most famous mountain of all, be omitted, where the Lord delivered the law to Moses, and revealed Himself to the children of Israel in the cloud upon the smoking mountain, and where other momentous events in the passage through the desert took place.

The mountain of which the Bible makes earliest mention is Ararat, and it is identified with an occurrence that renders it a testimony for ever of God's power and mercy. When the race which had provoked the wrath of Heaven by its wickedness had been destroyed in the waters of the deluge, the ark with its favored inmates was guided to rest and safety upon its heights. The Lord let loose the powers chained up in Nature against His enemies, and yet, "remembering mercy," preserved a remnant by which the fair earth was again filled with life. Mount Ararat forms the loftiest peak in the long ridge of the Taurus, rising 17,750 feet above the level of the sea, or nearly 2000 feet higher than the summit of Mont Blanc. It is situated in that corner of Asia Minor where the dominions of Russia, Turkey, and Persia touch, and from the circumstance that it is partly detached from the groups around it, the eye takes in nearly its whole outline from base to apex; hence in isolated majesty it stands forth among the most sublime mountains in the world. Its crest is mantled in snow, and so difficult is the ascent that, although often attempted, it was never achieved until 1829, when the feat was accomplished by Professor Parrot, of the Russian service. Since the days of Noah, perhaps, no other human foot had ever been planted on the top of that famous hill. Mount Ararat is an object of interest and veneration not only to Christians but to Mohammedans also, as well as to the inhabitants generally of that district of Western Asia. An Oriental traveler relates that when an Armenian for the first time beholds the well-known outline of the mountain after a long absence, he kisses the ground, makes the sign of the cross, and repeats certain prayers.

Stupendous though mountain masses be, they form but trifling inequalities when compared to the diameter of the globe on which they rest. Between the summit of Chimborazo, one of the highest of the Andes, and the deepest part of the Atlantic yet sounded lying to the south of Newfoundland, there is an estimated difference of level amounting to about nine miles. This may be considered as representing with near approximation the difference between the highest and the lowest spots upon the globe.

The loftiest peaks of the Himalayas hardly exceed an elevation of five miles above the sea, which is a height so inconsiderable in relation to the diameter of the globe that it is a great exaggeration to compare it, as is often done, to the rugosities on the surface of an orange. Proportionate inequalities on an orange would be invisible to the naked eye. According to other estimates the highest table-lands of the world might be fairly represented by the thinnest sheet of writing-paper, and the highest mountain by the smallest visible particle of sand laid upon a 16-inch globe.

Mountains play an important part in the economy of Nature, and they are the agents by which the Creator bestows many blessings upon his children. They act as loadstones to the clouds, and draw down from them the fertilizing rain. Often it is a mountain-range which determines whether a country is to be a garden or a desert, and points out the place where rain-bringing winds are to yield up their treasures. While considering the "waters above the firmament" it has been shown how the barrenness of the deserts of Thibet and Mongolia has been produced by the rain-intercepting ridge of the Himalayas, and how the southwest monsoon, which covers the wide plains of Hindostan with fertility, is the result of their combined action. As Maury has observed, the desert and the mountain are "counterpoises or compensations to make the machine perfect," and they are placed in certain selected situations over the earth for the general good, to regulate up to a certain point the course of the winds, and determine where the rains shall most abundantly fall. In relation to this important function, no less than to other cosmical considerations, it may be said, with literal truth, that "He has comprehended the dust of the earth in a measure, and weighed the mountains in scales, and the hills in a balance." Had the "dust" of the deserts of Central Asia been measured out either with greater or with less abundance than actually is the case, or had the Himalayan mountains been weighed in masses greatly differing from those they now present, the whole monsoon-machinery would have been thrown off the balance on which it has been so perfectly adjusted, and the wide plains of India would have been changed into a sterile desert.

Mountains "drink the waters of the rain of Heaven." They are the great water-sheds of the earth. On their tops the river-systems of the world are born, and the tiny rills thence first started on their way soon coalesce into streams, and then into rivers, to be poured back eventually into the sea whence they came. It is obvious that, if the earth had been a dead level, and if there had been no slopes and hollows to collect the moisture together, water would have lodged in stagnant pools over its surface, spoilt its fertility, and covered it with unhealthy swamps. As a general rule, to which for wise reasons there are some remarkable exceptions, mountains form the backbone or central ridge of continents; and Nature, by decreeing that the chief rains shall fall among them, has secured the greatest amount of fertilizing service which it is possible for them to render. As it flows downward to the sea, the rain-water, collected into streams, dispenses fertility on all sides. Had it been otherwise arranged, and had the chief rainfall occurred near the coasts, the course of the rivers produced by it would have been necessarily short, and the amount of good done by them would have been comparatively small.

Let us for a moment trace the influence which the position of mountains exercises on the climates of certain districts. The extraordinary fertility of the soil and the richness of vegetation found throughout the vast basin of the Amazon and in some regions to the south are produced by the absence of high mountain ridges running parallel with the eastern shore of equatorial America. The Trade-wind reaches the shores of Brazil saturated with moisture gathered up while sweeping across the Atlantic. If it now encountered lofty mountains, the rain would be drawn from it in quantities which, while they deluged the districts near the shore and made them comparatively useless, would have left little moisture behind to fertilize the vast interior. The Valley of the Amazon might then have been changed into a desert, instead of being adorned, as it now is, with the most glorious vegetation in the world. Let us consider what has actually happened on the opposite side of South America, where the conditions just mentioned are reversed. One of the most rain-charged winds in existence blows from the Pacific Ocean against the coast of Patagonia. But no sooner does it reach the shore than it encounters the lofty Andes; torrents of water are immediately drained off from the clouds, and one of the wettest climates of the earth is the result. The vegetation, however, is of a rank and not very useful kind, owing to the superabundance of moisture and the want of sun; and the whole country is covered with gloomy, impenetrable forests of pine. But mark what happens to the districts lying beyond. The interior of Patagonia is a vast desert; for the moisture, which otherwise would have fertilized it, has been already condensed out of the wind by the cold tops of the Andes. And the same fate would unquestionably have overtaken Brazil and La Plata had the Andes been placed upon the eastern instead of on the western side of the continent.

Many mountain ranges in warm or tropical countries, like prudent foster-mothers, hold near their summits vast reservoirs of water frozen into ice and snow, in order that they may pour down from their sides the needful supply of moisture when the plains below are parched by the summer's sun. Thus the glaciers of the Himalayas feed the Ganges, the Indus, and the Burhampootra; and the higher Andes roll down cool streams into the rainless districts bordering the Pacific. The Rhine and the Rhone, with many of their early affluents, issue from glaciers in

Switzerland, and they would dwindle into small proportions in the summer time were it not for the supplies given to them by these compensating reservoirs of ice. In winter, indeed, these alpine sources are partially locked up by the frost; and hence it is remarked that these rivers never have their channels better filled than during the hot summer months when the melting of the glaciers is most rapid.

In ascending lofty tropical mountains successive belts of vegetation are traversed, which represent in miniature the different climates of the earth as we pass from the Equator toward the poles. At the base of the Peruvian Andes, for example, the traveler finds himself in the glowing temperature of the tropics. For the first 5000 feet of ascent his way lies among pine-apples, cocoas, bananas, and other kinds of palms, with bright and fantastic-looking orchids clustering on the trees, and marking the equatorial character of the belt. While plodding his way up the next 5000 feet of ascent the traveler sees much to remind him of the vegetation of temperate climates: the vine flourishes, while crops of maize and wheat luxuriantly clothe the ground, as in Southern Europe. In passing through the next 5000 feet the temperature gradually chills into severe cold. At first vegetation wears the aspect of the higher "temperate" climates. The wheat has disappeared, and figuratively the traveler may be said to be as far north as John o'Groat's; but the potato still thrives, while barley and rye assimilate the climate to that of parts of Norway. The stately trees of the lower belts have disappeared, and the forests are thin and degenerate, until at length a scrubby pine or birch is their sole representative. Here, at an altitude equal to the summit of Mont Blanc, the first wreaths of perpetual snow and the last efforts of expiring vegetation come into contact. Plantal life as usual dies out with the moss and the lichen.

Mountain ranges and lofty plateaux form a natural sanatorium frequently established by Providence in the midst of hot, unhealthy tropical countries. The worn-out invalid finds on these cool heights a climate which soon restores him to health, and enables him again to encounter the less favorable influences of the plains. Recent improvements in traveling have enhanced the value of this blessing by enabling many to take advantage of the change who formerly could not profit by it. The Madrasian retires to recruit his exhausted vigor among the bracing Neilgherries; the citizen of Calcutta travels to the "upper country" to seek health among the slopes of the Himalayas; the Cingalese leaves the sultry coast to profit by the more bracing air of the coffee districts near Adam's Peak; the Mexican leaves the Caliente for the Templada or the Fria; and the Peruvian or Chilian of the coast finds cool air, verdure, and health on the lofty sides of the Andes. On the whole, there are few tropical districts so unfortunately placed as to be beyond moderately easy access to some mountain sanatorium.

Mountains exhibit wonderful proofs of the force displayed in the arrangement of the surface of the earth. Geology tells us that many of them — like the lofty peaks of the Andes, or Ailsa Craig, or Teneriffe — have been cast forth as liquid lava from the interior of the earth by the force of fire. Others, again, though deposited originally at the bottom of the sea, have been lifted as it were on the back of other rocks, so as now to form lofty ridges. There are limestone strata of marine origin, labelled with shells identical with others found in low-lying beds near Paris, which are now placed at a height of 10,000 feet above the ocean, crowning the summit of the Diablerets among the Swiss Alps. Examples of similar elevations are met with among the Himalayas, in Tahiti, and elsewhere.

Viewed under another aspect, mountains show forth the power of the Creator in a way still more marvelous. Many mountain masses and level strata consist chiefly of the remains of animals that formerly existed on the globe. The beautiful marbles of Derbyshire, for instance, owe their variegated markings to the shells which successive generations of creatures built up and left behind. One feels astounded at the profusion of ancient life revealed by those "medals of creation." Nearly the whole city of Paris has been reared out of the consolidated remains of microscopic Miliolæ quarried from the neighboring tertiary beds; and calculations show that every cubic inch of this stone contains not fewer than 2000 millions of individuals. The most famous of the pyramids are formed out of the remains of microscopic nummulites, cemented into a building-stone which is found abundantly in Egypt and in many other places. One of the most remarkable examples of the former profusion of life is to be found in the polishing slate of Bilin, in Bohemia, which is estimated to contain the remains of 41,000 millions of infusory animals in every cubic inch.

Look at those distant hills! We recognize the English Downs by their soft, wavy outline, by the marvelous brightness of their green, by their springy turf, by the white sheep specks that dot their gently sloping sides, and by the bracing air which sweeps over them with the crisp freshness of the sea. They undulate in a broad belt through England, from the shore of Dorset to the cliffs of Flamborough and Dover. In the north of Ireland the chalk has been broken through and almost fused by the volcanic fires which once formed the Giant's Causeway. It extends across the Continent of Europe in several directions nearly from end to end, and in other quarters of the world it is largely developed. The vast mass is heaped upon thousands of square miles of the earth's crust. Yet it is but the sepulchre of myriads of creatures that formerly existed, and the visible evidence of the profusion of life that issued in ancient times from the Creator's hand. Scattered throughout are the bones of reptiles and fishes, with corals, sea-urchins, sponges, and other marine remains. While surveying these relics we realize and seem to become familiar with the curious forms of life which then existed. But the tomb of chalk in which they lie is itself composed partly of crushed, compressed, or metamorphosed shells, partly of myriads of microscopic animalcules, whose structure and markings are often as beautiful and perfect as if they had only died yesterday. Who can conceive the abundance of the life which thus built up those hills? Yet every thing tends to show that there is not an atom of chalk in the world which did not once form part of a living animal!

I will remember the works of the Lord; and call to mind thy wonders of old time. — Ps. lxxvii.

THE EARTH.

O let the Earth bless the Lord: yea, let it praise Him, and magnify Him for ever.

IN those summer strolls amid rural scenes which now and then cast sunshine on the way of even the busiest among us, who has not rested on some river's bank or green hill-side, and in his heart humbly thanked God, both for having clothed the earth with beauty, and for having bestowed upon himself the faculty to appreciate and enjoy it? Which of us can estimate the sum of purest pleasure that would have been lost to man had he been created as unconscious of this beauty as the beasts that perish? But by the love of our Father — who careth for our pleasure as well as for our wants — a power to perceive the charms of Nature has been implanted universally within us, and none are shut out from its enjoyment. The savage and the civilized, the old and the young, the rich and the poor — all are capable of feeling its softening influence. This admiration awakens a taste which grows and strengthens by what it feeds on; for he who has once truly experienced the charm of Nature's scenery will ever afterward be on the watch to discover and enjoy it. In the midst of scenes like these let the thought now and then rise in the mind that in making Nature so attractive it was intended, not merely to please the eye, but to draw man on to the consideration of the work itself, and to move him by the aspect of its beauteous perfection to magnify the Great Artificer.

But while there are many whose delight it is to feast

upon such treats, spread out before them for enjoyment by the Father, there are some who pass on without caring to taste. The very commonness of the privilege dulls their perception, and they either see it not at all, or look on with apathy. There are others who ardently profess their love of Nature, but the feeling, though sometimes even extravagantly expressed, is nevertheless capricious and uncertain. They are ready to admire on great occasions; but they have little relish for Nature in its ordinary dress, and exact the stimulus of "fine scenery" before they will condescend to enjoy. Alas! what loss is theirs — and how thriftless they are in thus throwing away a pure and oft-recurring pleasure in a world where pleasures without alloy are all too few! It is, indeed, only reasonable that we should be most keenly impressed by the more rare displays of Nature's highest beauties; but surely that need not render us insensible to such charms as may with certainty be found in almost every landscape. In our daily intercourse with Nature out-of-doors it is wisdom not to encourage too fastidious a taste. A few earnest, sympathizing glances, however homely may be the scene on which they dwell, will rarely fail to gather up some grains of gratification, and Nature will surely smile back on us if we will but look with interest upon her. A little encouragement given to this appreciative disposition will return a rich reward, for it will bring within life's circle a thousand moments of enjoyment which would otherwise be wholly lost.

In other parts of this book some remarks will be found on the cosmical relations of our planet. Various illustrations of God's Goodness and Wisdom, as exhibited in the productions of the earth and in its physical geography, are likewise given elsewhere. In this place I shall endeavor to point out by some further illustrations how marvelously man has been able, by the favor of Providence, to convert many of the raw materials of the earth into great blessings. I shall also venture to make a few observations in regard to the principle on which the treasures of the earth are to be dedicated to His service, and on the mode in which they may be made to contribute to His glory.

> The Earth is the Lord's, and All that therein is. — Ps. xxiv.

The earth is, indeed, beautiful; but this is only the outside adornment lavished on a priceless casket. Earth is a fruitful mother, filled with the treasures of God's love to man! Its vaults are packed full of stone for building and marble for decoration — with metals of every kind for use and ornament — with coals for warming us and multiplying ten million-fold the strength of our arms — with fountains of oil for our lamps, and with countless other gifts that minister to our happiness. Who could succeed in exhausting the catalogue of the things with which the earth trumpets forth His praise and glory? For all our material wants this is the storehouse in which are laid up the gifts that will content them. Yet in the midst of riches that are inconceivable there is nothing that is superfluous, or which does not fulfill its appointed task in Nature's economy. With short-sighted rashness we sometimes call certain things worthless, and others precious; but in the system of Providence none are worthless and all are precious.

Within the wide range of scientific art there is perhaps no change more surprising than that by which sand is converted into glass, and there are few that are fraught with more advantage to man. Consider the abundance of sand, and how it covers the earth almost to redundancy. That this coarse, opaque substance should cast off its common nature so completely as to become bright crystal is a marvel which none could have anticipated, and which seems comparable only to the metamorphosis of the dull pupa into the beautiful imago of insect life. Intractable though sand may be when heated in the furnace by itself, the admixture of an alkaline substance with it in the crucible tames its obdurate nature, conquers its opacity, and fuses it into the precious, transparent glass which we apply to so many useful purposes.

Glass-making was one of the earliest of the arts. Its manufacture, as practiced 3500 years ago, is painted on the walls of the Egyptian tombs of Beni Hassen, and the mummy-chambers of that and subsequent periods have yielded up numerous articles in glass, of which an interesting collection may be seen in the British Museum. Not the least remarkable were the artificial gems which were turned out with a success rivaling the best modern productions of Paris. Fairholt tells us that "the green emerald, the purple amethyst, and other expensive gems, were successfully imitated, and a necklace of false stones could be purchased of a Theban jeweler with as much facility as at a London shop of the present day." During the early period of its history, indeed, glass-making was even more of an ornamental than a useful art, and it is curious to note how long it was before some of the most valuable applications of glass to the wants of man were discovered. A few of the windows in Pompeii appear to have been glazed. Some houses in England had windows containing foreign glass in the reign of Henry II.; but there was no manufactory of it in this country until the year 1557. Windows, before that time, were either open to the weather, or were closed with paper or linen made translucent by being soaked in oil. In some countries a natural but very inferior substitute for glass had been provided in the shape of thin scales of mica.

It has been remarked that, to a superficial observer, nothing appears to be of less value than sand, except it be its twin sister clay. But we have seen how God has inspired man with the power to turn sand into glass; and with equal goodness He has taught him how to convert clay into useful pottery. Let any one try to realize how much comfort and convenience would have been lost had our Father not impressed those substances with their valuable, secret qualities; or had He not with corresponding design, led man on to the knowledge of how to profit by them.

The making of pottery was one of the earliest arts practiced in the world. In its rudest state it seems an easy invention. On the one hand, the common wants of man urgently suggest it; on the other, the plastic clay impressed by his foot and baked in the sun obviously points toward it. It was impossible for man long to shut his eyes to such plain hints from Nature; hence pots and cups of rudest earthenware form the only record of many peoples who lived before history began, and few savages are found by travelers and voyagers at the present day who are destitute of vessels of some sort fashioned out of clay. The ancient Egyptians were clever potters. The wheel employed in the time of Moses and Pharaoh does not differ greatly from the one now in use, while it constitutes the earliest "machine" of which we have any record. As is well known, the Chinese were the first to make that finer kind of pottery to which the term porcelain is now restricted, and the art with them seems to have reached its highest perfection about the year 1000 A. D. With the "renaissance" in the 15th century, the coarse pottery of Europe began to be improved. In Italy it was raised into Majolica, Faienza, Raffaelle, and Robbia ware; in Holland improvement took the less beautiful and often quaint form of Delft ware; in England the well-known Queen Elizabeth ware was thought wonderfully fine, and, though extremely coarse according to modern standards, was at least an improvement upon the black-jack and drinking-horn which it superseded. All such works, however, owed their value, not to their quality as porcelain, but to the paintings enameled on them by Raffaelle or his pupils;

to the skill with which the clay had been modeled by Luca della Robbia and Bernard de Palissy; or to the quaint and fantastic forms given to them by the artists of Holland. And there is no saying how long a fine paste might have been wanting to enable Europe to produce porcelain rivaling that of China, had it not been for the occurrence of a lucky accident. About a century and a half ago it happened that Dr. Böttcher, of Magdeburg, devoted himself to the discovery of the philosopher's stone, and he was probably the last in the long list of alchemists. Dissatisfied with the crucibles then in use, he set about manufacturing his own; and, from the experiments he was led to make, he acquired a practical knowledge of the pottery produced from common clays. At this critical moment it happened that the Doctor one morning found his well-powdered wig unusually heavy, and on inquiry he learnt that his servant had ventured to introduce to his notice, without asking, a new kind of hair-powder which had just come into fashion, and of which the material, instead of being expensive wheat flour, was only a common white clay that had been well dried and finely pounded. Böttcher's crucible experiments instantly suggested to him that this clay would make an admirable white "paste" for pottery, and a few trials satisfied him of the value of the discovery. By means of this fine, white clay he in fact converted common earthenware into porcelain. Favored by the patronage of the Duke of Saxony, he was attached to the manufactory at Meisen, from which specimens of porcelain immediately began to be issued which astonished the world of art. From this Saxon root the most famous china-works in Europe gradually sprung up. For a long time the art was kept a profound secret, and the artists were as rigidly secluded in their manufactory as ever nuns were in a convent. They were prizes competed for by the different continental Courts; and, under the temptation of high bribes, some of them from time to time escaped from prison, carrying their secret with them. Most of the early porcelain manufactories owed their origin to these runaways. The most remarkable exception was that at Berlin, which was established by Frederick the Great by means of workmen whom he seized as prisoners after the successes of the Seven Years' War. Thus, as Fairholt observes, the last of the alchemists, though he did not succeed in finding the philosopher's stone for converting common matters into gold, made a discovery hardly less valuable, by which a substance as ordinary as clay might be changed into porcelain, the finest specimens of which are so precious as to be worth more than their weight in gold.

Clay consists essentially of silica, or sand, in union with the oxide of a bright metal which has assumed a homely working dress for the purpose of fitting it to take a most useful part in the composition of the soil. To the clay thus mixed up in it the ground is indebted for some of its best qualities as a producer of food. But when treated skillfully by the chemist, clay casts off this unattractive dress, and appears as the metal aluminium. For thousands of years clay had been handled and worked without its true nature having been suspected; nor was it until the discoveries of Sir Humphrey Davy had proved potash, soda, and magnesia to be metallic oxides, that a similar nature began to be theoretically imputed to clay. Great was the sensation in the chemical world when, in 1827, Wöhler announced the discovery of the long-looked-for metal in a pure state, although, from the difficulty of the process of extraction, it was for some years to be seen only in museums or at scientific conversazioni. But its useful qualities were, nevertheless, speedily recognized, and it at once took high rank among the metals. Aluminium possesses the quality of lightness which is so rare among metals, and it is hard and white like silver, though much less brilliant. It can be beaten readily into plates or rolled out into wire, and it is not tarnished by air or water under ordinary temperatures. The great, but assuredly only temporary drawback to the value of this new gift has been the cost of producing it; but even already the intelligent industry of man has to a considerable extent triumphed over that difficulty. In the Aluminium Works at Newcastle many tons of this metal are annually extracted by a process which admits of its being sold at a comparatively cheap price, and for many purposes it is fast coming into general use. In the Industrial Exhibition of 1862 there was a beautiful display of work, both useful and ornamental, in aluminium; and there is now scarcely a bazaar which does not offer bracelets, buckles, and other light productions manufactured out of this widely diffused metal.

To the oxide of this metal — alumina — obtained by an easy process from common alum, we are indebted for the permanence of some of the brightest tints used in calico-printing. It is found that many colors have little affinity for the cotton fibre, so that while they readily stain it, the stain is evanescent and disappears in washing. Luckily for the dyer, alumina has a strong affinity at once for the cotton fibre and the color, and holds them both firmly united in its grasp. In this way the color is fixed permanently, or becomes, as it is termed, "fast."

It is obviously impossible to find room here for a description of the many ways in which metals contribute to our happiness or comfort. It may be observed generally that there is even more marked variety in the properties of metals than in those of wood; nor can any one fail to perceive that this is not the result of accident, but is due to the forethought with which Our Father has provided for the wants of His children, by increasing the range of the purposes to which metals are applicable. Thus when strength is desired we have the giant, iron, at our beck and call. An obdurate, unwieldy servant in his rougher shapes, we tame him through fire, and make his dull force yield to our skillful weakness. Powerful in our knowledge, we summon this metal to sustain our houses and bridge our rivers, and we bend and roll and twist and fashion it as we please for a thousand useful purposes. Do we want a medium to help on commerce by making clumsy barter unnecessary? there is gold. Is heaviness required? it is to be found in platinum; or lightness? there is aluminium; or softness? there is lead; or brittleness? there is antimony; or fluidity? there is mercury; while for a combination of many qualities useful in domestic life, there are copper and tin. By the design of Providence one metal appears to have been created to supplement the deficiencies of another. Thus iron, strong though it be, yields to the combined attacks of air and moisture. But by sheathing it in a film of zinc or tin — metals which, though comparatively weak, are yet less sensitive to air and moisture — iron gains the priceless quality of endurance. By the skillful union of other metals the chemist knows how they may be adapted to almost every purpose. Thus the value of the metals as a gift to man can only be compared to that of wood and stone, to which it is supplementary. In bestowing these three blessings, what a provision has been made by Our Father for our comfort!

Let us pass to another compartment of the storehouse, and consider the beneficence and the knowledge of our wants with which the rocks of the earth have been treasured up. Fire and water, under the formative guidance of the Lord of Nature, have contributed their mightiest forces in preparing them for our service, and have split and blocked and layered them into shapes convenient for our use. Sometimes they are cemented into huge masses out of which colossal breakwaters and docks may be constructed. Some rocks cleave readily into slices for our pavements; others split into fine plates for our slates. Some are so soft that they may be cut with a saw, and yet harden firmly when exposed to the air; others are so hard that iron will scarcely scratch them, while they surpass that metal in endurance. The rocks yield lime, so useful as manure; and salt, which is a necessary of life. Vast strata of coal lie cellared in the earth. These blessings are so common, and are so intertwined in the daily experience of us all, that it appears almost to be trifling to recapitulate them. But should a gift be less formally acknowledged because it is given abundantly? Instead of withholding these blessings altogether, or bestowing them niggardly, He has diffused them everywhere; but, strange to say, it is this very lavishness which often dulls perception, and creates the danger of our passing by without a thought of gratitude. All occasionally make general admissions of their obligations; but how few ever stop before a quarry or a coal-mine to quicken their gratitude by thanking God specially for His good gift! Yet what abundant evidence is afforded by every quarry of God's providence toward us. Is it a small thing to be able to think and to know that long before we came into existence Our Father was already caring for us and for our wants, and was already "preparing the dry land," by storing it with good gifts to add to our happiness?

Let us for a moment pause to survey the famous quarry of Craigleith, and try to estimate the shelter, the comfort, and the happiness that have been dug out of that vast chasm. Stand on its brink, and it will make you giddy to look down into the fearful gulf. Far away in its lowest depths you descry busy workmen dwarfed by distance into pygmies. The birds, whom your approach has disturbed, hurriedly cast off, and seem by their long fluttering as if they never could reach the opposite shore of the abyss. Descend to the bottom by the climbing zigzag, which calls to mind some engineering triumph in the Alps; stand in the centre — look round — and then try to realize in imagination the vastness of the void that was once filled up brimful to the top with solid stone. Frowning precipices rise sheer from the bottom for several hundred feet. Perched high up on a projecting crag, in a spot which many a feudal castle might envy, the giant steam noisily stretches out his strong arms to help on the labors of the place. One stands amazed to think what could have consumed and swallowed up so much hard rock. Never did earth more opportunely bring forth her hidden treasures. An ancient capital hard by had outgrown itself. Cooped up by Nature within the limits of a narrow ridge, its streets, with a single, grand exception on its crest, had been squeezed together into wynds and closes, partly from scantiness of space and partly for the sake of aiding defense in troublous times. Dunedin was like a pent-up river whose waters were watching for a chance to spring beyond their old confinements. Suddenly the citizens broke through the spell of custom and tradition. The old gate was passed, the swampy North Loch was bridged over, the green fields on the other side were reached ; and then arose a city — the like of which had never been seen before. Nearly every stone that left this vast void was built into that new town of Edinburgh, whose glory, next to its matchless site, is the beautiful rock of Craigleith quarry.

From the observations just made it appears that the crust of the earth may be regarded as little else than a storehouse filled with good gifts from Our Father for the purpose of ministering to our happiness ; and surely the consideration of this truth ought to suggest to us the propriety, or rather the duty, of turning them if possible to account in His service, and of making them, as far as may be, the visible expressions of our thankfulness. Let us first endeavor, as carefully as we can, to clear the ground for the observations about to be made. God is a Spirit, and we know that the works of our hands, how perfect soever they may be, can have intrinsically no value in His eyes. But we are, at the same time, distinctly assured that it is possible to do every thing to His glory, and we are enjoined so to do it. "Whatsoever ye do, do *all* to the glory of God." Nothing is excepted — no act is either so great or so small as to be beyond the circle of this command. By it we learn that it is the motive which sanctifies. Unless the motive be God's glory, the finest work sinks into worthlessness; but, hallowed by that motive, the smallest offering is graciously accepted.

One way by which we endeavor to promote God's glory is the building of churches, and in this act especially we seem to be turning the materials of the earth to account, and to be dedicating them to His service. In what mind, then, ought we to undertake this duty? Is it consistent with the feeling of gratitude and propriety, or even of decency, that His temple should be raised barely and meanly when we have it in our power to do more? The widow's mite was highly valued because it was the utmost she could give; but if she had possessed more it would not have been so considered. Ought we not then to follow out this principle as far as we can, and to give our best? Can it be right that, while we deem no architectural beauty too good for our own dwellings, we should be satisfied with His House being only a little better than a barrack — when it is in our power to do more? While we adorn our palaces with every thing which good taste can obtain from the sculptor or the painter, can it be right to consider the carpenter and the plasterer good enough artists for the church — if we have it in our power to do more? Or while we fill our concert rooms with finest music, shall we celebrate His praise in the sanctuary in hymns that are often discordant to healthy ears — when we have it in our power to do more?

We would rather be among those whose rule it is to do their best for God's glory, than with others who are content to consider what is inferior or easy to be had as good enough for the adornment of His House. Scarcely do they seem to understand or appreciate their high privilege when they withhold what ought gladly and lovingly to be laid upon the altar. These services are in themselves true offerings, yet not less are they due on the lower, yet still high, ground of consistency and fitness, for they seem to be only the natural outward expression of our gratitude. Surely it will not be denied that the feeling is good, or that the principle of offering the best in our power wherever the service of God is in question, must be right and safe. Though paradoxical, it is nevertheless true that giving liberally for such purposes does not practically diminish the sources from which the means are drawn. There probably never was a case yet where one church remained unbuilt, because another had been suitably adorned; but, on the other hand, we think it may be safely asserted that the aspect of a church whose fitting adornments inspired devotional feeling has often acted as a stimulus to help on similar works. We may rest assured that, when our all has been done, we have equally fallen short of His glory and our own obligations.

Let us for a moment consider how our pious forefathers acted in this matter. They invariably built churches to the best of their knowledge of art, and adorned them to the best of the means that lay within their reach. The works that have come down to us from mediæval times attest how carefully they were originally built and set apart for God's service. The most skillful master-masons were employed, the most beautiful stone that could be procured was brought even from distant sources. The Norman Bishop Walkelyn built his new Cathedral at Winchester with materials brought from quarries in the Isle of Wight, and the beautiful white stone of Caen was in request for the decoration of God's House from a very early period. Our forefathers, however, were limited in their materials for decoration, and hence their architectural adornments chiefly took the form of column, arch, and tracery. When we consider the ecclesiastical works — the cathedrals and churches — erected in the 13th, 14th, and 15th centuries, in relation to the resources from which they were produced, we are equally impressed with the earnest purpose of our forefathers, and humbled at our own supineness. Happily in these latest days church architecture has revived, and all denominations of Christians now vie with each other in taking advantage of its taste and resources.

The internal adornment of churches has also much improved of late, although there is some difference of opinion as to the extent to which it ought to be carried. In a difficulty of this nature it is surely safe to apply the principle that we are to "do the best that lies in our power;" nor need we fear that we shall do too much, so long as ornamentation is governed by good taste, suitableness, and devotional feeling. To what more elevating use can man apply the woods and the metals, the stone and the marbles, with which this earth has been blessed for his sake, than in dedicating them to the service of his Maker? or how can man better employ sculpture and painting — the direct offspring of those talents which are the special gift of God — than by devoting them to His honor? It surely cannot be otherwise than right and consistent, when we are enjoined to "do all to the glory of God," that the best fruits of the talents with which God has endowed man should be humbly dedicated to the glory of Him who created them. Can we believe that Fra Bartolomeo was wrong when he studied painting in order that he might devote his art to the illustration of his Master's life; or that Michael Angelo was wrong when he dedicated the best years of his life to labor at St. Peter's as architect, sculptor, and painter, for the "love of God"?

Marbles were little known in this country in the olden time, but our forefathers were glad to make use of them when they fell within reach, as in Sussex and elsewhere; and there can be no doubt that they would have turned them still more extensively to account had it been within their power. Marbles are the flowers of the rocks, traced out and colored by God's own hand; and they serve to remind us that He has not stopped short in His beneficence at the point where our bare wants were supplied, but has been pleased to add the charm of beauty, over and above, in order to gratify His children. For what other purpose, indeed, is it conceivable that God should have made marble beautiful, since, of all creatures on this earth, man alone has been gifted with faculties capable of enjoying it. Considered under this point of view, the flowers of the rocks seem peculiarly suitable for church decoration.

Our forefathers in mediæval times liberally employed the best sculpture of their day; but while we admire the devotional feeling which often spread a charm over their works, even when poor art marred artistic success, it would surely be a great mistake in us were we to aim at reproducing any of their defects. In those days anatomy was almost unknown, and art was too often found in alliance with bad taste and incongruity. These errors come down to us softened by the lapse of time, and the motive which produced them covers them with our respect; but shall we, in our turn, be "doing our best" if, with better knowledge of anatomy and greater technical power, we aim at nothing higher than imitation? With still stronger reason figures twisted into impossible attitudes, exaggerations, monstrosities, and other inconsistencies ought to be avoided. The strange cloister-jokes and fancies often cleverly carved in wood or stone are scarcely excused by the want of refinement which then universally prevailed; but, if it were only because they are falsifications, they are clearly out of place in the House of Truth. One can hardly understand a sculptor hewing out grotesque impish figures as fit decorations for any part of God's Temple. Surely these cannot be held as suited in any way to promote His glory, and therefore they ought to be excluded from the Sanctuary, every part of which is consecrated to His service. If sculpture in churches be in any degree allowable, it can only be when it is calculated to excite emotions of reverence and devotion, not of mirth or levity. The Sacred Volume is an inexhaustible source from which subjects both suitable and beautiful may be selected. Wherever the standard of religious propriety is departed from, decoration in the sacred edifice easily degenerates into desecration.

A custom became common about the beginning of last century, which, viewed by the light of taste and consistency and not through the medium of sentiment and association, must be held to have done much to disfigure the interior of our churches. It had its origin in that praiseworthy feeling which loves to cherish the memory of the dead; but its effect has been to cause the walls to be stuck round with monumental records, in the framing of which more bad taste has been displayed than, perhaps, on any other feature within the church. Many a chancel has thus been fitted up in a style which brings to mind the workshop of a Kensal Green sculptor. Square, printed "bills" of marble, with deep, black edgings, are plentifully posted about. There are skulls — idealized in their repulsiveness, reposing on crossed thigh-bones of curious shapes not to be found in Nature, and flanked — supporter-wise — by monster hour-glasses. There are mantel-pieces let into the walls, with inscribed slabs where the grate should be. There are mortuary chests piled one on the top of the other; urns like overgrown soup-tureens, wine-coolers with sloping pail-lids, and tall pots that caricature Etruscan vases. It is no exaggeration to say that nearly all the objects here mentioned may sometimes be seen collected within the walls of a single parish church. In the nave of Westminster Abbey there are certainly some exceptions; nevertheless its general character is too much that of a museum of monumental rococoism. Out of respect for the dead let us accept what has been bequeathed, but it is surely time to substitute something better than this questionable custom for the future.

It seems strange that while the aid of sculpture in decorating God's House has been, more or less, almost universally accepted, the service of its twin-sister, painting, has often been altogether repudiated. We know not any good reason why this should be, or why the work of the pencil should be accounted evil, while that of the chisel is held to be good. The question is one to be decided by judgment, and not by the mixture of feelings engendered by association which is often mistaken for principle. There is nothing that can be said in favor of sculpture, or other architectural ornamentation, which cannot likewise be said in favor of painting; and if it be alleged that painting is disqualified for Protestant churches because it has been abused in other churches, the same thing may be said of sculpture and every other kind of embellishment. Both equally represent the employment in God's service of the talents with which He has blessed His children. Both come into the church by the same title — that they are done "to the glory of God." And if, in addition, the ideas they suggest penetrate to the mind and touch the feelings, surely they are both serving as innocent means toward a good end. The principle of the admissibility of painting appears, indeed, to be so generally conceded in practice that it seems inconsistent to deny it in theory. Nearly all denominations now consider themselves free to admire the paintings that adorn the windows of their churches, and we do not see how they can with consistency object on principle to representations of similar subjects painted upon the walls. Is it, for example, a right thing to depict the "Ascension" upon glass, and a wrong thing to take the very same drawing and the same colors, and lay them upon plaster? At all events, the principle which sanctions the one cannot logically be turned against the other. We give no opinion as to how far painting should be employed in decoration. Judgment and good taste, to say nothing of the difficulty of procuring it of a sufficiently high degree of merit, will always circumscribe its employment, and practically almost confine it to cathedrals and other great churches. Better, too, that it should be altogether omitted than introduced at the cost of congregational discord. No one would desire to see this or any other kind of church ornamentation pushed to excess, for it is extravagance which so often casts a blight over what is really good.

The inscription of illuminated text scrolls over arches and in other appropriate situations seems a very suitable kind of ornamentation. It produces a pleasing effect in the parish church by relieving the large bare spaces of white, and adding to the distinctness of architectural outline. Another advantage is that, while painting and sculpture must always be rare from their costliness, the suitable execution of these texts is seldom beyond the resources of a congregation, assisted by such art as may be found in almost every country town. Nor are these scrolls without a higher aim and use. They are read over and over by young and old; and every time this simple act is performed there is the chance that some good feeling may be touched. They are sacred words placed favorably to catch the eye, and appealing week after week to the hopes, the affections, and the consciences of the congregation. Often they arrest the wandering thought and turn it back more fitted than before to join again in the Service of the Church.

If it be right to sing unto the Lord in His House, surely it must be right not only to raise that "melody in our hearts" which is the most precious quality of praise, but also to make the outward expression of it the best that it is in our power to offer. What that best is must be left, as in the case of sculpture and painting, to be regulated by the standard of propriety and devotional fitness. The only limit that need be put to the style of music adopted is that it shall be devotional in its character, and within the power of the congregation to execute, or at least to join in. The difficulties and "effects" into which parish choirs are sometimes tempted are no less misplaced than excess in sculpture and painting, and while they display skill, have occasionally the result of excluding the congregation from the Service altogether. Within the limit above assigned there is range enough to occupy the best means that can be brought to bear. There is no grace in praising like fervor, and a too elaborate choral display, how beautiful soever it may be in itself, goes beyond the real aim of congregational singing, and, by checking or silencing it, tempts one to wish for another Gregory to sweep away redundancies, introduce simplicity, and impart devotional feeling.

It is unnecessary to make any estimate of the comparative value of these "aids" to devotion. Much depends on the peculiar mental impressionability and associations of the individual, and probably in no two persons would the standard be the same. We seek here to establish nothing more than the principle that, as they were all given for our use, not one of them should be neglected. A touching allusion to the Cross, for example, may excite the same religious feeling in the mind whether it be spoken, printed, painted, or sculptured. Who or what gave one sense the monopoly in things religious over all the others? What is there that so exclusively fits the ear to promote adoration, and which so rigidly excludes the eye? Does the whole substance of religion consist of creed only, and has feeling no part in it? Is there no such thing as love, pity, or sympathy in it? If such emotions form any part of religion, then every means that can rouse them becomes of use, and was given for the purpose.

Provided the idea reaches the mind it signifies little how it came there, whether its starting-point was a star, a plant, a statue, a picture, words spoken, or letters printed. They are all equally symbols and means to an end. If they fail to send on the idea to its goal, they are all equally worthless; but if they succeed in doing this, they are all useful. Were we more perfect we might possibly dispense with many aids; but, being as we are, we cannot afford to lose even the least of those that have been given to us. It is true that some feel the meaning of a symbol, and some do not; but why should they who can profit by such appeals be deprived of them because there are others on whom they are lost? Excess is always wrong, and a sparing use of symbolism in church adornment is perhaps expedient. We know with what force association molds conviction, and this is a point on which much may be yielded to opinion or even to prejudice. But supposing it were possible to surround ourselves in every direction with symbols of God's attributes, what other result than our advantage could arise? what monitors for good, what shields against evil they would be! Yet, if we look meditatively around, is not this in reality our own position? God *has* encompassed us on every side with symbols that recall Him to our thoughts, and it is habitual neglect alone which makes them profitless. What object is there in Nature which does not in some way suggest His Power, Wisdom, or Goodness? Thus were these objects used by the Three Children of old, and thus may they be profitably used by ourselves.

If there be any kind of adornment which more than another seems fitted to God's House, it is that thoughtful use of the "green things upon the earth" with which our churches are decorated at certain seasons of the year. Flowers are the painted sculpturings of Nature — the shapes and colors of beauty which the Creator has lavished upon the world, and surely they can never be employed for a better purpose. In the church flowers suggest thoughts that are in unison with the occasion. Who does not understand the signs of joyfulness which they express at Christmas and Easter; and do they not sometimes serve to quicken our sympathy for those who stand around the font? These are small matters; but let us throw nothing away that tends to good. The time and care thus bestowed on the adornment of the parish church are not without their reward. Pious thoughts arise while skillful fingers are busy with the work, which, as it is done for the sake of God's honor, must from its very nature be linked with good to all concerned in it.

Whoso offereth Me praise glorifieth Me. — Ps. l.

GREEN THINGS UPON THE EARTH.

O all ye Green Things upon the Earth, bless ye the Lord: praise Him, and magnify Him for ever.

IN considering the green things upon the earth we are in turn impressed by their beauty, their usefulness, and the wisdom of design displayed in their creation. Everywhere we see plants fitted to the different conditions involved in the various climates of the earth — to the length of the day, which regulates the amount of light and heat they are to receive — and to the duration of the year, within the compass of whose seasons the cycle of their functions — growing, flowering, and fruit-ripening — must be completed. If the axial rotation of the globe were a little quicker or a little slower, the length of the day would be different from what it now is, and the actual conditions of plants would be disturbed. If the earth under less perfect adjustment were placed nearer the sun, plants would be overwhelmed in a flood of heat and light. Or, again, if the orbital speed of the earth were greater or less than it is, the length of the year would be altered, and the whole routine of the annual functions of plants would be thrown into disorder. Even as it is, we know the confusion which arises in the garden from a summer prolonged far into autumn, or from a too early spring. In reality, we observe that the Creator has everywhere endowed plants, in regard to their external relations, with the exact constitution which insures their well-being.

Dr. Whewell has well pointed out the harmony subsisting between the functions and structure of plants and that law of gravitation which rules the universe. Had the earth been more or less dense than it actually is — had its size been a little larger or a little smaller — had its distance from the sun much exceeded or greatly fallen short of 92 millions of miles, the influence of gravity over every thing on the earth would be different from what it now is, and the whole machinery of animal and vegetable life would be thrown off its balance. The sap of plants, for example, rises from the root into the stem, and from the stem into the leaves, against the power of gravity. Now the force which urges on this stream is exactly adjusted to the weight that has to be lifted; but it is clear that if, from any of the causes mentioned, the gravity, or weight, of the sap were increased, the force which now suffices to raise it would be too weak for the purpose; or if the weight of the sap were less, the force now moving it would be out of proportion, and destruction of the plant would inevitably ensue.

We see also that the strength of the framework of plants has been nicely calculated on the same principle. The thickness of the stem, the tapering of the branches, the weight of the leaves, flowers, and fruit, are all modeled, to a grain, on the actual astronomical conditions in which the earth is placed. Were terrestrial gravity greater than it now is every thing would weigh more than it now does; or, in other words, the force with which the earth pulls every thing toward its centre would be increased. The trunk of the tree, which we now see towering into the air as a symbol of strength, would be unable to support the branches, and the branches would be overpowered by the leaves. The blossoms and the fruit would break down the stalks that hold them up, the valleys would no longer be adorned with wavy corn, for it, as well as the grass, would be dragged prostrate to the ground. But by the wise design of the Creator, stem, branches, leaves, flowers, and fruit have been framed in accordance with the weight they have to carry; the weight is regulated by the attraction of the earth; and this, again, is in exact proportion to the size, density, and distance of the sun and planets. Every minute microscopic fibre throughout the whole vegetable world has been created in exact relation to this principle, and in nothing, perhaps, is the fact more beautifully illustrated than in plants which, like the fuchsia, the arbutus, or the snow-drop, incline their flowers in graceful pendants. As a general rule flowers are erect, and the stamens are longer than the pistils, in order that the pollen, or fructifying powder, may naturally fall on the stigma, or germ. It is obvious, however, that if these relative proportions as to length had existed in drooping plants, the stamens would have been placed lower down than the pistils; and, consequently, the pollen when set free would have fallen to the ground without coming into contact with the pistil. But, by an obviously designed departure from the usual plan, the comparative length of the stamens and pistils has been reversed in drooping flowers, by which means the anthers are made to occupy their ordinary superior position; and, consequently, when the pollen is set free it naturally falls upon the stigma, placed below it. In noticing this exquisite adjustment Dr. Whewell observes, — "We have here a little mechanical contrivance which would have been frustrated if the proper intensity of gravity had not been assumed in the reckoning." "There is something curious in thus considering the whole mass of the earth from pole to pole, and from circumference to centre, as employed in keeping a snow-drop in the position most suited to the promotion of its vegetable health."

And all men that see it shall say, This hath God done; for they shall perceive that it is God's work. — Ps. lxiv.

The love of flowers exists within us almost as a part of our nature. It calls forth some of the first cries of admiration in the infant, and, by clinging to us through life, strews many an innocent pleasure on the way. In the daisies, the buttercups, the dandelions, and other wild flowers which the hand of childhood eagerly grasps, or twines into garlands and wreaths, we behold the earliest treasures of life. Even more especially do the "green things upon the earth" merit our regard for their usefulness. Plants give us houses for shelter and ships for commerce, and medicines with which to combat disease. They feed us and they clothe us. Often we may see the fields decked with the blue flowers of a plant which for its own beauty's sake obtains a welcome in many a garden border, but which is largely cultivated on the farm to yield a most useful clothing. It is the common flax. From the earliest days of Babylon and Egypt this plant has never ceased to be a blessing to mankind. Specimens of linen as old as the Pharaohs, wrapped in endless coils round shrunken mummies, have survived to our own time; while paintings on the walls of Theban tombs show us with minuteness the process of its manufacture, and prove that it was then essentially the same as now. In creating the flax-plant God gave to man a thread which by its tenacity and flexibility is particularly adapted to be made into clothing, while from its hardy constitution it is widely spread over the world. Thus it thrives on the mountain slopes of India, as well as in Northern Europe and America. In this wide distribution it has the superiority over its twin-blessing — cotton; for the latter is limited to the warmer regions of the globe, and attains perfection in comparatively few of them.

The cotton-plant was also from remote times known in the valleys of the Euphrates and the Nile, and was aptly termed by ancient writers the "fleece-bearing tree." From the more complicated preparations required for its conversion into cloth, it did not, however, come into such general use as flax at an early period. It was little known in

England till the reign of Charles I., when it was meritoriously introduced by the East India Company, which was then in its infancy. So long as it was manufactured into cloth by hand its use was necessarily much restricted; but at length Providence, in order to extend its usefulness, inspired our countrymen with the invention of the needful machinery. In the latter part of the last century three men arose within a few years of each other — Hargreave, Arkwright, and Compton — whose ingenuity produced the spinning-jenny (1767), the spinning-frame (1775), and the spinning-mule (1779), which have brought good and cheap clothing within easy reach of a large portion of the human race. There are, in fact, few inhabited spots upon the earth into which machinery-manufactured cotton has not penetrated, and more families, perhaps, owe their daily bread to it than to any other branch of industry. Distributed everywhere, this little plant has also become a great agent in the spread of civilization; and, as the missionary often enters with the merchant, it may likewise be considered as assisting in the propagation of true religion. Certain it is that the way to many a heathen tribe would have remained barred against every Christian effort, but for the opening which the cotton traffic prepared for it.

The history of the cotton-plant points to something more elevated than commerce and manufactures. When we consider that the time of its introduction into England coincided with the commencing expansion of our trade — that in the course of a century afterward, when the population of the world had much increased and had become accustomed to its use, the needful machinery was invented, by which the cloth might be produced to an extent somewhat in proportion to the demand — when we think of the perfection and cheapness of the manufacture, the wide penetration of modern commerce into every land, and the active zeal of missionary enterprise — each step being, as it were, a preparation for the one that followed — who can resist the conviction that these events are to be regarded not as unconnected and accidental, but as the planned working of Providence?

Various plants supply a soft white down which, judging by ordinary examination, appears as well adapted for manufacturing cloth as cotton itself. But there is a structural peculiarity inherent in the fibre of the latter which distinguishes it not only from flax-fibre but from most other downs; and, although so minute as to be microscopic, it nevertheless distinctly marks the purpose of the great Designer. It may here be observed that cotton is a vegetable hair enveloping the seed capsules, while flax-thread is a kind of fine woody fibre of which the stem of the plant is chiefly composed. Both are originally round in form; but the flax-fibre being strong continues to retain its shape, while the cotton-fibre being weak collapses in drying up. In the field of the microscope it will be seen that every cotton-fibre is flattened into a minute ribbon twisted round at intervals upon itself, while its surface and edges are roughened and unequal. From this roughness comes the invaluable property that when the fibres are twisted in the manufacture they cling and lock into each other, by which not only is the strength of the thread increased, but the inconvenient tendency to untwist observed in many other fibres is also obviated. The degree of fineness to which, from this peculiarity, cotton-fibres may be spun is almost incredible. A single pound weight of cotton has been twisted by machinery into a thread 4770 miles in length! Such fairy-like thread, it need scarcely be observed, cannot be applied to any useful purpose, for cloth made from twist many degrees coarser than this, by means of a machine as delicate in its action as a watch, was found to be as fragile as a spider's web, and would not bear handling.

Are we not too apt to take our good gifts as mere things of course, and to lose sight of the magnitude of a blessing in its commonness? The necessity for clothing is, for the greater part of mankind, only second to the necessity for food; and flax and cotton stand in the same relation to our clothing as wheat and other cereals do to our daily bread. If all the health and happiness which these two "green things of the earth" have diffused among mankind could be added up into one sum, what expression would be comprehensive enough adequately to represent it?

Praise the Lord, O my soul, and forget not all His benefits. — Ps. ciii.

The lower animals have their food given to them already prepared by the hand of Nature; but man requires not only to cook his food, but often to alter the original condition of the plant itself whence it is derived, and improve it by cultivation. Those cereals, for example, on which we now mainly depend for "the staff of life" were originally wild grass. They have been brought to their present state of perfection by long years of patient cultivation, but they would infallibly relapse into their original wildness if they were neglected even for a few seasons. The same observation applies to the potato, turnip, cabbage, and many other useful vegetables. How great the skill and perseverance expended in bringing them to their present state, and what gratitude is due to the King of Nature for having prompted us with the knowledge necessary to accomplish so great and beneficial a result!

In our comparatively cold climate Nature is, as usual, kind and bountiful, but she exacts a greater labor-payment than in warmer countries. The tax thus levied must not, however, be regarded as altogether without profit. If the climate bring the difficulty, it also brings energetic heads, well-braced muscles, and firmly strung nerves to cope with it. Hence, although our farmers are doomed to a constant struggle with the weather, the soil, and other adverse influences, they generally triumph in the end by skill and industry, and are able to produce both enough and to spare.

In tropical countries, on the contrary, the Creator, as if in compassion to that muscular relaxation and want of energy which heat engenders, has caused the earth to produce its fruits with comparatively little expense of labor, and has often multiplied in a wonderful manner the uses to which a single plant can be applied. The catalogue of products yielded by the date-palm includes, according to Humboldt, " wine, oil, vinegar, farinaceous food, and sugar, timber and ropes, mats and paper." An allied tree — the cocoa-nut palm — which grows without cultivation, is in itself a storehouse of every thing needful to sustain life in those climates. Thus it " forms a grateful shade from the vertical sun ; its timber serves to build huts, and its leaves to thatch them. The cut sheath of the flowers distils a sweet liquid, which by fermentation speedily becomes the palm-wine so eagerly drunk by the natives of hot climates. From this liquor sugar may be obtained by boiling, or, if it be long exposed to the air, an excellent vinegar is made. The nut is most valuable as food, and indeed forms the staff of life to the coral islanders of the Pacific ; it likewise supplies an oil, equal to that of almonds, which is extensively used in India. The strong fibres enveloping the nut are turned to numerous domestic purposes, while the shell itself may be made into cups or goblets."

The various climates of the globe have impressed a special physiognomy on the flora of its different regions. Within the tropics the great stimulants of vegetable growth — light, heat, and moisture — exist at their maximum, and consequently the glories of the plantal world are there developed in the highest perfection. Tropical forests surpass those of the rest of the globe in their beauty, color, size, density, and fragrance ; but their characteristic physiognomy is more especially stamped upon them by the bananas, cocoas, and other kinds of palm, and by the dazzling orchids which gem or garland the trees. No description can adequately portray the profusion of tropical vegetation. In the vicinity of the larger towns, where cultivation prevails, the rank exuberance of plantal life is of course kept within bounds; but in the jungles and in the recesses of the primeval forest its density is extreme, and the surface of the earth is packed with the abundance of its own richness. Through obstacles like these the serpent may creep, or the wild beast, sheathed in the armor of its thick fur, may force a passage; but man can only cut out his way with the hatchet in his hand. On either side of the passage thus driven through, vegetation tangled, interwoven, compressed by plant growing upon plant, builds itself up as solid almost as a wall. The density of the leafage overhead is in keeping with the requirements of such climates. Strong, protecting coverings are necessary to intercept and absorb the fierce rays of the sun, and shield the surface of the earth from their scorching touch; they are needed, also, to break the fall of the deluge which pours down like a water-spout from southern skies. The blackness of the shade may be measured when it is contrasted with the vivid points and lines of almost dazzling light which here and there pierce through chinks in the leafy canopy. The course of a river searching for a passage through the thick forests of South America seems hewn out among the trees; it has no shelving banks of green, but is cut clean out of the forest mass. "In descending the streams between the Orinoco and the Amazon," says Humboldt, "we often tried to land, but without being able to step out of the boat. Toward sunset we sailed along the bank for an hour to discover, not an opening, since none exists, but a spot less wooded, where our Indians, by means of the hatchet and manual labor, would gain space enough for a resting-place for twelve or thirteen persons." There must be something extremely captivating both to the eye and the imagination in tropical scenery. All travelers speak of it — both of its wild forests and its cultivated spots — with enthusiasm, and with that affection in which memory embalms only a few of the places one visits in a lifetime. Of the smiling environs of some Brazilian cities Darwin thus writes: — "While quietly walking along the shady pathways, and admiring each successive view, I wished to find language to express my ideas. Epithet after epithet was found too weak to convey to those who have not visited the intertropical regions the sensation of delight which the mind experiences. I have said that the plants in a hot-house fail to communicate a just idea of the vegetation, yet I must recur to it. The land is one great wild, untidy, luxuriant hot-house, made by Nature herself, but taken possession of by man, who has studded it with gay houses and formal gardens. How great would be the desire in any admirer of Nature to behold, if such were possible, the scenery of another planet! Yet to any person in Europe it may be truly said that, at the distance of only a few degrees from his native soil, the glories of another world are opened to him. In my last walk I stopped again and again to gaze on those beauties, and endeavored to fix in my mind for ever an impression which at the time I knew sooner or later must fail. The form of the orange-tree, the cocoa-nut, the palm, the mango, the fern-tree, the banana, will remain clear and separate; but the thousand beauties which unite them into one perfect scene must fade away; yet they will leave, like a tale told in childhood, a picture full of indistinct, but most beautiful figures."

Here is another sketch of southern vegetation, drawn by Piazzi Smith during his excursion to Teneriffe: — "When walking at midday in one of the basalt-paved streets, each glittering stone sending back the full rays of a vertical sun, and the gleaming houses on either side affording a steady, white, hot glare of unmitigated sunshine, what words in a northern language can express the delightful emotions, when at the open gateway of one of the semi-Moorish abodes we look in upon a grove of bananas! Throwing a tender green shade over the interior court, their grand and delicately structured leaves rise up aloft, catch the fierce rays of the sun before they can do mischief, receive them into their substance, make them give out the most varied yellow greens; pass them on from leaf to leaf subdued and softened — pass them on to the oleander's fountain of rose-pink flowers, to the dark-green of the orange-like myrtle and the bay; and leave just light enough at last in the green cavern below to show the bubbling of some tiny fountain — the welling heart of the fairy oasis."

In striking contrast to such pictures of tropical splendor, let us, for an instant, turn to those desolate tracts in the far north, where the physical conditions we have been considering are reversed, and where light, heat, and moisture are at a minimum. Still, even into this inhospitable climate a meagre vegetable life extends. There is, in fact, no latitude into which man has penetrated where plants do not exist; and it may be confidently predicted that, if land should be found under the poles, there also a flora will be seen to flourish. Covered up in its blanket of snow there is a lichen on which in the winter time the Esquimaux can contrive to exist when other provisions fail; and it was by means of this plant that a boat-party detached from Kane's expedition beyond Smith's Sound were saved from starvation. Some nutritious mucilage is also extracted from the Iceland moss, which from its mild, demulcent properties is favorably known in many a sick-room. But as the short, polar summer advances, and the ground is bathed day and night in warm sunlight, vegetation springs up upon the surface with a bound. Scarcely has the last snow-flake melted from the ground before the earth is carpeted with the softest, shortest, greenest grass.

In propitious spots the saxifrage, primrose, anemone, ranunculus, and wild thyme crop up and brighten the dull surface with their pretty flowers. With these are associated the scurvy-grass and the sorrel, — plants which may well be deemed providential in a climate of which scurvy is the direst scourge.

Between these two extremes there is a long series of gradations in vegetable life, which we have here barely space to notice. In general it may be said that there is a progressive increase in plantal abundance and richness as we pass from high latitudes toward the tropics. In Europe, tree life commences humbly round the bleak shores of the North Cape. The birch and the willow first appear, not with the graceful forms and foliage by which they are known to us in England, but as dwarfed and scrubby shrubs, — interesting only as the earliest efforts of Nature to establish forest life. Then come the hardy Scotch fir and the spruce; and these are soon joined by the sturdy sycamore. Among our favorite ornamental trees the mountain-ash, or rowan, is the first to show itself, robed in white blossoms in spring and covered with ruddy berries in autumn. The sandy soil of Denmark is now the great home of the beech. By the time our own belt of climate is reached, forest life has passed from scarcity to profusion, and our woods are distinguished by their variety no less than by their beauty. The oak, which began by struggling for a bare existence about Trontheim, in Norway, has by degrees grown stronger and nobler, until by the consent of all it has attained the rank of monarch of the wood.

In descending from the north, barley and rye are the first among cereals to bless the earth. They begin to be worth cultivation in Norway as far up as latitude 70°, where, under the stimulating influence of the constant summer sun, they are sown, reaped, and gathered within the short three months' interval that intervenes between the last snows of spring and the first of autumn. In our island the profitable cultivation of wheat barely reaches John o'Groat's, but it extends a little higher on the opposite coast of Norway. It attains its highest perfection in the south of Europe. A line passing through the northern provinces of France and Germany marks the limit beyond which the vine does not flourish in the open air. As we approach the extreme south of Europe we reach a plantal frontier, including only a few of the sunniest regions of Spain, Italy, and Greece, where the productions of temperate climes begin to be blended with those that characterize the tropics — where the olive, orange, and oleander are interspersed with the hardiest of the palm tribe. This sudden glimpse of the richness of southern vegetation is very delightful to a wanderer from Northern Europe who sees it for the first time, and it forms one of the most striking transitions in the aspect of plantal life which is to be found anywhere. Passing beyond the southern shores of the Mediterranean the temperature rapidly increases, and vegetation soon assumes a true tropical character.

It has been computed that the earth is enriched with at least 100,000 different kinds of plants. The seed is brought forth with a profusion which not only provides amply for the increase of the species, but which generally leaves a large supply over and above to serve as food for birds and other animals. It is remarkable what pains Nature takes to distribute the seed. The chief sower is the wind, which blows the seed about until a suitable spot has been found. Many seeds are furnished with feathery appendages, which may be compared to wings or sails, in order that they may more easily catch the breeze and be wafted through the air. Most frequently the seed-vessel opens after it has reached maturity, and casts its contents over the ground ; at other times it waits until it is touched by some passing object. Some, like the mahogany, open when they become dry; others wait until moisture and other circumstances are propitious for germination, when the seed-vessels open and the contents are scattered around. De Candolle tells us that the seed of the rose of Jericho does not ripen until the season is so far advanced that every drop of water has been sucked out of the soil. It would answer no good purpose were the seed to be allowed to fall upon such arid ground. The plant, however, is rescued from its dilemma by a curious device of Nature. Under the influence of the scorching sun the branches dry up and become rolled into an irregular, elastic ball. By and by the wind of the desert, as it sweeps along the dusty plain, catches the plant and tears it up by the root. The ball rolls easily over the surface, and is driven to and fro until it sticks fast in some little oasis or spot of moisture. During this rough journey the seed-vessels hold their precious contents firmly and safely; but no sooner do they perceive the "signal" of moisture than they open freely, and the seed falling on "good ground" springs up rapidly.

Though much seed is lost — or at least does not germinate — there is a providence which takes care that every spot of earth shall be supplied with the vegetable growths that suit it. What wonderful efforts are sometimes made to stock new land with plants! An eminent naturalist, after describing the beauty of the cocoa-nut groves that flourish on the Coral Islands of the Pacific, has suggested the chapter of designed accidents to which they owe their origin. When the island emerges from the deep it is a barren reef of limestone rock, glittering white and bright under a tropical sun. In process of time patches of chalky mud and sand, formed upon its surface by the action of rain and waves, are washed into clefts and sheltered places along the shore. The island now begins to be fit for vegetation; and, strange though it may seem, the cocoa is usually one of the first plants to appear. How does the seed get there? The bulky nut is too large to be carried by birds, and ships avoid the reef as a source of danger. A stray cocoa-nut that grew in far-distant groves, after being the sport of storms and currents, has hit the new spot in the lone ocean. Cast ashore by the surf, it has become fixed in one of the muddy clefts, where it finds enough of nourishment for its growth. By and by a young plantation of descendants is established around. The fall of the leaves and the decay of each generation add to the stock of mold and supply the soil for more varied vegetation, until at length the bare, white reef is changed into a scene which sailors describe as an earthly paradise.

With what orderly providence all the steps of this long operation succeed each other. There is, first, the emergence of the bare rock, and the preparation of a little store of mud. Then some palm-tree, growing perhaps hundreds of miles away, drops a nut, which, rolling into the neighboring stream is carried downward into the sea. It is thus launched upon a seemingly random and useless voyage — a waif of the ocean, unseen by man, but guided by the hand of Providence. Encased in its armor of shell, against which wind and wave beat in vain, it seems as if constructed on purpose to carry a life-freight across stormy seas. Soon the current takes it in possession — slowly it drifts along — months roll on, and the cocoa-nut is still sailing on its mission. Rocks are avoided against which it might have dashed, and shores on which it might have been stranded, until it arrives at last at the lonely spot in the wide ocean, and then the surf casts it ashore into its destined cleft where the little patch of mud is ready to receive it.

As a protection against the accidents to which seeds are exposed, Nature has endowed them with wonderful tenacity of life. Passing over the assertions that have been made about the vitality of Egyptian wheat after a 3000 years' slumber in Theban tombs, there are other cases sufficiently wonderful, about the authenticity of which there can be no question. In some parts of the country "dykes" or mound-fences have existed from time immemorial; but no sooner are these leveled than the seeds of wild flowers, which must have lain buried in them for ages, sprout forth vigorously, just as if the ground had been recently sown with seed. Plants, too, which formerly flourished in the district, but which had long disappeared from it, have sometimes been recovered in this manner. In a well-authenticated case, a house that was known to have existed for 200 years was pulled down, and no sooner was the surface soil exposed to the influence of light and moisture, than it became covered with a crop of wild mustard or charlock. Instances might easily be multiplied almost indefinitely, but we shall be satisfied with noticing one of a very extraordinary kind. In the time of the Emperor Hadrian a man died soon after he had eaten plentifully of raspberries. He was buried at Dorchester. About thirty years ago the remains of this man, together with coins of the Roman Emperor, were discovered in a coffin at the bottom of a barrow, thirty feet under the surface. The man had thus lain undisturbed for some 1700 years. But the most curious circumstance connected with the case was that the raspberry seeds were recovered from the stomach, and sown in the garden of the Horticultural Society, where they germinated and grew into healthy bushes.

There is a period of helplessness in the life of a plant when it is dependent on the provision that has been made for it by its parent, and which corresponds very closely to a similar condition in the life of animals. A seed may be compared to an egg. The greater part of the bulk of an egg consists of nutritive matter, which the embryo chick absorbs until it is sufficiently developed to break its prison shell and shift for itself. In like manner the greater part of the seed consists of nutritive matter, which is absorbed by the embryo plant until it is sufficiently developed to provide independently for its own growth by sending its root down into the soil and its stem up into the air. How strikingly the providence of the Creator is displayed in the different phases through which a seed passes! The old plant, before parting with its tender offspring, softly envelops it in a thick, warm blanket of starch, and covers this over with the tough, dense wrappers of the seed, in order that the life-spark within may sleep in safety through the winter, until Spring awakens it with her signal calls of light and heat. This starchy substance is insoluble, and, therefore, easily preserves itself, in most cases, against the melting influences of damp or rain. But this very quality, which protects it so well during the winter, is a fatal bar against its being used as nourishment by the embryo plant, whose delicate powers of assimilation enable it to feed only on substances that are soluble. To meet this necessity a process of vital chemistry is instituted on the approach of spring, by which the insoluble starch is converted by a kind of fermentation into a soluble saccharine substance called "diastase." On this the germ can act readily, and thus obtains abundance of food. Every body has observed how potatoes change as spring comes on. Their mealiness, that is, a portion of their starch, is gone, and they have become waxy and sweet. Their value for the table is impaired, but their fitness to serve as seed has been secured. There is no "spoiling," as is often thought. The covering which kept out the rain now splits to allow the passage of stem and root; and the blanket which kept out the winter cold, being no longer needed, is put off at the command of Nature, or, rather, it begins a new course of usefulness by converting itself into a soluble substance on which the young plant can feed.

How happens it — is it from contrast merely, or from revived association, — that "green things" never seem more attractive than when they greet us unexpectedly in the midst of crowded cities? Buried though the Londoner be in his labyrinth of bricks, he is yet happily within reach of those beautiful parks where Nature blends itself so charmingly with Art, and where at leisure hours he can relax the tension of his thoughts and watch the annual return of spring and summer. But did the reader ever stumble upon a patch of verdure in the midst of the noisy, bustling city, closely hidden between streets and gables, with, perhaps, the not unfrequent plane-tree rising in the centre and diffusing shade and freshness all around? The hum of London traffic breaks softly there upon the ear, like the hollow sound of a distant sea, and soothes rather than disturbs. All is wrapped in almost cloister silence. In summer, besides the shade, there is the grateful coolness produced by the evaporation going on from the beautiful broad leaves. Instead of flinging back the hot glare of the sun, like the stony desert in which it is set, the plane absorbs a portion of the light for its own use, and then sends back to the eye the rest, softened into refreshing green. It is curious to think how many of those verdant oases still survive in the old heart of modern Babylon, even where the bricks are thickest on the ground; and never do they disappear at the summons of the architect or the engineer without leaving behind them remembrances of regret.

We have often thought that one of the most pleasing sights to be seen in St. Giles's or Spitalfields are the flower-pots, including broken jugs and battered, lidless coffee-pots, in which many a decent family tries, not unsuccessfully, to coax a little verdure to abide with them throughout the year. So also, when we escape by rail from London, and skim over the house-tops of some densely peopled suburb, what eye does not dip with kindly glance into the little gardens marvelously wedged in between the backs of humble streets. There the busy workman contrives to find time and heart to wage constant war with city dust and falling "blacks." There, in the intervals of toil, he changes the scene, and finds himself face to face with Nature. There he can note how plants grow, how seeds germinate, how the root grasps the soil, how the foliage bursts forth, how summer ripens the fruit and autumn strikes down the leaves. Thus, though fate claims him for the town, he is not absolutely cut off from the "green things upon the earth;" and in his cherished spot of garden he finds ideas that link his thoughts with country scenes. Nor is our rapid survey less pleasing when we reflect that such pursuits for leisure hours have a moral value to the workman beyond the mere interest that lies upon the surface, for they are antagonistic to dissipation, and lead straight from the dram-shop.

<blockquote>Let all the trees of the wood rejoice before the Lord. — Ps. xcvi.</blockquote>

Among "green things" trees stand out preëminently as the grandest of God's works. In beauty they are surpassed by no other kind of plant, while in height, size, and strength they have no rival among living things. When polished, many kinds of wood exhibit a variety of color and figure which may compete with the finest marble. In its physical qualities wood is admirably adapted to our use. Thus many kinds are soft, like pine or poplar; others hard, like oak or holly; some light, as cedar or lime; others so heavy that they sink in water, like ebony or lignum vitæ. The yew has a durability expressed in the proverb that "a post of yew will outlast a post of iron." Some are remarkable for their toughness, like the ash. In short, there is hardly any quality rendered necessary by the thousand purposes both of use and ornament to which wood is applied which is not to be found in one kind or another. How much this variety contributes to the comfort and resources of our daily life need not here be pointed out, but we cannot fail to see in it an evidence of the kindness with which our Father has foreseen and provided for all our wants.

Some of the giants in the forests of Northwestern America attain a height of upward of two hundred and thirty feet, and they are said to have a girth of one hundred and twelve feet, which represents a diameter rather exceeding thirty-seven feet. In tropical forests the great cable palm has a stem five hundred feet in length. Favored beyond most other living things, there is for trees no age that excludes beauty — not even the period of decay. What a goodly sight it is to see an old oak battling with Time! The sturdy monarch yields only inch by inch to the power that conquers all things, and he protracts his fall with dignity and picturesqueness. The bole is rugged with the scars that were left ages ago, when the huge arms of his strong days were torn from his side by the storm; and it is breached here and there with gaps and fissures which it has taken centuries to chisel out, but through which all-conquering Time, baffled elsewhere, is fain to enter in and gnaw out a way to the heart. Of the trunk that once formed an emblem of strength but a shapeless fragment remains; yet in the midst of ruin the brave old oak still sends forth to every spring its accustomed tribute, whose green freshness stands out in curious contrast to the withered stem that bears it up. Following the universal law the old tree instinctively fights for life, and shrinks from ceasing to exist.

Trees are full of interest as the broadest living links that bind us to the past. There is nothing else with life that bridges across the Middle Ages and carries us back into remote antiquity. The oldest forest patriarchs were planted long before history occupied herself with chronicling such events, still there are other means by which the age of trees may be approximatively determined. There are, perhaps, in England as many oaks named after William the Conqueror as there are old feudal towers attributed to Julius Cæsar, and there are at least some trees to which even a higher antiquity may be indubitably assigned. The oldest and largest tree of which Windsor can boast is the "King Oak," which Loudon tells us is said to have been a favorite with the Conqueror when he inclosed the forest. It is twenty-six feet in circumference, and is supposed to be a thousand years old. More famous still is the Winfarthing oak, near Diss, in Norfolk, which tradition asserts was known as "the old oak" even in the Conqueror's time. Immediately above the root its circumference is seventy feet, and forty feet at the middle of the bole. According to the best authorities this oak is believed to be not less than 1500 years old! Not many buildings now existing, except in ruins, are so ancient as this tree. In the Conqueror's time it might well be called "old," for it had then seen some seven hundred summers. It was an old tree when Alfred the Great was fighting the Danes and founding the English monarchy; in fact, it may be said to have lived through the whole "History of England." Another tree, the sober-mantled yew, — associated in our thoughts with the peaceful parish church-yard, — attains a remarkable size and longevity. Numbers are to be found with a girth of 25 or 27 feet; and there is one at Ankerwyke, near Windsor, which is believed to be 1000 years old, and which, therefore, must have been flourishing in ripe maturity when King John was signing Magna Charta on the neighboring Runnymede. Another famous yew grew near Fountain's Abbey, whose age, as indicated by the concentric rings of its trunk, must have been about 1214 years. Scientific deduction was in this instance corroborated by history; for it is on record that, while the abbey was being built in 1133, the monks were accustomed to take shelter under it from the rain. Mention is likewise made of another yew, which, one would think, must have been the Methuselah of its tribe, for its age, as was inferred from the usual structural evidence, reached back over a space of 2880 years. Admitting this estimate to be true, the tree must have been planted about the time when Solomon began to reign in Israel. The great botanist, De Candolle, believed that the age of the famous Baobab of the Cape de Verde Islands, whose circumference is 109 feet, reached far beyond the period mentioned.

Hardly less interesting than these celebrated trees are the lineal descendants and last existing remnants of the primeval forests which in the time of Cæsar and Tacitus covered our island. A few of these oaks, with the badge of their ancient pedigree strongly stamped upon them, still linger on in several places; and their venerable aspect never fails to suggest that they belong to an older race of trees than the new-looking generations that flourish around. Such are the noble oaks of Cadzow, near Hamilton, the true descendants of those Caledonian forests which root back beyond the beginnings of Scottish history. In various parts of the "middle south" of England, near Croydon, for example, one stumbles now and then upon a group of patriarchal oaks, living apart by themselves, and far out of the way of woods and parks. It is impossible for a moment to doubt their ancient descent, or not to recognize in them the last survivors of the forest of Andred's Weald, which in days of yore spread widely over this southern district of England.

Among all the "green things upon the earth" which crowd around to attract our notice there are none which creep in about our hearts like certain individual trees. They stand apart by themselves, and are regarded by us with what we must call a sentiment of affection, if such an expression may be used toward a tree. We have come to know them so well, that we begin almost to fancy that they must know us. Trees, moreover, are objects around which memory twines some of her firmest cords, and not unfrequently they appear among the starting-points of our recollections. With advancing years the scenes of early life grow dim in spite of every effort to retain them; and in looking back at the vanishing picture we often see the form of a tree in the remote distance. Some of our own earliest remembrances happen to be associated with an old laburnum. In those far-off days it was our ship. In growing it had spread quaintly into three stems — these were the masts; and the branches, by which we swung ourselves from one to the other, were the ropes and rigging. Sometimes it was calm, and then we reposed lazily among the leafage; at other times, a gale was supposed to blow, which we gallantly rode out among the waving branches. But the invariable climax of our enjoyment was to fancy ourselves shipwrecked, and then with loud shouts we swung and clambered about from one branch to the other in all the pleasurable excitement of imaginary danger. There is nothing that brings back the treasured feelings of early boyhood with greater freshness than the sight of that old tree. Most people, no doubt, have their laburnum.

How wonderful is the circulation of the sap! Look at a huge tree. Let the eye girth its full proportions, glance up the stem, follow the branches, and try to estimate the twigs and leaves. Then let imagination trace the corresponding labyrinth of root and fibres underground. How wonderful to reflect that, during the greater part of the year, a stream of sap gathered in the soil is actively flowing upward through root and stem, branches and twigs, to every single leaf in all that tower of foliage. How mighty the intelligence which has adjusted the atmospheric pressure and the power exercised in the vessels and cells so that they exactly produce the force required for carrying on the circulation all through the plant, and which has accurately meted out to each microscopic current its proper strength, so that it shall neither flag from want of impulse, nor, like an ill-regulated torrent, burst its channel and destroy instead of supporting life. In the higher classes of animals, with a circulation that is both shorter and less opposed to gravity, there is a central heart to pump, and elastic vessels to convey the blood; but here there is no heart to urge on the current, and the vessels are, for the most part, stiff, unyielding tubes. It is now many years since Hales first demonstrated the force with which the sap is propelled in plants by dividing a vine in spring and connecting the lower end with a tube. He then found that the sap was urged upward with a power equal to a column of thirty-eight inches of mercury, or nearly five times greater than the current in the crural artery of a horse. The forces that produce this startling result are somewhat obscure. Transpiration from the leaves may exert a suctional action. Chemico-vital agencies are doubtless busily at work. Capillary attraction assists, and in particular that curious power by which thick fluids attract thin fluids through membranes such as cell-walls, and to which the term endosmose is applied.

In all that relates to the "green things upon the earth" we see evidences of design and care not less striking than those we admire in the animal kingdom. It may be said that leaves and roots have a power which reminds us of the instinct possessed by the lower animals. Leaves cannot perform their functions without light; hence they invariably seek it out, one might say, intuitively, and present to it their upper surface. In whatever position the seed is placed in the ground the root will turn downward, while the future stem will grow upward. Again, the roots of plants contain numerous absorbent vessels, of which the ultimate extremities, or "spongioles," are surrounded by a mass of tender cells, forming a kind of spongy membrane through which the nutriment derived from the soil must pass in a state of solution. Now these rootlets possess a certain discrimination, or power of selecting food, and of rejecting what would be poisonous or hurtful to the plant. Besides this they seek out the nourishing patches of the soil, and have a way of divining, as if instinctively, where the richest food is to be obtained. The root of the famous vine at Hampton Court once fell under the attractive influence of a neighboring sewer, and actually forced its way through solid masonry in order to reach it. A case even more remarkable is related by Dr. Carpenter, in which a drain at Thoresby Park was found blocked up by the roots of some gorse growing at a distance of six feet. Another instance of what we are tempted to call the instinctive sagacity of roots in their efforts to obtain nourishment is given in the "Gardener's Magazine" for 1837. Near the river Leven, in the West Highlands, a shoot was thrown out from the bole of an old oak, about 15 feet from the ground. Receiving, as it would appear, insufficient nourishment from the tree, the shoot sent a root first down to the ground, and then about 30 feet onward across a bare rock, until it met with a patch of suitable soil, in which it imbedded itself. Few things connected with plants are more remarkable than the certainty with which they detect crevices in walls or other solid obstacles, of which they take advantage and pass through in search of food. The tender rootlet first insinuates itself, and then, under the thickening and hardening process of subsequent growth, it becomes an ever-widening wedge, which forces its way through the densest soils, loosens blocks of masonry, and rends even solid slabs of rock.

Leaves are the lungs, or gills, of plants, where, as in the higher orders of animals, the nutritive fluid or sap is perfected by the action of the air for the purpose of forming the different tissues and secretions. They might equally be termed aërial roots, for they extract from the air the chief portion of the carbon, or charcoal, of which the wood and the other solid parts of plants mainly consist. In respect to this important part of their nutrition, therefore, the atmosphere forms an inexhaustible reservoir of supply in which the leaves are always plunged — a pasture-field in which they browse all the day long.

As carbon is a solid substance, it is obvious that the

leaves could not have obtained it in that form; and in order that it might be brought to them by diffusion through the atmosphere, it was essential that it should assume the gaseous state. The Creator, therefore, combined it with oxygen, so as to convert it into carbonic acid, in which condition it readily diffuses itself through the air, and sweeps over the surface of every leaf. In a matter so important Nature has left nothing uncertain, but has so arranged it that the mixture shall not only be most intimate, but that it shall be of uniform strength, and that no part of the atmosphere into which plants can penetrate shall be without its due proportion. This supply of gaseous food, as has been elsewhere pointed out, is lavishly provided from many inexhaustible sources. When stimulated by light, therefore, plants are always at work upon the carbonic acid of the air, decomposing it into carbon, with which they build up their tissues, and into oxygen, which they set free into the atmosphere.

It is ever the thrifty plan of Providence to combine the performance of the functions of one order of living things with the necessary wants of another; and thus all parts of the animated world are linked together by the beneficial interchange of good offices. Not for their own advantage only do plants pick out the carbon from the atmosphere; for in setting the oxygen at liberty they purify the air and render an essential service to the whole animal world. The carbonic acid which the plants so eagerly imbibe is a poison so deadly to air-breathing animals that a very few inspirations of it, in a concentrated state, are sufficient to destroy human life; while an atmosphere containing even so small a proportion as ten per cent. would be fatal if used in ordinary respiration. Yet, as is elsewhere pointed out, the air is being continually flooded with this poison. It is given off abundantly from the lungs of man and all other "air-breathers." Volumes of it are poured into the air during the combustion of substances used for light and fuel. Occasionally it streams from cracks in the earth, especially in volcanic countries, and it is continually rising from certain mineral waters. It is, therefore, most obvious that had no provision been made for removing the poison, the accumulation of carbonic acid resulting from all those sources would have gradually contaminated the air to an extent incompatible with life. But the Great Architect has so admirably constituted the living world that what would be death to animals is life to plants, and that what we get rid of as a poison, they necessarily seize as food, while by that very act they restore to us the atmosphere in healthy purity. Thus the alternate conversion goes on in an endless chain. Nothing is lost or created in vain; for the waste and refuse of one kingdom becomes the life of the other.

Although oxygen is liberated by plants during the day, the process is of course invisible when it is performed in the air. It is different with aquatic plants, for as they necessarily operate on the carbonic acid gas diffused through the water, the bubbles of oxygen when liberated are seen rising to the surface. The process, indeed, forms one of the attractions of the vivarium, in which the plants are studded all over with myriads of bright air-bells. On a larger scale the same operation may be observed going on, while the sun shines, in every pond and brook in whose waters vegetation is found. In every one of these bells there is a minute contribution toward the purity of the atmosphere; and the resulting aggregate of oxygen obtained from all the plants in the world is just sufficient to counteract the action of the various causes constantly tending to deteriorate it. Thus no plant on which the sun shines — whether it flourish on the surface of the earth or under the water — exists in idleness or passes a useless life. All work for Nature in their appointed way.

Under certain circumstances, and more especially when the air is moist, leaves absorb much invisible vapor and grow rapidly. Some plants, even when they are removed from the ground and hung up in the conservatory, absorb enough of carbon and water to keep themselves in a tolerably healthy state; but the chief supply of moisture is taken in from the ground. The excess that is absorbed is transpired by the leaves, and thus the juices of the plant are maintained at the healthy degree of concentration. In hot weather the balance between the absorption and transpiration of water is destroyed; and as more water passes off than comes in, plant-life languishes and droops. At the close of a long sultry day in July there is an enjoyment to be derived from watering plants, which in a certain far-off way reminds us of giving drink to a thirsty man. It is one of those pleasing labors which we do not like to see thrown away upon any body who finds nothing in them but the fatigue. Is it extravagance to say that our sympathy is touched when we mark the signs of suffering which our favorites so naturally express? and is it not difficult to divest ourselves of the impression that plants enjoy the refreshing shower in some mysterious way of their own? Never do they fail to repay the little service with ready gratitude. Scarcely have the drops fallen before they begin to raise their drooping heads, and to signal their thanks to us out of every stiffening leaf and flower. Their whole being freshens and breathes, expands, inhales, exhales. Their air of flaccid languor disappears as if by magic, and they charm us once more by their look of renovated vigor.

There is a grassy-looking weed that grows among the sand near the sea-shore. Thousands in their rambles pass it by unheeded, or notice it only as an unattractive emblem of sterility. It is so coarse in texture that even hardy cattle turn from it with disdain. Yet this sea-reed, Arundo arenaria, as it is called, performs such signal service to man that its presence in this particular situation cannot be deemed less than providential. Many low-lying coast-lands require to be defended not only from the sea, but also from the sand cast ashore by the waves. This loose sand gradually accumulates, is driven hither and thither by every gale of wind, and has a tendency to encroach upon the fertile fields, and convert them into desert wastes. The threatened danger is averted by this humble plant, and the slightest consideration of its habits demonstrates that it was specially created for the purpose. While most plants instinctively seek out the richest soils, this one prefers the driest sands. The "gritty" storms so often raging around, which would overwhelm or destroy the tender organization of other plants, beat harmlessly against the silicious coverings of this hardy reed. In striking its roots into the sand it binds the loose particles together; and, as its sapless-looking tufts appear above the surface, they arrest the stony current as it is driven along by the wind, and consolidate it into little mounds. In process of time these are piled up into the well-known hillocks by the growth and decay of countless generations of tufts. Such sand-hills are common in various parts of Britain where the coast is low; but they are seen on a more extensive scale in the rugged "dunes" which stretch in almost endless succession along the shores of Holland. Not only do they intercept the devastating progress of the sand, but they likewise form the stoutest bulwark against the encroachments of the sea.

The common broom has long been employed in the Landes of Aquitania as a means of binding the low-lying tracts of sand, and preparing them for the growth of pine-forests. Professor Piazzi Smith informs us that there is a kind of mountain-broom which grows on the sterile, shifting lava-sands of the Peak of Teneriffe, more than a vertical mile above the level of the sea. "How wonderful," he eloquently remarks, "the adaptations of Nature to the necessities of various regions! For here, where the ceaseless motion of the sliding particles composing a hill's sides destroys every other living thing; where the aridity of the soil during many months is only surpassed by the aridity of the air, which is drier than that of the Sahara, Nature has produced a plant that on the mere remembrance of winter rain long since evaporated, can furnish no contemptible supply of wood; and with its richly stored white flowers, arranged in close rows along its smaller branches, affords illimitable honey-making materials to all the bees of the country."

There is, perhaps, no better way of estimating the value of God's gifts than by trying to realize what the world would have been without them. Conceive the variety of uses to which wood is daily applied, and for which no other substitute could be found. There is, in fact, hardly a work of construction that goes on anywhere into which wood does not almost necessarily enter. The growing employment of its rival, — or rather let us with thankfulness say its twin-blessing, — iron, serves happily to economize the world's decreasing stores of wood, but it does not detract from the value of this inestimable gift.

The most serviceable properties of wood, hardness and strength, have been secured by the peculiar way in which it has been ordained that wood should grow. If the myriads of sap-vessels and cells contained in the tree had been equally dispersed through its whole thickness, the condition of the timber would necessarily have been soft and prone to rot, and the formation of that dry, hard, and central part, which from its soundness we call the heart-wood, would have been prevented. Nature, therefore, with the intent of making her work more useful to man, has collected the chief channels of the sap immediately under the bark. It is here that the layer of mucilaginous cells and vessels is found, to which the term cambium is given. Here is the chief laboratory of the tree, and here the principal formative operations are carried on. Thus, on the outer side of the cambium the cells are periodically laid in the order which qualifies them in due time to assume the functions of the bark; while, on the inner side of the layer, the cells are arranged so as to form new wood. The annual time of wood-manufacture corresponds to the season of the year during which the circulation of the sap is active; and it stops in winter when the flow of the sap has been reduced to the lowest degree compatible with the preservation of life. Every year's increase is a distinct and separate contribution to the thickness of the tree, and is represented ever afterward by one of those "concentric rings" with which all are familiar in cross sections of the stem. From their mode of formation, therefore, each concentric ring indicates a period of one year, and the entire number forms one of the most reliable data from which the age of the tree may be calculated. At the same time this rule does not apply under all circumstances. In trees that are evergreen, for example, the circles are indistinct, because, as the leaves are always present, the interruption to the circulation of the sap, on which the line of separation between the circles depends, does not at any season occur in so marked a manner as in trees that are deciduous. In some equatorial countries with peculiar climates there are, it is said, several distinct periods of growth followed by intervals of repose during every year. It has been asserted that, in certain parts of tropical America, rings in trees are sometimes to be found for every month in the year.

From the way in which the wood-mass of the tree is thus built up year after year in regular "courses," it follows that the worst, or at least the softest timber, is found towards the outside of the trunk. Within this layer, and more especially as the centre is approached, the hardness of the wood increases, because no new growth is being carried on there, and because the old lignite cells, which were comparatively soft when originally deposited, have in the course of years gradually become blocked up, solidified, and hardened by the thickening of their walls. On this account the timber of the tree has been divided into the soft, external sap-wood, or alburnum, and the hard, internal heart-wood, or duramen. Between these two parts of the tree the color is often very conspicuous. As familiar examples may be mentioned the well-known heart-wood of the ebony and the laburnum. Besides these the black-walnut is remarkable for its dark-brown centre. In the barberry the heart-wood is yellow; in some kinds of cedar it is purplish red, and in the guaiacum-tree, or lignum vitæ, it is greenish. When we reflect that, in the roots of trees, the sap-vessels are distributed through the whole substance, making the wood soft and useless; while, in the stem, this order has been changed, and they have been collected under the bark, by which means the chief bulk of the timber remains hard and serviceable, it is impossible not to perceive that there is here the clearest evidence of that beneficent planning to satisfy our wants in which we recognize the hand of our Heavenly Father.

One of the most mysterious properties of plants is that of regulating their temperature. The twigs of the tree are not frozen through in winter, neither does their temperature mount up in summer in proportion to the external heat. Their vitality protects them equally from both extremes. The bark, moreover, with its loose texture and included air, is a bad conductor, and forms, as it were, a great-coat in which the plant is wrapped up. Many trees perish from cold when stripped of their bark. Winter berries differ in their power of resisting cold. White of Selborne tells us that the haws are spoilt by the first sharp frost, while ivy-berries do not seem to freeze, but "afford a noble and providential supply of food to birds in winter and spring." The surface evaporation in summer produces, no doubt, a certain amount of freshness in the leaves, and we know how cool they feel even in hot days. But evaporation does not explain this circumstance in regard to many kinds of fruit which are encased in an envelope of closest texture through which evaporation is difficult if not impossible. The coolness of fruit in hot climates is remarkable. Dr. Hooker relates that the juice of the milky Mudar, growing by the side of the Ganges, was found to have a temperature of 72° Fahrenheit, while the damp sand on which it flourished was scorching in a heat that reached from 90° to 104°. But, in order to enjoy the coolness of tropical fruit in perfection, it must be eaten soon after it has been gathered. With the extinction of life its power to resist heat ceases also, and by falling under the same laws as other dead matters, it soon acquires their temperature. In our survey of the "green things upon the earth" let us ever gratefully remember the means with which they providentially supply us for combating most of the diseases to which flesh is heir. Herbs possessing medicinal virtues are, like mineral waters, widely distributed over the globe. The most valuable drugs may, perhaps, be considered as limited more especially to tropical countries, where the stimuli of light and heat, being at their highest power, develop in perfection the various vegetable principles; but commerce has abundantly placed most of them within our reach. Yet even to countries situated in higher latitudes Providence has been bountiful. As for ourselves, it may be said that, were the supply of foreign drugs to fail, we could still obtain from our native plants a "materia medica" of the utmost value. Time was when every abbey and monastery in the land had its "physic garden" and its stores of simples; and when the priest, on whose skill the whole district was dependent, searched the woods and meadows in quest of the herbs with which he was to assuage suffering.

As autumn draws on, the leaves begin to prepare for a new sphere of usefulness; for as yet they have been passing through one phase only of their mission in Nature's economy. Yet what a life of beneficent activity has been theirs since they issued from the bud in spring! First, let us thankfully acknowledge how much they have contributed by their beauty to gladden the aspect of the earth. They have moderated evaporation from the soil, and shielded it from excessive heat and cold. Under the thick foliage cattle have enjoyed a welcome shelter from sun and storm, and many a timid creature has found there a safe refuge against pursuing enemies. Every single leaf has done its part in the work of perfecting the sap of the plant on which it lived. Leaves have purified the atmosphere which was contaminated, and have prepared it anew for the respiration of the animal world. But now "the turn of the year" is upon them. Their pleasing tints of green are passing into warning shades of red and yellow. The flow of sap grows languid in their veins, and the sharp night frosts shrivel and crisp them up. The melancholy "fall" is at hand. The vitality of the shed foliage is gone, and it is about to be made subject to the action of another Power of the Lord. Upheld no longer by life, the leaves must yield themselves, like the other dead matter around, to the inexorable laws of chemistry. Wind and weather will soon break up their delicate texture, until, reduced at length to mold, they will mix with and enrich the soil, and serve in their turn as food for other plants. Not a leaf will be lost, for each will contribute something toward the general good. Thus amid the boundless profusion of Nature economy is ever the ruling law. The fragments are gathered, and nothing is wasted. Bountifulness and thrift go hand in hand.

Great is the enjoyment associated with the hours spent among the "green things of the earth," when every sense we possess was gratified in its turn. There was beauty for the eye, perfumes floated in the air, and sounds that were sweet and fascinating broke pleasingly upon the ear. The treat was one we could not prize too highly, for our Father himself spread it out before us for our enjoyment. Nature might have been made dull, colorless, silent, and ugly, or we might have been formed without the power to appreciate it; but the Creator has made it lovely, and has given us minds to see and feel its loveliness. Shall we not, then, cherish the gift? Can we for a moment doubt that if we neglect or despise it we are to a certain extent frustrating the purpose for which it was bestowed?

Our Lord Himself illustrated many of his precepts by examples derived from the vegetable kingdom. The lilies, the wheat and the tares, and the grain of mustard-seed, are all associated in our minds with His teaching. Moral lessons — calls to duty — causes for thankfulness — reasons for praise — the desire to adore, flow gently in upon our thoughtful contemplations in field and forest. In surveying "the green things upon the earth" we see how unspeakably our Father has blessed and cared for us. We look and analyze, we trace, calculate, and study the All-merciful and the All-wise, and our hearts are filled to overflowing with "wonder, love, and praise."

"Let all Thy works praise Thee, O Lord," or, as it might be expressed, Let Thy children, inspired by the contemplation of Thy works, praise Thee, as the Psalmist exhorts, "with understanding." Viewed in this light the plantal world is no longer silent, but justifies through us the invocation of the Benedicite. It speaks in a language almost infinitely varied, but the lofty theme it proclaims is ever the same. Like the "voices of the stars," the green things upon the earth are truly a fair Hymn of Praise, written all over the land, not in words, but in living characters of beauty. May we not also regard them as smiling monitors placed everywhere around our path to whisper to us thoughts of God's greatness and love?

Delight thou in the Lord; and He shall give thee thy heart's desire. — Ps. xxxvii.

BEASTS AND CATTLE.

O all ye Beasts and Cattle, bless ye the Lord: praise Him, and magnify Him for ever.

OF all the scientific pursuits that can form the object of man's study, that of Natural History is, after Astronomy perhaps, the most fascinating. Its class-room is the fair field of Nature, its facts charm us by their intrinsic interest, and its revelations not only contribute to our enjoyment, but, by exhibiting the perfection with which every creature has been constructed with reference to its way of life, lead our thoughts adoringly upward to the Creator. No pursuit forms a more healthy relaxation for the body, or a better training for the mind. It exercises memory, patience, judgment, and reason; it cultivates the habit of observation, and confers a taste for order and exactness. The frequent contemplation of the harmony, wisdom, and beneficence therein displayed surely accomplishes an improving effect upon the mind. If, indeed, Natural History were to be followed for its own sake merely, and if we were to rest satisfied with intelligently admiring its many pleasing marvels, its highest purpose would be overlooked, and it would lack its crowning value.

Nowhere is God's beneficent consideration for man's wants more conspicuously seen than in the class of animals to which "Beasts and Cattle" belong. In the natural exercise of that dominion over them with which we have been intrusted, we derive from them one of our most important supplies of food. There is, indeed, scarcely any thing entering into the structure of cattle which does not, directly or indirectly, minister to man's comfort. Their hides form the best protection to the feet, and are applied to a thousand useful purposes besides; we get glue and parchment from them; out of their horns are made a variety of serviceable articles; and we grind down their bones to fertilize the fields. Nor are they less valuable gifts while living, and the exactness with which they respond to many of the most obvious requirements of man cannot be regarded otherwise than as providential. Man needed an assistant to carry his burdens, to work for him in the fields, to bear him swiftly on his journeys — and finds that assistant in the horse. It is unnecessary to pause here, to point out the thousand other ways in which the horse is serviceable to man, or how much would have been lost to the comfort of life had this single creation been omitted. Either naturally, or under the fostering care of man, the horse is to be found in almost every land outside the polar circles. Yet there are a few spots in the world, like the Arabian desert, for which the horse is unfitted, and for which special requirements are necessary — so God created the camel.

In no animal are the evidences of design more conspicuous than in the camel. In it we see the good qualities of the horse, as it were, supplemented, and various structures modified, with the obvious intention of adapting it to the special work it has to perform. Not only is the "ship of the desert" docile and strong to qualify it to be a beast of burden, but its feet are cushioned with elastic and expansile pads, which spread out into broad flat surfaces when pressed on by the weight of the body. It is evident that the camel has thus been shod in order that it might stalk across the loose sand without sinking into it. Nor is it constructed internally with less careful reference to the special nature of its work. One great danger which animals incur in crossing the desert arises from the want of water; but the camel carries its own supply in a sort of internal tank. Thus a part of its complex stomach is set round with deep cells or sacs — little barrels, they might be called — which are filled with water as opportunities may occur, and they are then by the constriction of their orifices shut off from communication with the rest of the cavity. When the camel requires to draw upon this store the orifices are relaxed, and the cell compressed so as to empty out the water. By means of this special contrivance the camel can journey in the desert several days without drinking even in sultry weather. Its adaptation to its work has been further perfected by the remarkable acuteness of the sense of smell, by which it is said to scent the presence of water at the distance of half a league. Its power of subsisting on such hardy fare as the coarse herbage of the desert, and the leaves and twigs of trees occasionally met with in the oases, as well as the sharp, strong teeth fitted for cutting and grinding them, are additional proofs of wise design. As no organ is more apt to suffer from the heat and glare of the sand than the eye, the camel has prominent, overhanging eyebrows, and this light-shield is made still more perfect by long thick eyelashes. During the wild tumult of the simoom every thing living tries to keep out the clouds of hot dust that are borne along by the wind. On this account the nostril of the camel is not wide and patent, as in the horse, but a mere slit, which can be firmly closed at will as with a lid.

In a certain sense the camel may be said to carry with it a supply of meat as well as drink, for the hump on its back is chiefly composed of fat stored up in time of abundance to be drawn upon in time of scarcity. In the course of long journeys, if food be wanted, the hump wears away, and it requires a course of good feeding before it is restored.

In loading the camel it is made to kneel down to facilitate the operation, and in order that its knees may not suffer from rubbing or pressure, they are naturally defended by callous pads placed where the chief pressure is sustained. These pads, as well as another situated on the chest, serve for the camel to rest upon in reposing.

An animal very analogous to the camel is seen in the llama of the Andes; but a point of difference in their structure may be here noticed, as it has an obvious relation to the field of labor designed for each. The camel travels over the flat, loose sand, and has a broad expanded foot; but the llama is intended to climb the steep mountain slopes, and is furnished with a cleft hoof, the ends of which are prolonged into a kind of hook or claw, by which its foot-hold is made more certain.

In tropical countries, where excessive heat in some measure disqualifies man for severe exertion, and where more aid in performing the heavier parts of labor is required, he finds an invaluable servant in the docile elephant. Whole volumes have, ere now, been written to illustrate the sagacity and usefulness of this animal. His structure, too, offers many points of admirable contrivance, into which want of space prevents us from now entering.

In northern countries, beyond the natural limits of horse and donkey, a substitute was needed which might carry on the work of transport, and yet live amid the snows on the roughest fare. The elk and, more especially, the reindeer fill up the gap, and place their strength and fleetness at the service of man. The range of the reindeer is very extensive. From the northern parts of Sweden and Norway it extends deep into the polar regions, and this animal is said to flourish in perfection among the inhospitable regions of Spitzbergen. Its very appetite and powers of digestion are molded on the productions of the home which Nature has given to it. Though the climate is unfavorable to grass and cereals, many of the forest-trees, and much even of the most barren land, are abundantly covered with lichens, of which the animal is fond. A Lap who is fortunate enough to possess plenty of ground whitened over with lichen, surveys it with feelings akin to those with which a farmer might regard his promising fields of wheat or barley. He regulates his movements by the wants and likings of his precious reindeer. In winter, it lives amid the rough shelter of the woods: in summer, when the mosquito drives the herd from the forests, he repairs with it to the higher grounds, where it finds food and coolness. Its acute sense of smell guides it to where the lichen grows, where it "routs like swine," or clears away the snow with its fore-feet. In case of need Nature has armed the reindeer's head for a part of the year with a shovel and a pick conveniently placed just over their muzzle. No one can look upon those brow antlers, of which at least one is flattened out like a spade and tipped with horn almost as hard as ivory, without the conviction that they were designed for this special purpose.

The hardy Laplander's riches centre in his reindeer. It is his beast of burden, and his carriage-horse. Seated in his sledge he traverses long journeys with great rapidity. A distance of 150 miles in 19 hours is not considered a great feat, and many most marvelous exploits are recorded. The reindeer supplies his owner with milk and cheese for the winter, and with an ever-ready store of venison. Like cattle elsewhere, every thing about this animal is of use. The hide makes shoes and the warmest of winter wraps. The skin of an allied animal, the cariboo of North America, supplies a cloak so warm that it enables its wearer to defy with safety the rigor of an Arctic night. Consistently with the established order of things the Laplander could not have horses or cows, wheat or hay; but Providence has given him a kind of "Cattle" substitute, which in itself supplies all his requirements, and has combined with this gift the growth of a hardy lichen which is better adapted for its food than the finest hay.

Man needed, moreover, a confidential friend to guard

his house and property, to lighten his labors by sagacious activity in tending flocks and herds, and to help him by instinct and fleetness in the chase. Such a friend is found in the dog, the most loyal and trusty of the brute creation. For man's sake the dog has forsaken its gregarious instincts, and the company of its fellows, in order to become his attached servant and companion. The dog is brave, intelligent, honest, unselfish, and submissive. The camel is a substitute for the horse, and the reindeer is in some degree a substitute for both; but nowhere on earth could a fitting substitute be found for the faithful dog. Beyond the limits of the reindeer the Esquimau is carried swiftly and safely in his sledge over the frozen seas of Greenland by the aid of his team of dogs, and many a life is saved by their untiring exertion. Thus the geographical distribution of this "good gift" has been made almost universal, and from the Equator to Kamschatka the ubiquitous dog is found doing his appointed work.

Not only are the animals of polar regions wrapped up in thickest fur, but they are generally clad in white — a color which economizes the internal heat by diminishing radiation from the surface. Many animals in Northern countries, as ptarmigan and hares, which are of a speckly or bluish color during the summer months, change more or less to white in winter, and for the same reason. Animals living in polar climates are remarkable for the abundance of their fat, which acts as a blanket to keep them warm when living, and, when killed in the chase, affords large supplies of carbonaceous food to the natives to maintain the needful temperature of the body in winter by being burnt in the lungs. These are points with which most persons are familiar, but they illustrate very strikingly how, even in minute matters, the peculiarities of animals are adjusted and designed according to the necessities of their position, and with reference to the special wants of mankind around them.

How widely, also, another of God's best gifts — the sheep — has been distributed over the world, partly by the hand of Nature, partly through the agency of man. The wool which it supplies so abundantly for clothing takes equal rank with flax and cotton. Originally coarse and harsh, it has by degrees been brought to its present perfection by the persevering skill and industry of man. The wool of neglected flocks soon degenerates, and would ultimately resume the coarseness of the rough-haired, primitive wild sheep of Siberia.

When our colonists first went to New South Wales it was remarked that no representative of the tribe of oxen was to be seen. Pastures were there of the richest kind and of almost unlimited extent, but in so far as cattle were concerned these resources appeared thrown away. A little further observation, however, seemed to indicate in this anomaly a wise and benevolent design. The climate in many parts of Australia is peculiar, and subject to droughts of such severity as to dry up the rivers, as well as the deep natural water-tanks hollowed out in their course. At other times the withered, tinder-like grass takes fire, and the conflagration rapidly spreads itself over extensive districts. Let us imagine what would most probably have occurred in such a case had there been cows and calves on these pasture grounds. The dams might perhaps have escaped by abandoning their young; but the latter, not having the strength to migrate, would have been overtaken by swift destruction. Instead of oxen, the settlers found an animal of a different and peculiar type in possession of these prairies, which seemed as if it had been designed to cope with the difficulties of the climate. The Kangaroo has locomotive powers very superior to the cow, but its distinguishing feature is the marsupial pouch destined for the reception and preservation of its young. In case of necessity these could take refuge in the pouch, and, holding on firmly with their mouths, could be safely transported by the mother to a place of greater abundance or of safety. But when civilized man appears upon the scene, a new page is opened in the design of Providence. The mission of the Kangaroo is drawing to a close, and it must give way to more valuable tenants. An intelligence is now on the spot which can in a great measure overcome the difficulties of the climate. The farmer can dig tanks in which the water will not easily dry up: he can in some measure circumscribe the conflagration; in time of drought he can lead the cattle to streams by whose banks green herbage is still to be found; and he can lay up stores of hay and other provisions against the winter's scarcity. Had cattle been previously introduced, they might often have been exposed even to worse tortures than those which Humboldt describes as overtaking the wild cattle of South America in seasons of inundation.

The buffalo and the bison afford striking examples of the way in which the normal structure of an animal is often materially modified in accordance with necessities arising from the physical character of the country it inhabits. In dry districts their feet are compact and have comparatively narrow hoofs; but in swampy districts, and by the side of low marshy rivers, this kind of hoof would be a serious defect. In process of time, therefore, it flattens and expands considerably, so as to counteract the tendency to sink into the mud.

In tropical countries the elephant has got a skin which is nearly destitute of hair. The climate supplies the necessary amount of warmth. But in the extinct Siberian elephant or mammoth which lived upon the verge of the ice, the skin was doubly covered with a thick, short fur, and with long hair. This structure is clearly shown in the famous specimen obtained from the ice of the river Lena, and of which the skeleton is preserved at St. Petersburg. A piece of skin from the same animal is likewise exhibited in the museum of the Royal College of Surgeons.

We do not always judge wild animals fairly. We are apt to regard their savage nature as almost a blot in the plan of creation, and we feel puzzled in our attempts to reconcile it with universal benevolence. Ferocity in such animals is invariably the result of a structure which has been carefully designed for a good purpose, and is by no means an indication of innate cruelty. When considered in relation to their obvious mission of checking such an increase of animals as would be fatal to the general welfare, and with reference to their necessary mode of living, this ferocity, so far from tending to augment suffering, tends directly to diminish it. The habits of an animal may be said to depend upon the shape of its teeth, or, to speak more correctly, both have been consistently adjusted to each other. If we examine the mouth of a tiger or hyena, nothing is more clear than that it is designed to seize and rend a living prey. Now the more ferocious animals are, the more effectively they will use their teeth, and the sooner will death relieve their victims from suffering; but had such teeth been engrafted upon a milder nature, the prey might have been killed in a way that would have been slow torture. Hence there is designed mercy in their savageness, and Nature in putting those fearful weapons into their mouths has aimed at shortening the pang of dying. Not forgetful of the evil which the unrestrained exercise of such power for destruction might bring upon weaker animals, the propensity to kill has generally been subordinated to the calls of hunger. A lion or a boa constrictor reposes peaceably as soon as its appetite has been appeased; a lion-tamer is careful not to enter the den until the half-subdued monsters have been fed; and even a pike, whose disposition has been more especially branded with cruelty, seems to inspire little terror among surrounding fishes as soon as he is gorged.

For wanton cruelty we must go, alas! to civilized life. It is probably unknown among animals in a wild state, although, in carrying out certain purposes of Providence, all the appearances of cruelty are sometimes assumed. To take an instance from the class of insects : — what at first sight appears more repulsively cruel than the wholesale slaughter which goes on in a wasp's nest at the approach of winter? Wasps labor under a bad character, but, whatever their failings may be, nobody ever accused them of want of tenderness for their offspring. They tend the cells where the eggs are hatched, and they nurse the newborn grubs with a devotion quite equal to that displayed by their more esteemed neighbors the bees. Yet no sooner does the first sharp pinch of frost nip them in the autumn, than their whole nature undergoes a change. Their love, by some mysterious impulse of instinct, is then converted into fury, and, falling on the young brood of the nest, they ruthlessly destroy them all. But, we may ask, if these grubs had been spared, would their fate have been improved? The summer mission of the wasps was ended, food was getting scarce, and starvation was in immediate prospect, so Nature sent the voracious grubs a speedy death, instead of a lingering torture. Few of the executioners, however, long survive the desolation of their home, and in the extinction of both man may recognize a mercy to himself. The progeny of a single wasp in spring mounts up to 20,000 or 30,000 before the end of autumn, and if most of these were to survive the winter, the species would increase at a rate which would be incompatible with man's comfort, if not with his existence. What food is there which he would have been able to preserve from their ravages?

His mercy is over all His works. — Ps. cxlv.

Among the influences most injurious to the health of man are the emanations arising from animal and vegetable substances in a state of decay. To mitigate this evil, we enforce our sanatory laws, we build sewers, we fumigate and whitewash. But there are nooks which brushes cannot reach, and our war with the inevitable results of decomposition would have been unsuccessful had not Nature herself come to the rescue with her powerful aids. There are winds which search our streets and courts, and dissipate many a gathering animal poison wherein pestilence is secretly breeding; there are rains which wash our walls, scour our ways, and flush our sewers, and float away the seeds of disease. In polar regions, where life is comparatively scarce, and decomposition is limited to the brief interval of summer, nothing is needed in a general way to purify the air. But in tropical climates, where life teems and heat and moisture stimulate decomposition, scavengers are especially needed; and while man has done least, Nature has there done most, to carry on the necessary work. Without Nature's aid many a village in hot climates would scarcely be habitable. Some Indian towns have no other scavengers than the wild beasts which lurk in neighboring jungles during the day, and carry away all the offal of the place in nightly razzias. Every body has heard of the snarling, howling, mangy mongrels of Stamboul and other Eastern towns, which range through the streets at night, and purify the tainted air by snapping up the animal refuse of the town. Further to the south the hyena and other kindred animals prowl round the lone African village, waiting for the time when the inhabitants shall have retired to rest, in order that they may venture within the precincts and feed on any garbage they may find. Judging by the extent of the machinery employed and the imperious instincts with which, to secure performance, this service has been combined, there can hardly be any more important work within the circle of the world's economy. From man himself downward every class of animals and all plants take their appointed share of labor in keeping Nature's common household clean and pure. According to the kind of work to be done, Providence appoints with unerring wisdom the kind of workman to be employed.

With all her boundless variety Nature is the most consistent of artificers, and so strict is the relation subsisting between the various organs of the body, that from a single tooth or other bone can often be inferred the chief points connected with the habits and structure of the animal to which it belonged. In this manner Cuvier, by his knowledge of Comparative Anatomy, was able to reconstruct with approximative accuracy many fossil animals of which mere fragments only had been preserved in the strata of the rocks; and his system has been followed up with success by Professor Owen and others. Cuvier tells us that there is an extreme pleasure to be found in thus tracing the structural harmonies established between the different parts of animals, and in noting how one organ entails another. "None of these parts can change without the whole changing; and consequently each of them, separately considered, points out and marks all the others."

In many cases animals have been sent into the world for certain obvious purposes, and it is instructive to note the perfect way in which they are fitted for their task. It is the highly necessary mission of the Ant-eater of South America to keep within bounds the enormous profusion of that form of life by destroying myriads of ants as food. It is, in the first place, armed with strong claws to tear up the houses or earth-galleries in which the ants live. Having disinterred its active prey, how are the ants to be seized? An ordinary mouth would be of little use, but Nature has provided the animal with a prodigiously long tongue, which it smears over with a viscid, adhesive mucus, derived from enormously developed glands surrounding the throat, and it then thrusts in this fatal trap among the little insects. The ants adhere in thousands, and are thus conveyed into the mouth with marvelous rapidity. The next point is that the ants should be crushed; for the hard, parchment-like covering in which they are encased offers great resistance to the gastric juice. The mouth is ill adapted for the purpose; for it is, in fact, little else than a tubular case for the long tongue. In the next place, it is destitute of teeth; and, indeed, teeth would have formed far too powerful a mill for such tender food, while many of the active little creatures would certainly have escaped from the mouth during mastication. The crushing, therefore, goes on in the stomach; and, as Owen has expressed it, the Ant-eater has borrowed the gizzard of a fowl for the purpose. In this muscular stomach or gizzard, therefore, myriads of ants are reduced to a pulp, out of which their arch-enemy extracts abundant nourishment. How clear the evidence of the special design with which claws, tongue, glands, mouth, and stomach are mutually and in a very peculiar manner adapted to each other!

A whole series of structural adaptations is displayed in the Aye-aye, a quadrumanous, or four-handed, animal found in Australia. It is nocturnal in its habits, therefore the pupil of the eye is large to admit as much light to the retina as possible. The organ of hearing is also greatly developed, for the purpose of enabling it to detect the scraping operations of its favorite food, which is a kind of grub that bores and burrows in trees. Having found the spot under which the grub is at work, it chisels down upon it by means of strong jaws and teeth specially constructed for the purpose. But no sooner does the grub find its dwelling broken into than it retreats to the other end of its burrow; and all the labor of the Aye-aye would probably have been in vain, had not Nature anticipated this difficulty by bestowing on it a peculiar and most odd-looking contrivance in the shape of an enormously prolonged slender middle finger having a hook at the end, with which it probes into the recesses of the burrow and extracts the impaled grub.

In ancient Bible times herds and flocks constituted the riches of the wealthy. Jabal was "the father of such as dwell in tents and of such as have cattle." A great herdsman was equivalent to a great proprietor, and he was qualified for the highest offices. Abraham and Lot possessed much wealth of this kind, and they separated because it was difficult to find sufficient pasture for their united herds. Moses was a shepherd after his flight from Egypt, while he tended the flocks of his father-in-law, Jethro, in the land of Midian; Amos, the prophet, was a herdsman. Among "cattle" were included many of the beasts useful to man for feeding, clothing, and other purposes; in this group, therefore, were to be found oxen, sheep, goats, horses, asses, and camels. Hence it seems most natural that the Three Children, while enumerating the blessings sent from above, should have specially dwelt on this "good gift."

In the preceding pages we have endeavored to point out a few illustrations of the goodness and wisdom with which God has adapted "Cattle and Beasts" to the requirements of that sphere in creation where he has placed them, but we have done little more than open up the subject. It is one which grows in handling, and the more we look the more thickly illustrations flow in upon us. With such a theme it is difficult to know where to begin, and it is equally difficult to know where to leave off. Every animal is a text by which creative wisdom is admirably displayed.

<blockquote>The Lord is my shepherd; I shall not want. — Ps. xxiii.</blockquote>

FOWLS OF THE AIR.

O ye Fowls of the Air, bless ye the Lord: praise Him, and magnify Him for ever.

IT may be truly affirmed that Birds are not surpassed by any class of animals in the illustrations they afford of the Power, Wisdom, and Goodness of the Creator. Their shape and plumage attract our admiration. Their voices fill our woods in spring with sounds of cheerfulness and life. The grace, boldness, and endurance of their flight excite astonishment; the unerring certainty with which, at the period of migration, many of them traverse seas and continents exceeds our comprehension; while the industry, faithfulness, and devotion displayed by them in the construction of their nests and the rearing of their young claim for them our sympathy and protection.

The song of birds has evidently the closest relation to the period of breeding, and common sense plainly tells us that it must be one of the chief attractions between the mated pair. The mistress of the future nest listens complacently to the notes poured forth in her honor, which, in a language she well understands, both encourage her in her preparations, and add to the pleasure with which she sets about them. At other seasons of the year, unless incubation be going on, there is comparatively little singing. It has answered its purpose, and the presence of the loved young ones in the nest is Nature's guaranty that the parents will tenderly bring their offspring up, and send them forth into the world when they are ready to cope with its difficulties.

The importance of the organ of voice to birds may be inferred from the details of its structure. The windpipe is comparatively wider and stronger than in any other class of animals. In man and other mammalia there is a single organ, or larynx, but in birds it is double; or it may be considered as divided into two parts, one being placed at the top, the other at the bottom of the windpipe, or trachea. The sound is produced in the lower larynx by a mechanism which is generally compared to the reed in a clarionet, and it is subsequently modified in passing through the upper aperture into the bill. There are, moreover, dilatations frequently found at the lower larynx, the air in which adds to the sound by its vibrations. We shall have occasion to point out that there are also air-sacs abundantly dispersed over the body with which the organ of voice is in communication, — a circumstance which serves to explain how so small a creature as a bird can pour forth its loud stream of song uninterruptedly for so long a period. From these reservoirs it can supply itself with wind for its instrument of voice, in the same way as the Scotch "pipes" are supplied with air from the "bag," or the organ from the bellows. The sound thus produced is often remarkable for intensity. The nightingale, according to Nuttall, can be heard farther than a man, while the cries of storks and geese are said to be four times more powerful than the human voice. Flocks of these birds may be heard during their migratory flight from an altitude of three miles, and when they themselves are scarcely visible.

Let us not pass on without a tribute to the skylark, which sings to us nearly all the year round. When other birds leave us, he never forsakes his home; when others become mute, his cheery voice may still be heard. Scarcely are the noise and dust of the busy city left behind before he salutes us with his song; as we walk onward the gladsome carol is caught up by others of the band; and as our stroll ends it still lingers in our ears. Of all the feathered songsters he is the most constant companion of our rambles, and ever seems as ready to sing as we are to listen. Poised as a dark speck in the clear air, or rising on quivering wings above his nest, his song gushes out as if from an abounding fountain. Upward — upward — higher and higher! until at length the songster himself sometimes vanishes from sight, and the notes, softened and faintly heard, seem to come out of the depths of the firmament. There is no bird we could not sooner spare, or whose absence we should feel so much.

The singing of birds may be considered from another point of view. It is something more than a language between themselves, for it is likewise a contribution toward the pure enjoyments of life. To thousands it brings a pleasure which, though small perhaps in itself, must be added to the list of the little enjoyments scattered abundantly around, which in reality make up so much of the happiness of daily life. These concerts of Nature's choristers form one of the attractions of the country; but even to the inhabitants of cities birds bring much pleasure, if we may judge by the number of feathered songsters tenderly preserved by them. In reflecting upon such things, do we not find that their value consists less in the direct pleasure they bring than in the proof they afford that even in little things "He careth for us"?

The natural history of birds is a captivating study, and has given rise to some of the most delightful volumes in our language. The limits of the present work, however, forbid us to do more than briefly point out a few of those structural contrivances, and peculiarities of nature and habits, which exhibit to us in the most striking manner the power of the Great Artificer.

It will be generally admitted that no animals possess a covering which in beauty is comparable to the plumage of birds; and yet, as always happens where Nature is the artist, this beauty has not been purchased at the cost of any useful quality. On the contrary, what lighter clothing could have been devised for creatures whose aërial flights render lightness indispensable? The entire plumage of an owl weighs only an ounce and a half! Or what clothing could be warmer than the feathered quilt in which they are wrapped? And how essential a warm covering is to shield them from the heat-robbing currents of air and water to which they are exposed! No air is too keen for those cold-defying feathers, nor can the chill even of polar seas, where so many pass their lives, strike through this non-conducting blanket. To make the clothing perfect it was only necessary that it should be waterproof. The other qualities of the plumage would be useless if the water could penetrate among the feathers, and convert them from a dry, impermeable armor into a sodden mass clinging to the skin. Unable to resist the cold, the bird would then have perished. But the plumage has been perfected by giving to birds, and especially to water-fowl, the power to secrete an oily matter, which being smeared over the feathers renders them impervious to moisture. All must have observed that when a bird is dead, and can no longer diffuse this oil over its feathers, the water soaks in and soon spoils the plumage. The feathers are so arranged over the body of the bird that in flying or swimming the pressure of the air or water keeps them closely applied to the skin, so as to offer the least resistance to motion. Thus may we with admiration perceive how perfect in all points is the feathery covering of birds in relation to the purposes it is required to serve.

The wings of birds exhibit some beautiful proofs of creative design. In rapid flight the wings beat so forcibly against the air, that it is obvious that, unless the feathers were strongly bound together, the weaker parts would give way, and allow the air to pass through, by which the power of flight would be impaired. But this danger has been obviated by furnishing the barbs of the vane, or more pliant part of the feather, with what are called "barbules," forming on either side minute hooks, curved in contrary directions, which by intercrossing and locking with each other knit the feather into a strong compact paddle, so firm in most birds that it may be driven without yielding against the air, with a force that often produces a whistling sound. It is a further proof of design that certain birds, such as owls, which are in the habit of stealing slyly upon their victims, do not possess this structure, as it would be attended with the great inconvenience of giving their prey notice of their approach. The wings of owls are consequently loose and soft, but by allowing much of the air to pass through they are not adapted for rapid flight. Hence the slow, noiseless, almost mysterious gliding of these birds.

Another interesting example of design in relation to feathers is afforded by the woodpecker. When this bird is at work, excavating its house in the substance of some soft tree, or hunting for food in the crevices of the loose bark, it supports itself upon the perpendicular stem by planting its claws firmly into it, and then using its tail as a sort of third leg to lean upon behind. It thus stands firmly supported as it were upon a tripod. But as feathers of the ordinary kind would have been too weak for this "propping" service, the tail of the woodpecker is made of unusual strength and thickness.

The prominence of the keel of the breast-bone, with which all are familiar in poultry, gauges the size of the muscles which move the wings, and indicates the flying power of the bird itself. In those whose flight is rapid this projection is large, while in others not intended to fly the keel is shallow or wanting, and the pectoral muscles small in proportion. The speed of birds offers great variety. When the flight does not exceed 30 miles an hour, they are considered slow flyers. The speed of the swallow is computed at 90 miles, the hawk 150 miles, while that of the swift is said to attain the astounding velocity of 180 miles an hour.

The endurance displayed by birds upon the wing is wonderful, and many instances are recorded which almost exceed belief. In the time of Henry IV. of France there was a falcon which became famous in Europe by flying from Fontainebleau to Malta, 1350 miles, in 24 hours. But, without going so far back, we may on a summer's afternoon watch a flock of swallows for an hour without detecting the briefest interval of rest. Their skimming, busy, rapid wings never seem to tire. What strength of flight, too, must be required in those annual migrations which bring our winter water-fowl across the North Sea from frozen Scandinavia, and our summer visitors, the nightingales and swallows, from Southern Europe or Africa. Longer feats of flight are performed by some others, such as the Frigate or Man-of-war bird, which is sometimes found hunting for food in the Atlantic more than a thousand miles from shore. Yet it never seems to tire, or to seek rest either on the surface of the sea or in the rigging of the ship. It is said indeed never to visit the shore from choice, but only when the return of the breeding season renders a short sojourn on land indispensable.

Feathers are of considerable value in arts and manufactures. Since the seventh century nearly the whole literature of Europe has been written by means of quills, though in these latter days all-pervading iron threatens to drive them out of the field. When feathers are alluded to in connection with dress, they are usually suggestive of the vanities of life, but they have other uses of greater importance. Among savages, and especially among the Esquimaux, warm coverings are made of the skins of wildfowl, the feathers being turned inward. The great point in warm clothing is that the texture shall be loose enough to contain sufficient air to make it a bad conductor, and yet not so loose as to permit currents of cold air to circulate through it. Now it is found that the feathered skin of the Eider-duck fulfills these requirements in a very perfect manner, while it possesses in addition the valuable quality of lightness; hence it is regarded as the most complete model of warm clothing in existence.

Birds supply the civilized world with the luxury of soft beds and warm coverlets; and, indeed, there are few houses above the line of poverty which are not indebted to birds for some of their comforts and attractions. Goose feathers are the most esteemed for beds on account of their combined softness and elasticity; while Eider-down is best adapted for coverlets, because, although it is superior in softness, it is less elastic and does not bear heavy pressure so well. It is painful to think how cruelly the geese are treated from which we obtain our supplies. Unfortunately the best feathers are considered to be those which are taken from the living bird, and for this reason the poor creature has in many districts to undergo the torture of partial plucking several times a year. The Eider duck parts with its plumage on terms which, if less cruel, must still involve much suffering. It abounds on the coast of Norway, and in various parts of the Baltic, where the feather trade employs a number of men and produces a considerable revenue. In preparing her nest for the expected brood, the mother plucks the soft down from her breast, and lines her habitation with it. Soon afterward the hardy "fowler" appears upon the scene, suspended by his rope, and scrambling along the face of the cliff. The eggs are taken for food, and the feathers for commerce; and then the poor bird, after doubtlessly passing through her season of grief, sets to work to repair the mischief by plucking off another supply of down, and laying another set of eggs. Once more the spoiler visits the nest, and carries off as before the eggs and the down. But the instinctive courage and perseverance with which Nature has inspired the bird are equal to the trial. For the third time she fits up her habitation as before and again she lays her eggs. But now the sagacious fowler leaves her in peace. He knows that, in making this final effort to refit the nest, the Eider-duck and her mate have torn the last shreds of down from their breasts, and that were he again to rob the nest, the brood by which he hopes at some future day to profit could not be reared.

The weight of *dead* birds is familiarly known to every body. There is, in fact, no very striking difference in this respect between them and the other animals that live upon the ground, and it is obvious that mere wing-flapping alone would be insufficient to sustain them in the air, were they not aided by other means. As bones are the heaviest of the structures which enter into the composition of birds, it might naturally be expected they would offer the chief impediment to flight; and such would undoubtedly have been the case, had not Nature, by a slight deviation from the general rule, converted what would have been a drawback into a source of assistance. Animals whose movements are on the rough surface of the ground, require to have bones of great strength and density to enable them to withstand the shocks and strains to which they are liable; but birds, whose chief movements are in the air, do not require bones of such solidity. Nature, therefore, by forming them into hollow cylinders, has given them the shape which mechanically combines the greatest strength with the greatest lightness; and after every particle of superfluous bony matter has been thus removed, the interior of the bone is generally filled with air instead of marrow, by which the weight is still further reduced.

Not only does air pass freely into the bones of birds, often down to the ends of the small bones composing the toes, the tips of the wings, and even into the quills of the feathers, but, by means of a peculiar system of air-cells or receptacles, it is diffused all over the body, with an abundance which corresponds to the flight-power of the bird. These air-cells are in free communication with the air-passages of the lungs, and many of them can be inflated or emptied at will. They are of large size in the thorax and abdomen; occasionally they reach high up in the neck, forming as it were a balloon in front of the body, and they are generally very widely distributed under the skin. In birds distinguished for their power of flight, such as the Solan-goose, Albatross, and Pelican, the air not only fills the bones but surrounds the viscera, insinuates itself between the muscles, and buoys up the entire skin. The whole body is inflated like a balloon.

The circumstance, however, which chiefly promotes buoyancy, and gives to this remarkable arrangement its lifting power, is the comparatively high temperature of the included air. Birds are warmer blooded than mammalians; thus while the internal temperature of man seldom exceeds 98° Fah., that of birds varies from 106° to 112° Fah. This higher temperature is an indispensable requirement of their great muscular energy; and it, no doubt, also helps to counteract that tendency to cold which necessarily arises from their rapid movements both in air and water. But the purpose served by this high temperature to which we now draw attention is that it acts as a furnace to heat the air within the bones and cells. In circulating round the walls of the cavities containing air, the blood imparts to the latter a portion of its own warmth, just as a service of hot-water pipes heats the air in a room round which it is carried. The heated air, of course, renders the whole bird buoyant, on the principle of a fire balloon or caoutchouc ball, both of which readily rise into the air on being warmed. When the weight of the bird has thus been brought more or less into equilibrium with the surrounding air, the action of the wings easily lifts it from the ground. How completely this equilibrium is sometimes attained, even in the case of very large and heavy birds, may be inferred from the fact that the gigantic Condor of the Andes is occasionally seen wheeling in circles for hours together without the aid of a single flap from its wings. The perfection of buoyancy is even more wonderfully displayed by the Frigate bird of the Atlantic, which is said not only to rest its wings, but even to slumber as it floats in the air like a balloon.

The comparison just made may be carried a step further. If an opening be made in the balloon or the caoutchouc ball, through which the warm air can escape, they will collapse and fall to the ground. And in like manner, if the bone of a bird be fractured, or an opening be made into it at a place that is favorable for the escape of the air, the buoyancy of the bird is destroyed and it tumbles to the earth. So easy is the communication between the air-cavities of the bones and the lungs, that when the windpipe of a bird is closed, respiration can still be carried on for a short period through a broken bone, which serves as an artificial windpipe to convey the air to the lungs.

Many birds, instead of seeking for their food on shore, skim over the surface of the sea, and dive after their prey, or even pursue it under the water. It might reasonably be expected that the inflation of the body with air, which has just been described, would unfit them for diving and swimming under water, exactly in proportion as it promoted their power of sustaining themselves in the atmosphere. It is a singular fact, however, that the birds most remarkable for flight are sometimes no less distinguished for the ease with which they dive and glide about under water! The Solan-goose, for example, whose usual haunts in this country are the lofty heights of the Bass Rock and Ailsa Craig, is a most expert diver, as is proved by its being sometimes accidentally caught in fishing nets that have been sunk from 10 to 30 fathoms under water.

How happens it, we might reasonably ask, that a bird which at one moment is soaring buoyantly in the light air, can at the next be diving and swimming through the dense water? It is obvious that some rapid adjustment of its weight, or specific gravity, must take place in order to enable it to accomplish such a feat. This is achieved by simply giving to the bird the power of emptying more or less completely many of its principal air-cells, by means of muscles variously disposed in different parts of the body, which in contracting squeeze the air out of the cells, just as water is squeezed out of a caoutchouc bag when compressed in the hand. In this employment of air-cells to lessen or augment the specific gravity of birds, we are reminded of the function performed by the swimming bladder of fishes.

In regard to the movement of birds their general shape must not remain unnoticed. It will be observed that they are invariably formed like a wedge, of which the head and beak represent the apex. It is easy to understand how this must facilitate their progress both through air and water.

The beak of a bird is to be regarded not merely as a mouth, but also as an instrument of touch and prehension. In shape and strength it differs widely according to the nature of the work it is intended to perform. So closely, indeed, is this constructive relation observed, that, as Cuvier pointed out, you may tell from the beak of a bird what it feeds upon, what are its habits of life, and whether its disposition be gentle or ferocious, with as much certainty as you can decide the same question in regard to a quadruped, whether living or fossil, by the examination of its jaw. Some bills are excellent fly-traps, gaping widely and sweeping the air as with a net. Others, as in the snipe, are long and narrow, that they may probe the marshy ground, and they are supplied with nerves in order that they may feel the food which is often hidden from their view. Some bills, as in the Flamingo, are veritable scoops to ladle up the food into the mouth. Not the least admirable adaptation is to be found in the common duck, whose bill is soft, expanded, and sensitive, while the margins are supplied with horny transverse plates which act as a strainer to separate the particles of food from the turbid water in which it searches for them. The woodpecker's bill is a finely pointed chisel of great strength, tipped with horn almost as hard as ivory, to enable it to splinter the decayed bark of trees while hunting for insects, or to excavate the substance of the wood itself in nest-building.

Not unfrequently the beak serves as an organ of locomotion. A parrot, for example, uses it in climbing as dexterously as in cracking a nut and separating the kernel. The anterior extremities being appropriated for wings, the bill serves as a kind of hand with which birds lift, carry, and build. What human fingers could unhusk the seed with the nimble dexterity of some of our caged birds? There is, it is true, no arm to wield this hand, but Nature has made the neck of birds long and flexible, on purpose that it might act as an arm to apply this "bill-hand" wherever it is wanted.

As birds usually swallow their food the instant it is taken into the mouth, any particular development of the sense of taste would be superfluous. With few exceptions the tongue is stiff, cartilaginous, or even horny. In humming-birds and woodpeckers it is usually thought to be of great length, but this appearance is in reality due to a peculiar structure connected with the hyoid bone, to which the tongue may be regarded as attached somewhat as a spear-head is fixed to the end of the shaft. By this means the tongue may be darted out far beyond the limits of the mouth. In the humming-bird the tongue consists of a pair of narrow muscular tubes, resembling the double-barrel of a gun, and it divides at the tip into two spoon-like blades, or fringes, with which the bird adroitly seizes its food. In the woodpecker the tongue is a veritable spear, tipped and barbed with horn, by means of which it transfixes its prey, and bears it securely to its mouth.

Birds are no less characteristically distinguished by their power of vision than quadrupeds are by the sense of smell, and man by the sense of touch. Nuttall observes that a kite soaring beyond human ken detects a small bird or a mouse upon the ground, and descends upon it in almost a perpendicular line. The clearness of their vision is no less wonderful than its extent, for by slightly altering the shape of the eye it can be adjusted to distances and light, as if it were a telescope.

Many birds live on seeds which, being protected both by their vitality and their dense coverings, must be broken up before the gastric juice can act upon them with effect. To have crushed them in the mouth would have required grinders fixed in heavy jaws moved by bulky muscles; and these, in their turn, would have entailed the necessity for extensive surfaces of bone to afford attachments. It is obvious that such an apparatus is out of the question in birds, because it involves weights which are incompatible with flight. But the difficulty has been overcome by giving them a triturating machine, so admirably contrived that it dispenses with the use of teeth altogether, and forms a part of the stomach itself. The thin, membraneous stomach which we usually see in most animals would have wanted the requisite crushing power, and, therefore, it here takes the form of a muscular gizzard. Yet, even a gizzard, strong though it be, would not be able to cope with the hard texture of seeds, but for certain supplementary aids which perfect the action of the machine. Let us observe what happens. When the grains are picked up they are first received into "the crop," where they are moistened, and macerated, and kept back until the rest of the digestive apparatus is at liberty to attend to them. They next pass into the "ventriculus succenturiatus," or true stomach, where they are exposed to the solvent action of the gastric juice. And, lastly, after having been thus soaked and softened, they slip on into the gizzard, where they are ground into a pulp. As this process is continued, the food passes onward, and the nutritious portion is soon absorbed.

The gizzard is truly an instrument of astonishing power when its small size is considered. The force applying the triturating pressure consists of strong opposing muscles, and the cavity lying between them is lined by a tendinous expansion almost as hard as horn, on which the grain is ground as in a mill. There is a kind of petrel found far to the north, in which the cavity is inlaid with a hard tuberculous pavement, forming no inapt representation of the rough surface of a millstone. The gizzard of some mollusk-feeding birds, as ducks, is strong enough to crunch up shells with ease. In experiments on turkeys and common fowls, in which they were forced to swallow sharp, angular fragments of glass, metallic tubes, and balls armed with needles, and even lancets, all these substances were found to be broken or compressed by the powerful action of the gizzard, without having produced any wounds, or apparently even any pain. The chief bulk of the gizzard being made up of the muscular walls, the cavity is necessarily small, and only a little can be taken in at one time; hence the presence of a gizzard requires the aid of the other receptacles just described, to act as "hoppers," and by their special vital tact furnish a gradual supply. Graminivorous birds habitually swallow sand or pebbles to facilitate the grinding operation of the gizzard; and if the ear be applied to the side of a fowl while the gizzard-mill is at work, the sound of the "stones" rubbing against each other is often to be heard. In a certain sense the gravel may be said to act as teeth to pierce and lacerate the food in the stomach, and it has been remarked that fowls grow thin when it is rigidly excluded from their diet. They are, as it were, suffering from the loss of their teeth.

Although true crops are seldom found except in graminivorous birds, it is often desirable that there should be a receptacle in which food may be temporarily stored, either because the supply is precarious, or in order to facilitate its transport to the nest. In the pelican, the skin under the lower jaw forms a capacious expansile bag, in which fishes and other food may be carried to the young ones. Our favorite, the Swift, has also a jaw-pouch in which it deposits its insect prey until it is convenient to hand it over to the eager mouths in the nest. It is a curious circumstance that this pouch is found only in the breeding season, and then only in birds old enough to have a home and a family to provide for. So minutely are details attended to by Nature. But when we think how busily these birds feed their young throughout the day, we may form some idea of the time and trouble saved by means of this game-bag. In other cases the gullet is expanded into a receptacle, as in the vulture, which is thus enabled to lay in a stock of carrion, both for itself and its young, as opportunity offers. A similar arrangement exists in certain waders and swimmers. Bishop Stanley says that "in watching cormorants at a distance through a telescope, they may be sometimes seen quietly reposing with their mouths half-open and the tail of a fish hanging out, the remainder gorged in their capacious gullet; and sea-gulls will swallow bones of three or four inches in length, the lower end only reaching their stomach, while the rest continues in the gullet, and slips down gradually in proportion as the lower ends are consumed."

There are some wildfowl whose whole substance is, as it were, infiltrated with oil. It makes them buoyant on the water, and, like a blanket wrapped round the various organs, serves to retain the animal heat. It is also a store of fuel, to be drawn upon in times of scarcity for combustion in the lungs. The oil, moreover, sometimes forms a welcome addition to the "lighting" resources of communities placed far out of the way of gas and candles. Thus the hardy inhabitants of St. Kilda, a solitary island in the Atlantic, lying about fifty miles west of the Hebrides, are in the habit of levying on the Fulmar petrels frequenting the rocks an oil-tax, which is collected by making them disgorge a quantity of "pure oil" by means of the skillful application of pressure.

The number of the different kinds of birds known to exist is four times greater than that of quadrupeds; but it is the multitude of individuals that most astonishes us. They immeasurably exceed both mammalia and reptiles, and we must descend to fishes before we find tribes comparable to them in this respect. Strolling on the sea-shore of the Isle of Wight on an October afternoon, we have seen swallows flocking away to their winter homes in numbers that seemed countless, and in a broad stream which required ten minutes to pass by. Illustrations of the astounding multitudes of birds are to be found in every book on Ornithology, but we will here only refer to one given by Audubon. Among the Rocky Mountains flocks of migrating pigeons are often seen moving in a stream more than a mile broad, and although their speed probably exceeds a mile in a minute, three hours are sometimes spent before the long procession has ended. At the moderate estimate of two pigeons to each square yard, Audubon calculates the number in one such flock to be one billion one hundred and fifteen millions.

Such dense clouding of the air with birds leads the mind back to a scene that occurred in the wilderness, near Mount Sinai, more than three thousand three hundred years ago. We read in the sixteenth chapter of Exodus that the Israelites, dispirited and mistrustful, bitterly upbraided Moses for having led them so far away from Egyptian plenty to perish miserably in the desert: "Ye have brought us forth into this wilderness to kill the whole assembly with hunger." But the Israelites were rescued in their need, and the King of Nature fed them with quails and manna. "And it came to pass that at even the quails came up and covered the camp."

In the eleventh chapter of Numbers we read that on another occasion quails were sent in even greater abundance, — but sent this time in wrath to punish the murmuring Israelites. They had become discontented with the manna miraculously provided for them, and longed for the flesh and fish, and other good things to which they had been accustomed in Egypt. So the anger of the Lord was kindled, and He made the granting of their desire the means of their punishment: "And there went forth a wind from the Lord, and brought quails from the sea, and let them fall by the camp." For a day's journey round the ground was covered with birds in heaps: "And the people stood up all that day, and all that night, and all the next day, and they gathered the quails." "And while the flesh was yet between their teeth, ere it was chewed, the wrath of the Lord was kindled against the people, and the Lord smote the people with a very great plague." Yet this was the same kind of food which had before preserved them in the wilderness of Sinai. It had been eagerly desired, and had been granted abundantly; one thing, however, it lacked, without which neither food nor any other gift can profit — it lacked God's blessing. Deprived of that the seeming good became evil, and instead of bringing health and strength, it brought the deadly plague.

There is no denying that birds necessarily consume some of the fruits of the earth; but, on the whole, they well repay the tax thus levied, both by feeding on the seeds of weeds, and by the havoc they make among crop-destroying grubs and insects. The truth of this is sufficiently proved by the fact that, wherever crusades have been made for the extirpation of birds, success has invariably been followed by repentance. A few years ago sparrow-clubs for the indiscriminate slaughter of our familiar companions — the only birds that follow us into towns — came into fashion in some English counties, but enlarged experience and observation have sufficed to put them down. The last phase of the bird-crusade has been a fierce attack on rooks. While the balance of the argument is decidedly in favor of their protection, it must, nevertheless, be conceded that it is possible to have too much even of a good thing. On the one hand, the farmer may justly consider rooks as a natural police to keep within moderate limits some of the worst pests of the field; but, on the other, the force must be maintained with due relation to the work that is to be done. If the hands — or bills — be too few, grubs and other insect-vermin will increase destructively; but if the rooks be too numerous, the supply of grubs will be insufficient for the demand, and they will be driven to support themselves on other kinds of food. The wise course, therefore, is to keep them within proper limits, and then they will seldom be found feeding at the farmer's expense.

Nothing more conclusively demonstrates the bad policy, no less than the cruelty, of destroying little birds, than the experiment recently made by our neighbors in France. Until a short time ago small birds were absolutely without protection, and as every thing that flies is there apt to be accounted game, they were shot, trapped, and netted, until at length they were nearly extirpated. In many parts of France the silence that oppresses the woods and shrubberies in spring is melancholy. But by slow degrees farmers discovered that in killing little birds they had lost a willing band of active servants, whose absence from the field was marked by the rapid increase of insect-vermin; and they are now anxiously endeavoring to repair the evil that has been done by protecting birds by every means in their power. There is no reason to doubt that all birds have been created by Providence to perform some useful part in the economy of Nature; and that, while it is often expedient to keep their numbers in check, extirpation almost invariably turns out to be an act of folly.

It is not without interest to remark that in the Jewish Law promulgated by Moses nearly 1500 years before the Christian era, a law with which the Three Children were doubtless familiar, the case of the poor bird had been carefully considered, and some degree of protection legally afforded to it. In the twenty-second chapter of Deuteronomy it is enjoined: "If a bird's-nest chance to be before thee in the way in any tree, or on the ground, whether they be young ones or eggs, and the dam sitting upon the young or upon the eggs, thou shalt not take the dam with the young; but thou shalt in any wise let the dam go." The restriction doubtless referred to the allowable appropriation of the contents of the nest for the sake of food; but it evinces the same spirit of kindness to the lower animals generally by which the enactments of Moses were distinguished.

It would be easy to fill a volume with stories about the affectionate ways of birds, but it is impossible adequately to portray them in a few paragraphs. The genuine, unselfish, almost self-immolating tenderness they display toward their young is proverbial, while the contemplation of it always affords to hearts open to such influences a large amount of pleasure.

The very names of some birds are a testimony to their gentle nature; thus the word "Stork" both in Hebrew, Greek, and English expresses affection and kindness. It has been said that the young retain their love for their parents long after the usual nest-ties have been dissolved, and even cherish and feed them when they have become helpless through old age. What truth there may be in this popular tradition need not here be discussed, but every body must at least wish that so pleasing a trait of bird-nature should be true. It can excite no surprise that creatures about which such things are said should be favorites all over the East, and indeed in every country where they are found. Among Mohammedans more especially the stork is a welcome visitor, and is privileged to build its nest in whatever spot it may choose to select. Its habitation is held sacred, nor does it fail to show by its tameness that it understands the friendly footing on which it has been placed. It, moreover, repays the consideration it receives by waging incessant war against snakes and various other kinds of vermin; and by thus checking their undue increase, it fulfills its part in the appointed business of the world.

In Holland the stork is held in such reverence that it is protected by law. All travelers in that part of the world must have observed its grave, statue-like figure perched on roof or gable. There was a certain stork whose fame has spread far beyond its native Holland, as an example of devotedness to its offspring. It had taken up its quarters in Delft, and had the misfortune to build its nest on a house which was subsequently burnt down during a fearful conflagration. As the fire raged round the nest, the poor stork was seen anxiously yet vainly endeavoring with her wings to protect her young. Nearer and nearer swept the flames, the thatch crackled and blazed, but the faithful mother would not desert her post, and perished with her young ones.

The Pelican, so associated in our minds with Holy Writ and Eastern story, abounds in Palestine and in the wilderness spreading beyond the Tigris and Euphrates. This is another bird whose affection for its young has become classical. It is a most dexterous fisher, catching up with sure aim its finny prey, which it deposits for a time in the mouth-bag, formed by the dilatable skin under the lower mandible, until it can be conveniently conveyed to the nest.

Tradition long would have it that the affection of the pelican for its young induced it in periods of scarcity to lacerate its breast in order to feed them with the blood. Later observations, however, have shown this to be an error, arising from the habit which the bird has of pressing the mouth-pouch against its breast for the purpose of emptying its occasionally red-tinged contents into the nest. The pouch itself is an example of the considerate contrivance of Nature, by which she facilitates the transport of food-supplies to the young brood.

The examples we have cited are, so to speak, classical and historical, and they are so beautiful and characteristic that they never fail to be read with interest. But the experience of almost every body can recall instances which illustrate the affectionate ways of birds toward their young with equal truth, and, perhaps, with even greater force, since they have happened within his own knowledge. Who does not recognize the expressive cries of birds when their fears are excited by danger threatening their young? How fiercely the shy blackbird menaces and almost assails the prowling cat which an evil chance has brought too near her dwelling! With what cunning sagacity the lapwing, the wood-pigeon, the partridge, and a host of others, imitate the struggles of a wounded bird, in order to decoy the sportsman from the nest where the young ones lie hidden. And the fidelity with which in the midst of their terror most birds cleave to their young in the nest, up to the very moment when the hand is about to seize them, is a spectacle of devotedness which none can have witnessed without interest.

The tenderness of birds is not limited to their young, but is often lavished upon their mates also. Let us not forget that faithfulness in union is nowhere more conspicuous than in those birds that are notorious for fierceness and rapacity, as eagles and hawks. Ravens and crows generally pair for life. The dove, known in Scripture as the emblem of innocence and of the calm happiness it imparts, is also distinguished in this respect. The pigeon devotes her life to one companion, and the union is only dissolved by death. When bereaved she mourns her loss, and long refuses to accept another mate. "The black pigeon of the East, when her mate dies, obstinately rejects all others, and continues in a widowed state for life." Among thousands of examples few are, perhaps, more touching than one given in a note to White's "Selborne." " Lord Kaimes relates a circumstance of the canary which fell dead in singing to his mate while in the act of incubation. The female quitted her nest, and finding him dead, rejected all food and died by his side."

The affection of birds is frequently extended to their old haunts, and they cling with constancy to the place where they were born. Nightingales, swallows, and many others find their way back to the spot where their early days were spent, and often to the very nest-homes with which their joys are associated. Every body knows with what fidelity rooks cleave to their native trees, and how doggedly they resist every effort to dislodge them. With all the trees of the country open to their choice, rooks sometimes strangely prefer a nest in a solitary tree in some great city, because it is the home where they were born. For eight months of the year not a bird, perhaps, except the universal sparrow, is to be seen there; but with commencing spring the constant rooks, winging their way over streets and houses, once more appear, and set about patching up the old nest.

It is remarked in White's "Selborne," a rich quarry in all that relates to the habits of birds, that "even great disparity of size and kind does not always prevent social advances and mutual fellowship. For a very intelligent and observant person has assured me, that, in the former part of his life, keeping but one horse, he happened also on a time to have but one solitary hen. These two incongruous animals spent much of their time together in a lonely orchard, where they saw no creature but each other. By degrees an apparent regard begun to take place between these two sequestered individuals. The fowl would approach the quadruped with notes of complacency, rubbing herself gently against his legs, while the horse would look down with satisfaction, and move with the greatest caution and circumspection, lest he should trample on his diminutive companion. Thus by mutual good offices each seemed to console the vacant hours of the other."

Many who turn with interest and sympathy toward them complain that birds do not know how to reciprocate their affection. But this accusation appears to be disproved by facts. The means which birds have of expressing their liking toward us are, of course, very limited, and are often obscured by that natural distrust bestowed on them for their preservation. Still if any one will expend a little time and patience in trying to win their regard, it is wonderful how much may be accomplished. Caged birds often become very tame. They droop and pine in our absence; they revive, know us, and welcome us with a flutter of excitement when we return. They feed from our hands, respond by sympathetic movements or cries to the sound of our voice, and show confidence and affection in a thousand pretty ways. On the lawn or about the shrubbery we may soon collect round us troops of feathered friends. They will come when we call them, or sing when we whistle to them; in many cases they will pop down within notice the instant we appear in the garden, as if they had been on the outlook for our arrival. A bright-eyed robin will attend us on a short winter's walk almost as faithfully as a dog. Instead of not reciprocating attention, many birds seem only waiting to be made friends. If thoughtless little boys could be induced to try, they would soon find out that there is more enjoyment to be got by making friends with birds than by frightening them, or throwing stones at them, or robbing their nests. When once they have realized this pleasure, and begin to understand the feathered tribes, they will regard all marks of confidence shown toward them by birds as so many claims upon their sympathy and protection.

Singular stories are told of the fancies which birds have sometimes taken to particular individuals ; we shall here give two examples, all the more readily because they bring to favorable notice certain familiar inmates of the farm whose mental powers are generally underrated. Bishop Stanley in his delightful book tells us of a goose which used to follow a citizen of Elgin about the streets with as much fidelity as a dog. When visits were made to neighbors' houses, it waited patiently outside, and joyfully rejoined its master on his reappearance. No change of dress for a moment deceived its keen affection. It liked to hear his voice, and responded by its own peculiar cries of satisfaction.

The Bishop also relates the story of an aged woman, in Germany, who was habitually led to church by a sagacious old gander. Her attendant laid hold of her dress with its beak, and gently tugged her onward. Having seen her fairly seated in her pew, the wise bird decorously withdrew to the church-yard, where it enjoyed a well-earned repast until service was finished, when it reconducted its charge home. The family regarded it as the safest of escorts, and were accustomed to declare that they felt no anxiety on the old lady's account " so long as they knew that the gander was with her."

We all desire to think well of the cuckoo. The day on which it is first heard in spring is a marked event in country life, and we listen to the soft, mellow notes as a sure call toward the coming pleasures of the summer. Yet the character of our favorite is generally believed to break down upon a point on which it is thought that bird-nature is strongest, namely, in maternal affection. It certainly is proved, on evidence which cannot be disputed, that the cuckoo, instead of taking the trouble of building a nest for herself, stealthily drops her egg in the nests of other birds, and then leaves it to its fate. Such a habit seems a libel on Nature herself; but, instead of at once accepting the inference that seems to follow from it, we shall act wisely if we suspend our judgment for a moment, in the conviction that Nature would not thus strangely depart from her usual kind ways without some good and sufficient reason. Let us first consider what the facts against the accused really are, and then let us see what may be said for the defense.

It appears that this strange deception is practiced upon a variety of unsuspecting little birds. Yarrell gives a list of fourteen, among which are to be found the robin and blackbird, the skylark and the hedge-sparrow. The cuckoo chooses her time with great adroitness, generally after one or two eggs have been laid in the nest; and as the plot is favored by an unaccountable obtuseness on the part of the intended foster-mother, it never fails of success. The conduct of the young cuckoo by and by only makes the matter worse. Although the title of the other occupants of the nest is so much better than its own, scarcely have a few hours elapsed after its birth before it begins to take forcible measures to secure the whole nest to itself, and monopolize all the little bird's feeding attentions. Dexterously insinuating its head and shoulders under any unhatched eggs that may still remain, or under the bodies of its foster-nestlings, it raises them up on its back, and ruthlessly pitches them overboard. Let us now see what can be said in excuse for this apparently bad case. How a hedge-sparrow or any other bird can be so stupid as not to perceive the gross fraud thus practiced on its maternal tenderness, is difficult to explain upon any other principle than that, throughout the whole affair, Nature herself has been in league with the deceiver. First, it may be remarked that the cuckoo's egg is singularly small in proportion to the size of the bird. It is no bigger than that of the skylark, although the cuckoo is four times as large. In regard to size, therefore, the egg may pass muster in a small bird's nest. Secondly, it is observed that the newly born cuckoo has a peculiarity in its back, which is proportionally broader than in other birds, and has a depression in the middle, formed as if expressly to facilitate the process of ejectment. This view is further confirmed by the fact that this selfish propensity of the young cuckoo gradually subsides and disappears completely about the twelfth day, when the peculiarity in the back is no longer to be seen.

Besides the circumstances mentioned, the old cuckoo remains too short a time in this country to admit of its rearing its offspring to maturity. The eggs are laid at intervals from about the middle of May to the middle of July, and at the end of that month the old birds take their departure. It was therefore necessary that the young should be left in charge of other birds, which might take care of them and feed them when the parents left. By September or October the young cuckoos have attained strength sufficient to enable them to set out toward their winter-quarters. From the evidence now adduced we infer that a verdict must be given in favor of the cuckoo, as it clearly appears that when the bird drops her egg into a nest which is not her own, she is neither cruel nor destitute of maternal affection, but is only obeying an instinct of her nature, which is, perhaps, absolutely necessary for the safety of the future brood and the preservation of the species.

Nowhere is the vulture regarded with friendly eyes, and nothing that can be said in his favor will ever make him a lovable bird. But, though his appearance be fierce and sinister and his occupation repulsive, it must not be forgotten that his work is of very great utility in the countries where he is found, and that he is admirably adapted for its performance.

In our survey of Nature we are frequently reminded how necessary the removal of dead matter is to the salubrity of the air by the care which the Creator has taken to provide for it. In another part of this book it has been seen how innumerable infusorial animalcules are day and night at work in cleansing away minute animal rubbish. Insects and larvæ labor for the same purpose; and, in continuing to ascend the scale, we find that many of "the fowls of the air" have been appointed to discover where bulky animal matters are left to decay, and to arrest decomposition by converting them at once into food. In this useful band of Nature's scavengers vultures occupy a foremost place.

No charge of cruelty lies against vultures. They rarely attack any thing with life, and confine themselves closely to their own special work. They follow the movements of the camp and the caravan, and attend upon travelers and hunting parties. If a man take a siesta in the desert, observes a writer, he may find on opening his eyes that some of those birds are hovering around, evidently speculating on his death-like immobility, and the chances it seems to hold out of a speedy banquet. The great Condor of the Andes is likewise a scavenger in his habits. The height to which he soars and the acuteness of his vision doubtless assist him much in his search for food.

Vultures and other scavenger-birds are found to be most numerous in warm climates, where the speedy removal of dead animal matter is more especially necessary on account of the rapidity of its decomposition. In our own country, also, the hooded and the carrion crow, as well as some other birds, perform a little work of the same kind. Numbers of these birds were seen to follow in the wake of the Danish army in its retreat from the Dannewerke during the late war.

The quickness and certainty with which vultures divine where carrion is, or is likely to be, appears very remarkable. Hardly has the breath departed from the dying horse or camel, before they may be seen gathering in the air to the banquet. The power by which they thus almost invariably congregate where carrion is to be removed is not clearly ascertained. By some it is attributed to the sense of smell. But that sense is little developed in birds, and in the vulture it appears to be remarkably obtuse; for that bird has been known neither to perceive nor suspect the presence of carrion in a covered basket placed by its side, although the odor emanating from it was overpowering. With greater reason the faculty has been ascribed to the acuteness of their sight; but although this may account for it in general, it hardly appears sufficient to explain every case. To a certain extent, therefore, the subject still remains a mystery.

When gathered together at the scene of their work, let us observe how admirably they have been fitted for its performance. The bill of birds has been elsewhere compared to a hand; in the vulture it is a hand armed with a very formidable weapon. The bill is both strong and hard, and equally well fitted to cut, to lacerate, or to be thrust into the mass about to be devoured. Elsewhere, too, the long neck of birds has been compared to an arm to apply the hand-beak where it is wanted. In the vulture this arm is strong, flexible, and muscular, and both it and the head are naked or destitute of feathers. Should we not think the better of a workman who, in handling offensive matters, laid aside his coat and tucked up his sleeves? Now this is precisely what Nature has done for the vulture! Its bare arm facilitates the performance of its work. Under every aspect the service is repulsive, but how much more repulsive it would have been if the "arm" had been covered with feathers, to be soiled with the foul matters with which it must necessarily come into contact.

Occasionally the vulture exhibits qualities that entitle it to rank among the most sagacious birds. A recent traveler in the East tells us that "in the middle of the day ostriches leave their eggs in the sand, forgetting that the foot may crush them, or the wild beast break them. High in the air about this period of the day a white Egyptian vulture may be seen, with a large stone clutched between his talons. Having carefully surveyed the ground below him he suddenly lets fall the stone, and then follows it in rapid descent. If the hunter now run to the spot, he will find a nest of probably a score of eggs, each equal in size to twenty-four hen's eggs, some of which have been broken by the ingenuity combined with the good aim of the vulture."

The raven is another bird which has the misfortune not to be a popular favorite; but, admitting a few imperfections, he is certainly no worse than many other birds which pass muster with a fair character. In the East he is said to share the repulsive occupation of the vulture and the adjutant, a kind of crane from which the beautiful marabou feathers are derived, but in this country at least his diet is less objectionable. He is, we fear, occasionally in the habit of plundering the farm-yard; but if at rare intervals he make free with an ill-guarded duckling, the loss is amply atoned for by the war he is always waging in the farmer's interest against some of the worst kinds of vermin. In other respects the sober-tinted bird is distinguished for many excellent qualities. He is affectionate and faithful to his mate, attached to the tree or the tower of his birth, and capable not only of great tenderness to his offspring, but also of attachment toward various animals, and even to man himself. Superstition has unfortunately cast its debasing shadow upon the poor bird. There are people whose comfort for the day would be destroyed were they to meet a raven in a lonely spot, and its "ill-omened croak" even yet possesses terror sufficient to pale many a cheek. Surely it is time for the wide-spreading knowledge of the day to dissipate such puerile fancies, more especially as they are often suggestive of cruel acts against these harmless creatures.

Ravens were chosen on one remarkable occasion to show forth God's power and mercy, by conveying to Elijah the food on which he lived when he was a fugitive: "And the word of the Lord came unto him, saying, Get thee hence, and turn thee eastward, and hide thyself by the brook Cherith, that is before Jordan. And it shall be, that thou shalt drink of the brook; and I have commanded the ravens to feed thee there." "And the ravens brought him bread and flesh in the morning, and bread and flesh in the evening." — 1 Kings xvii. Ravens are also interesting to us from their having been selected by Christ to inculcate upon all men the lesson of trustfulness in God: "Consider the ravens, for they neither sow nor reap, neither have storehouse nor barn; and God feedeth them. How much better are ye than the fowls."

In the periodical migrations of birds we have a source of never-failing wonder. As certainly as winter approaches and the first icy blasts begin to blow over the land, our feathered visitors from the north swarm in upon us; while with returning spring they wing their way back again to their summer haunts. In this migratory circle many of our winter wildfowl annually revolve. In the land to which they repair they mate and build their nests and rear their young, until the passing season once more warns them that it is time to depart for the south. There is a corresponding southern migratory circle, in which the seasonal movements are just reversed — our visitors coming in the spring and leaving in autumn — but which is even more interesting to us than the former, since it brings the nightingale, the swallow, the cuckoo, and the other favorite birds with which we more especially associate the bright days of summer. Migration, indeed, strictly considered, goes on to an extent hardly suspected, as it is calculated that five sixths of all the feathered tribes shift their quarters more or less according to the change of season. Practically, however, the term is restricted to the few birds which take long flights.

The regularity with which migration occurs has been known from remote times, and is frequently alluded to in Holy Writ: " The stork in the heavens knoweth her appointed times; and the turtle and the crane and the swallow observe the time of their coming." So fixed is the advent of some of these travelers that, in certain Eastern countries at the present day, almanacs are timed and bargains struck upon the data it supplies. Nor is the period of return less remarkably punctual in some of our British birds. About the middle of April the nightingale makes its appearance in many localities, and there is seldom a difference of more than a day or two in the date of its annual return to the same place. Keen is the contest then between friendly neighbors as to who shall first enjoy the pleasure of hearing the expected note. Most frequently, perhaps, the nightingale is first heard in the morning, because his journey ended only during the previous night; but little time is lost before he salutes with his song the garden or the copse of his early days. At first his notes are low and interrupted, and he seems as if reserving himself for the arrival of his mate. Like a prudent pioneer he comes first by himself, as if to see that the old ground is clear, and that all things are propitious for taking up house. In a few days thereafter he will be joined by his mate, and then the work of the breeding season will begin. There is something extremely pleasing in the idea of birds seeking out not only their native clime or country, but even their native garden and the nest in which they were born. Storks invariably return to their old quarters; swallows not unfrequently occupy the same nest during several consecutive years, and the same remark applies to many other birds.

The distances traversed in migration are enormous. Certain little birds in America annually pass and repass from the Arctic circle to the Equator. Africa appears to be the great winter home of the "southern migration" in the Old World. Birds from the southwestern districts of Asia, from Syria, and ancient Babylonia, as well as from Russia and Turkey, pass, like the quail, into Egypt and parts adjoining; while those with which we are familiar on the western side of Europe return to Barbary, Algiers, and countries still further to the south. Swallows are resident throughout the year in the neighborhood of Sierra Leone, but their numbers greatly diminish in the summer, which is the period corresponding to their journey into Europe. Taking this point as the southern limit of their migration, the length of their flight may be estimated at from one to three thousand miles. Not without cause, therefore, do we see bestowed upon swallows a strength of wing that is extraordinary in proportion to their size, and a rapidity of flight unequaled in any other class of birds.

All migratory journeys are not performed upon the wing. Some birds, as coots and rails, migrate partly on foot. The great penguin, the guillemot, and various divers migrate partly by swimming. Some American water-birds, according to Nuttall, swim across the lakes, and then flounder over the intervening land which separates them.

The causes of migration and the means by which it is so unerringly accomplished have always been a puzzle to naturalists. Most frequently the cause has been ascribed to seasonal changes of climate and temperature, and in regard to these matters birds are believed to be more weather-wise than we are; or as due to the failure of the customary supply of food, involving the necessity of seeking it elsewhere. Both circumstances are probably not without influence in inducing migration, but there must be besides some powerful natural impulse. Nightingales and swallows confined in cages begin to be restless and agitated as the usual period for migration approaches, although they be kept warm and carefully supplied with food. The same thing happens even to birds that have always been in confinement, and which, therefore, cannot be influenced by the example of companions. With futile efforts the little prisoner beats the cage with its wings and tries to break through the bars; and when at last it sees the struggle is in vain, it often in despair pines away and dies. The impulse to migrate is so irresistible that it sometimes conquers the feeling of parental affection which is so strong in birds, as every year cases occur of swallows leaving their offspring to perish miserably in the nest in order to troop off with their companions to the sunny South. These unlucky broods have been hatched so late in the year that they have not had time to attain size and strength sufficient for their journey. It is, therefore, not without wise design that the early period of spring has been fixed as the breeding season for most birds. By this arrangement not only have the young ones the long period of summer abundance before them, during which they may grow and become hardy against the approach of winter, but time is also afforded to those that are migratory to acquire the requisite practice and strength of wing for their long flights.

The power which so unerringly guides the migratory bird across strange seas and continents is mysterious, and, indeed, at present incomprehensible. None of the senses with which we are acquainted, even though they were developed to the highest perfection we can conceive possible, would suffice for the purpose. As birds are so seldom seen when actually on their journey, it is supposed they fly chiefly during the night, and often at such an immense elevation in the air that they readily escape notice. From these circumstances it may perhaps be inferred that the lamp which guides them — whatever it may be — is not dependent on external objects.

Our limits prevent us from doing more than merely touch on Ornithology, yet enough has been said to indicate some of the many ways in which the "fowls of the air" magnify the Creator. In reflecting on this subject we are no less struck by the wonderful things that are achieved than we are by the simplicity of the means that are employed. What could be apparently a more difficult problem than to fit animals, formed chiefly of such solid materials as bone and muscle, to fly with ease through the light air? Yet this has been accomplished without the introduction into the plan of creation of any new type of structure, but merely by the skillful modification of structures already existing. The feathers, the claws, and the beak are only modified hairs or horn. The same bones which support fins in fishes, legs or paddles in reptiles, or legs or arms in mammalia, have by slight changes been made the framework of wings. The jaws, for reasons connected with the food, form a horny beak instead of teeth. This beak is not only a mouth but a hand, with the great advantage for birds of having the eyes set closely behind it. The neck is modified so as to be a long, supple, dexterous arm to wield this hand. Mastication was inadmissible in the mouth, so the weak muscular fibres usually found enveloping the stomach of vertebrate animals are developed into a powerful gizzard to crush the food independently of any assistance from the mouth. The anterior extremities being required as wings, the posterior are admirably placed to support the centre of gravity, and there are few animals which are such excellent balancers as birds. Many birds rest by perching on one leg, but notwithstanding their skill in balancing, they would be in danger of falling off every time they went to sleep, were there no self-acting contrivance to assist them in holding on. The bulky muscles which move the toes are placed for convenience' sake out of the way high up in the leg, but they send down narrow tendons, or cords, which, passing behind the joints at either end of the shank, popularly called the leg, are inserted into the bones of the feet. As the fowl stands erect these tendons are to a certain extent relaxed; but the moment the legs are bent, as in the act of settling to roost, the tendons are stretched tense over the joints, or pullies, so as to draw the toes and make them mechanically clasp the perch. If the tendons in the shank of a fowl after it has been severed in trussing be pulled, the nature of this admirable contrivance will be at once comprehended.

In some birds, as in parrots, the claws are arranged so as to grasp like a hand; hence, considering the use they make of the bill, they might be called "three-handed." The legs and claws of birds are planned in accordance with their varying habits of life. Some are made for wading, others for scratching; some for tearing, others for swimming. The swimmers are web-footed, and the paddle, after having delivered its stroke, folds up, or as it might be technically called "feathers," so as to impede as little as possible the progress of the bird through the water. By hollowing out the bones into cylinders, not only has the solid material been disposed so as with least weight to afford the greatest strength, but by causing the interior of the bones to communicate with the air-passages, great lightness has been given to the entire bird. The numerous air-cells distributed over the body have also contributed toward bringing the weight of the living bird into equilibrium with the weight of the atmosphere. The simplicity of the means, the perfection with which they are applied, and the admirable results accomplished, equally strike us with astonishment.

The evidences of creative design are nowhere more beautifully displayed than in the eggs of birds, which can be watched with facility from the earliest appearance of the germ up to the fully developed chick. The future bird first shows itself as a short white line, or "primitive streak," as it is called, lying on the membrane that contains the yolk. This germ gradually grows and develops itself, forming in succession a spinal column, brain, and heart, with blood which is at first colorless and then red. The other organs appear simultaneously or in succession. The egg itself, like a seed, is stored with abundance of food for the embryo; and, in proportion as this food is absorbed, room is made for the growth of the chick. A certain amount of aëration is required during development, and, therefore, the shell has been made porous. It is essential, also, that the rudimentary chick should always lie uppermost in the egg, in order that it may thus be placed next to the warm body of the hen during the process of hatching. To secure this end the yolk is made to float freely in the "white," and the side *opposite* to the germ is weighted or "ballasted," so as always to lie lowermost. Therefore, no matter how an egg is laid down, the germ will always be found to correspond to the side that is uppermost. There is, moreover, a little reservoir of air at the thick end of the egg, easily recognized by its translucency when held before a candle, from which the chick slightly inspires before emerging from the shell, and is thus enabled to emit the feeble chirps by which the act is sometimes preceded. Any one who has looked at the newly born chick must have wondered how such a soft creature can deal with so hard a substance as its containing shell; but if the upper part of the beak be examined, a few hard, horny scales will there be noticed. Thus Nature has not forgotten to supply the chick with a hammer for the purpose of breaking open its prison.

How truly, then, may it be said that the "fowls of the air" magnify the goodness and power of the Creator! Heartily may we respond to the invocation contained in this verse of the hymn for the sake of their beauty which gladdens the eye, and for the sake of their songs which delight the ear. Birds bring us vast stores of food to nourish us, clothing to keep us warm, comfortable beds on which to rest, and oil to cheer the gloomy winter nights. Before the lightning was pressed into our service, pigeons were our swiftest messengers. Birds scatter and sow seeds all over the world. When their numbers are maintained within reasonable limits they are valuable friends to the farmer, repaying him for the grain which they consume by picking up the germs of weeds, and by keeping insect life within due bounds. In the great work of intercepting and utilizing animal matter hastening away to destruction through decay, they take their full share. Their nest-building is a lesson in neatness, industry, and often in mechanical construction. Books on Ornithology are full of delightful stories of their affection toward their mates and their young ones. The interest they inspire dates almost from the dawn of Sacred History. It was a dove which signalized to Noah in the ark that the waters were subsiding, and it thus became for ever associated in our minds with good tidings, and the passing away of wrath.

In glancing at the bright green lawns which are so pleasingly characteristic of English country homes, a shrewd guess may sometimes be made as to the disposition of those who are accustomed to walk about on them. The differences to be observed are obvious and full of meaning. There are a few dull lawns, like the "desolate regions" of the ocean, on which birds scarcely ever seem to venture. Incessant persecution in some form has banished them from its borders, and the garden has thereby lost a charm for which no mere floral beauty can adequately compensate. On other lawns birds make their appearance like timid intruders. Seldom do they dare to lower their heads to feed, but with startled look and outstretched neck they seem to be always suspicious and uncomfortable. But on more genial lawns the little visitors alight as wel-

Fowls of the Air.

come and protected favorites, hop about familiarly as if they felt themselves at home, cheer and vivify the aspect of Nature around, and recognize in a thousand pretty but indescribable ways the friends who are accustomed to feed and pet them.

A bird's-nest, with its eggs or callow brood, is no bad lever with which to cast out from the young heart any seeds of cruelty which ignorance or thoughtlessness may have planted there. Among children it is universally an object of the greatest interest. With what delighted curiosity they fix their keen glances on the nest to which they have been softly and with bated breath led up, and how eagerly they peer at the pretty eggs, or the helpless creatures lying huddled together in their home. And if, perchance, the mother has been surprised at her duty of incubation, with what astonishment they behold the very bird which used to be so timid on the lawn now grown bold through maternal affection. Rooted to the nest, with body motionless, with eyes fixed and glassy, she appears as if turned to stone. Seldom, indeed, does the sight fail to touch the good feelings of the child, and to bring them into that plastic state in which they may be readily molded to humanity and gentleness. This is the propitious moment when the cruel impulse to seize and destroy may be easily changed by a few judicious words into the abiding desire to foster and protect.

 Teach me to do Thy will; for Thou art my God. — Ps. cxliii.

WHALES, AND ALL THAT MOVE IN THE WATERS.

O ye whales, and all that move in the waters, bless ye the Lord: praise Him, and magnify Him for ever.

WE need not here inquire critically into the meaning of the word to which the term "whale" has been applied in the Benedicite, since the invocation is obviously intended to include every inhabitant of the deep. It is well known that the whale, although in reality a mammiferous animal, and belonging, therefore, to the same class as man himself, was always considered a fish up to the time of Linnæus; and, indeed, in the minds of not a few it continues to be regarded as a fish up to this very day.

The Three Children, in their earnest desire worthily to praise God, passed in review all His greatest works; and it must be admitted that, had they been masters of the whole knowledge of Natural History accumulated since their time, they could not have selected any creature "moving in the waters" more fitted to display the power and wisdom of the Great Artificer. The whale, it is true, must have been comparatively little known at Babylon, still we may presume that the Three Children had heard enough concerning its immense size and strength to justify them in singling it out as the grandest representative of marine life. It is recorded that they were eminent for their attainments; and therefore they might easily have become acquainted with this animal from the descriptions of merchants whom commerce had made familiar with the productions of the Eastern and Mediterranean Seas. There was a time when whales frequented that great Atlantic inlet, and the circumstance of their having now forsaken it is probably due, not to any difficulty in regard to food or climate, but to their having been hunted off the ground. It is well known that seas which afforded rich whale-fishings even a century ago are now barren and profitless, and this timid, harmless creature is year by year driven further away from the haunts of man, and deeper into the recesses of the polar regions. He fights a losing battle with his human foes; for, from the more perfect appliances of modern skill, the chances are ever growing worse against him. It is the opinion of many naturalists that the Great Northern Whale is destined to disappear altogether from the earth at no very distant date; and then, like the Ichthyosaurus and the other extinct animals of bygone days, he will be known only by the bony relics he may have left behind him.

There are many different kinds of whales. Some, like the Cachalot or Spermaceti Whale, are almost peculiar to the southern hemisphere; others, as the Great Whalebone Whale, inhabit the northern seas. It is well to recollect that the latter is known by a variety of names. Thus it is often called the Right Whale, or the Mysticete, or the Baleen Whale; again, it is familiarly termed the Greenland, or simply the Common Whale. We shall here direct attention chiefly to the Mysticete, because from better acquaintance with its structure and habits we shall be able more clearly to perceive the fitness with which it illustrates God's power and beneficence.

The whale is the leviathan of creation. The Rorqual, a species which sometimes gets stranded on our coasts, is a moving mass of life often more than a hundred feet long and of extraordinary girth, with a weight which has been known to reach two hundred and forty-nine tons. The common whale seldom exceeds seventy feet in length. In looking at the skeleton of the latter preserved in the Museum of the London College of Surgeons, we perceive with astonishment a spinal column which in thickness and strength might be compared to the trunk of a goodly sized tree, and which in its thicker parts is built up of massive vertebral blocks, tied together in the living animal by the toughest ligaments and cartilages. Yet every organ reared upon this huge frame displays the same wonderful and perfect workmanship throughout. Every single fibre of the muscle-masses that wield these ponderous bones, and every nerve and blood-vessel, down to structures so fine that they cannot be seen without a microscope, or handled without the risk of being broken, have been finished with a delicacy and beauty not surpassed in any department of creation.

The head of the whale seems of monstrous size, especially when the animal is viewed out of the water and stranded on the beach. In the Cachalot, which is often seventy or eighty feet long, the head forms about a third of its whole bulk, a circumstance which is chiefly owing to the spermaceti lodged in a hollow on its upper surface. The jaws of the common whale are the portals of a mouth capacious enough to ingulf a boat; and, when brought home as curiosities from Arctic regions, they are sufficiently long and strong to serve as piers for gates and as supports for swings in play-grounds. Had the nature of this enormous creature been ferocious, these jawbones would doubtless have been armed with teeth of corresponding size, and he would have been the most fearful tyrant of the deep which it is possible to conceive — a monster more formidable than the Ichthyosaurus or Megalosaurus of ancient times. Happily the nature of the common whale is timid and gentle, and he is formidable to nothing except the small fry, medusæ, and various little mollusks which swarm in the polar sea.

Though living in the water, the whale, like the dugong,

porpoise, dolphin, and other cetacea, belongs to the mammalian or highest class of the Animal Kingdom. The term whale-fishing, therefore, is misapplied, though now fixed by custom beyond recall; whale-hunting would be a more correct expression. It is distinguished from fishes by many very clear marks. Fishes breathe by gills, which require the air to be conveyed to them through the medium of water. They seem always to be gulping or swallowing water, while in reality they are only propelling a current of it over the vascular fringes which form the gills. On the other hand, whales breathe by lungs, to which the atmosphere must be directly admitted. From this cause a fish dies if it be kept long out of the water, and the whale would be drowned if he were kept very long immersed in it. The fish has "cold blood," a heart with only two chambers or cavities, and what is termed "a single circulation." The whale is a "warm-blooded" animal, has a heart with four cavities, as in man, and has a "double circulation." In the fish, therefore, the blood which is sent from the heart passes to the gills, and, after receiving the small amount of aëration it requires, continues its course onward to nourish all parts of the body. In the whale the blood is *first* propelled from the *right* side of the heart, through the capillaries of the lungs, to be thoroughly aërated, or arterialized, and then returns to the *left* side of the heart, whence it is propelled to circulate generally over the body, for the purpose, on the one hand, of carrying nutriment to the various organs and building them up; and, on the other, of conveying away, in the returning current of venous blood, the rubbish or waste of the different organs to the lungs, where it is finally got rid of by being burnt. Fishes, moreover, have no external ear-openings; whales have them, and hear well in the water. Lastly, fishes multiply by spawning; whales bring forth their young alive, and suckle them with the greatest tenderness.

The whale, being an air-breather, requires to rise at intervals to the surface for respiration; but, as its hunting operations are chiefly carried on under water, it would obviously be a great hindrance were it obliged to come to the surface very frequently for that purpose. This circumstance has not been overlooked by the Great Artificer, and has been met by special modifications of structure, which are no less beautiful than wonderful. It may be here remarked that the absolute quantity of blood in a whale is greater in proportion to its size than in most other animals. The arrangements for its reception and circulation are on a corresponding scale. Hunter tells us that the heart and aorta of the cachalot "are too large to be contained in a wide tub," and that ten or fifteen gallons of blood are pumped out by every pulsation, through an aorta measuring a foot in diameter. Paley estimated this torrent as greater than the stream "roaring" through the main pipe of the water-works at old London Bridge! Now, in order to afford stowage-room for all this blood, it is found that, at various parts of the circulation, both arteries and veins have been made to assume a peculiar tortuous or plexiform arrangement, by which their capacity to contain blood is so increased that they may be considered as forming collectively a tubular reservoir. When the whale is breathing at the surface, the arterial reservoir naturally becomes filled with what may be called a supplementary store of highly aërated blood, upon which the whale draws, as it were, while under water, until it is exhausted by being changed into venous blood in the course of circulation. The whale must then return to the surface for a fresh supply. The diver, when working at the foundations of our piers or forts, carries down with him the air which is to renovate his blood; but the whale carries down a supplemental stock of blood which is already renovated. By means of this simple but wonderful adaptation, whales usually remain from five to ten minutes under water be-

All that move in the Waters. 343

tween the breathing periods; while some of the larger kinds are said to be able to remain for an hour and a half without coming to the surface.

The whale does not breathe through its mouth, but through the nostril or "spiracle," placed conveniently for the purpose at the very top or apex of the head. At such times it is to be seen spouting or "blowing." The mechanism of this act is admirable. In the passage leading to the nostril there is a sac which, inferiorly, communicates with the back of the mouth, and, superiorly, with the external surface by means of the spiracle. When the whale is about to "blow," the sac is filled from the mouth with water mixed with air, and the opening between the two is then closed. The sac is now forcibly compressed by a muscle spread over it like a net, by which action the water, unable to escape downward, is forcibly driven through the upper aperture, or spiracle, so as to spout into the air like a water-work. It is as if a caoutchouc syringe filled with water were suddenly grasped by a powerful hand. To make this structure perfect, the spiracle when not in use is closed partly by its valvular margin, but still more effectually by a hard, tendinous structure, like a plug, which, being drawn into the orifice by means of a special muscle, is held there by the pressure of the outside water, and the greater that pressure, the more firmly is the plug wedged in.

The skin of the whale is of extraordinary thickness, and, under several points of view, illustrates very remarkably the wise design of the Creator. The blubber which yields the oil is not collected in a layer under the skin, as is commonly thought, but is distributed through the substance of the skin itself. To form a correct idea of this structure we have only to suppose ordinary skin loosened or opened out into innumerable interstices or cells, in which the oily matter is lodged. In this manner fresh blubber acquires a firmness and elasticity which enables sailors, in "flensing" the whale, to cut it up into conveniently sized pieces with their spades, when it becomes necessary to stow it away in barrels for the homeward voyage.

The oil thus lodged in the meshes of the skin invests the whale with a covering which in many places is two or three feet in thickness, and from its non-conducting qualities, no blanket could be conceived better calculated to preserve the temperature of a warm-blooded animal exposed to the chilling influences of polar seas. Without some aid of this kind it is difficult to imagine how whales could exist in such climates.

The blubber renders another important service to the whale by acting as a float. Were there no special contrivance to assist in buoying up the enormous weight of muscles and bones which chiefly compose its bulk, it would be difficult for the whale to support itself at the surface of the sea for the purpose of breathing.

The blubber-skin is likewise of essential use in protecting the whale against the enormous pressure to which it is occasionally exposed when swimming at great depths. On the surface of the sea the pressure is equal to about fifteen pounds to the square inch; but at the great depths to which the whale is known to descend, it may be a ton, or even more, on the same superficial extent, a pressure sufficient " to force water through the pores of the hardest wood, so as to make it afterward sink like lead." It is needless to observe that such a degree of compression on the internal organs of a mammalian would be fatal to life. No mere skin, though it were twice as thick as the hide of a rhinoceros, and no mere layer of fat, though twice as thick as the coating of blubber found in the whale, would suffice to intercept it. But the strong, elastic combination of both constituting the blubber-skin answers the purpose admirably, and, like a barrel, or circular arch built round the body of the whale, defends the vital organs from injury.

The whale is an expert swimmer. Though usually moving at a gentle pace, it can skim over the surface in a way which has procured for it the distinction of being called "the bird of the sea." When harpooned, it can dive into what are termed "unfathomable depths" with startling rapidity. Scoresby tells us that on one occasion a whale which had been struck carried the line sheer downward for nearly a mile with almost the quickness of an arrow. With equal ease and velocity it can lift itself up again to the surface. In all these movements it depends on the strength of its tail. The extremity of this wonderful scull is flattened out into a blade, which often has a surface equal to a hundred square feet; and, for the sake of acting more effectually in diving and lifting movements, it is spread out horizontally, not, as in fishes, vertically. The power of the muscles which wield this scull is enormous. When excited the whale lashes the sea all around into foam, and can sink or crush a boat with a single stroke. Darwin tells us that while sailing along the coast of Terra del Fuego, he "saw a grand sight in several spermaceti whales jumping upright quite out of the water with the exception of their tail-fins. As they fell down sideways, they splashed the water high up, and the sound reverberated like a distant broadside." When we think of the weight of those whales, we may form some idea of the force that must have been required to lift them up from the sea in the manner described. Who can feel surprised that whaling should be considered a service of danger? The wonder is that, in the encounters which occur with the leviathan, he should so generally be worsted.

In some whales, as in the Cachalot, the lower jaw is furnished with powerful teeth, which enable them to prey upon large fishes, seals, and porpoises. The common Whalebone Whale feeds chiefly on the myriads of diminutive mollusks, jelly-fishes, and crustaceans that abound in the polar ocean. The scale of abundance on which this food is provided will be found described at page 138, and will again be immediately noticed. The gullet of the whale is singularly narrow in relation to the size of the animal, and more especially does it appear diminutive when contrasted with the vastness of the mouth. A good authority affirms that the gullet does not exceed an inch and a half in width; from which it may be inferred that a morsel which could be easily managed by a cormorant or a pike might possibly choke a whale. This circumstance, taken in connection with the fact that it has neither teeth nor claws, sufficiently indicates that the whale is not formed to attack or seize a large and active prey; nor, if the prey were caught, could the whale rend it into pieces small enough to permit of its being swallowed.

On the other hand, the whale is supplied with a most efficient apparatus for catching the peculiar kind of food on which it is destined to live. All round the mouth, instead of teeth, closely set plates of whalebone, terminating in thick, coarse fringes, project from the upper jaw in such a way as to convert the spacious cavity within into an enormous sieve. And, as if the size of this food-trap were not ample enough, it has been increased in several species of whale by dilating the floor of the mouth into a large bag. When the whale closes his jaws upon a mouthful of food-containing sea-water, he passes it, as it were, through the strainer; the superfluous water being expelled through the fine whalebone meshes, while every thing that is fit for nourishment is retained.

One of the duties assigned to the whale in Nature's economy is to check the inordinate increase of certain kinds of animal life. Piazzi Smith mentions that, when sailing along the margin of the Trade-winds, he fell in with a group of three whales feasting upon a shoal of medusæ, or jelly-fish. The shoal was from thirty to forty miles in length, and was computed to contain not fewer than 225 millions of individuals. Here, indeed, was a case where Nature's lavishness obviously required pruning; so the three whales had been "told off" to do the work.

And yet, strange though it may appear, the actual number of living creatures swallowed by the whales at their banquet was as nothing compared to the countless millions of organisms that are sometimes required to make up a feast for a single medusa! On examining the stomach of one of these inert-looking lumps of jelly, it was found to contain myriads of microscopic diatoms on which the medusa had been regaling when surprised by the whale. To arrive approximately at the aggregate of life here indicated, one would have to multiply the 225 millions of medusæ by that infinitely greater figure represented by the included diatoms. The latter were enveloped in their siliceous shields, and thus exhibited a singular instance where animals — if such they really are — so hard that they may be described as cuirassed in flint, were selected as a banquet by the softest animals in creation. Jelly though the medusa be, these flinty substances cannot resist the vigorous action of its digestive power.

Circumstantial evidence of the strongest kind suggests that the great mysticete should be added to the list of distinguished arctic discoverers; for, at a time when the existence of a northwest passage was still in doubt, the question was virtually solved by a Greenland whale. In the "fishery" it is customary to mark the harpoons with the name of the ship and the date of the voyage. On one occasion it happened that a whale was killed not far from Behring's Straits, and in its body was found a harpoon labeled with the name of a Greenland ship, by one of whose crew the weapon had been implanted at an early period of the same season. The question that naturally arose was — How did the whale get to Behring's Straits? Now it is ascertained that the common whale never crosses the line; for the warm sea-water and the hot climate of the Equator form a barrier across which it will not pass. Moreover, the interval since the whale in question was harpooned near Greenland was too short to have afforded time for it to come round either by the Cape of Good Hope or Cape Horn. The conclusion, therefore, which almost necessarily followed was that the whale must have traveled by the short, direct route of the northwest passage. The circumstance seemed equally to indicate the important fact that the intervening Polar Sea must have been almost, if not quite, open throughout, for, as we have seen, the whale cannot remain long under water at one time.

The whale appears to have been anciently captured in the Bay of Biscay by the hardy fishermen of the coast, and by the Norwegians in the German Ocean, less for the sake of its oil or whalebone than as an article of food. We are assured in the Naturalists' Library that when the flesh of a young whale is cleared of its fat, and then broiled and seasoned with pepper and salt, it eats somewhat like coarse beef. Even the blubber, when pickled and boiled, is said to be "very palatable." We know that the Esquimaux generally regard it with great favor. A stranded whale is truly a rich treasure to the ill-supplied inhabitants of the polar regions. They banquet on the flesh, and carry the oil about with them as a refreshing cordial. When some of the internal membranes are dried, they become sufficiently transparent to serve as windows for huts. The sinews are separated into filaments to be used as thread for sewing. Some of the bones are fashioned into spears and harpoons for killing sea-birds and seals. Various parts of the whale are likewise turned to account in the construction of tents and boats.

The English whale-fishery began at Spitzbergen in 1598, where it had been previously carried on by the Dutch. Until recently from 1800 to 2000 whales were annually caught; and, indeed, the fishery has been prosecuted with a perseverance which threatens the annihilation of the Northern whale altogether. In the arctic seas this inoffensive animal has no other enemy than man; but in those of Australia the whale, which some assert is the same as the Northern, has to encounter the attacks of a kind of porpoise, which are locally termed "killers." These animals hunt in company, and worry the whale, like a pack of dogs. Sometimes they bring the chase to bay, and thus incidentally serve as "pointers" to ships engaged in the fishery. Though smaller than the whale, many of these killers are 25 feet long, and, considering their strength and their terrible armature of teeth, must be very formidable enemies.

The whale is seen to greatest advantage when floating lazily on the surface, or skimming lightly over it, and spouting its curving stream of water into the air. But viewed as he lies stranded on the shore, he is, perhaps, the most monstrous and ungainly beast to be found in creation. Yet this huge lump of life is animated with a very warm and affectionate heart. The whale nurses her young with tenderness, and carries it about under her flappers until it is weaned, or until the growth of the whalebone sieve in the mouth is so far advanced as to enable it to catch food for itself. Often may the pair be seen disporting themselves and gamboling in the water; and, when danger threatens, the mother either hastily bears its young one off to some place of safety, or defends it bravely against assailants. Seldom can she be made, even when wounded, to seek her own safety in flight, and sometimes she has been known to perish rather than desert her offspring. The affection which the mated whales display for each other is no less remarkable. "Captain Anderson relates that having struck one of two whales, a male and a female that were in company together, the wounded one made a long and terrible resistance; it struck down a boat with five men in it by a single blow of the tail, and all went to the bottom. The other still attended its companion and lent it every assistance, until at last the whale that had been struck sunk under its wounds, while its faithful associate, disdaining to survive the loss, stretched itself upon the dead animal, and shared its fate." Every old sailor familiar with the "fishery" has something to tell in honor of this peculiar trait of whale-nature. With such stories present in our mind, we think less about the whale's ugliness than we did before, and experience all the pleasure of recognizing the play of those warm affections which always interest and delight, whether they be exhibited by the most beautiful or the most homely of God's creatures.

In Holland a considerable quantity of glue is manufactured from the mysticete, but its chief value consists in the whalebone found in the mouth and the oil contained in the blubber. Speaking anatomically, whalebone is of the nature of horn, and the loose fibres with which it is fringed closely resemble a very coarse kind of hair. The numerous uses to which it is applied are familiar to all. The skin of a "good fish" will generally yield about thirty tons of oil. The whale-fishery, including that of the southern hemisphere, has been ranked as "the most valuable industrial pursuit of the sea," and gives employment to vast fleets of ships.

If the productiveness of the whale-fishery be decreasing it may be considered providential that the falling off is only of recent date, and that the discovery of many other sources of artificial light has been coincident with it. Thus the seal-tribes are rapidly becoming rivals to the whale in an economical point of view. Oil extracted from the liver of various kinds of fish is now well known in the market. Many new kinds of vegetable oil are in use. Vegetable wax is largely imported. Camphine yields a bright and economical light. Of greater importance is the recent manufacture of paraffine, or mineral oil, from waste coaly matters and bituminous shales, which is being developed in this country with extraordinary success. But unquestionably the greatest addition made to our light-giving power in these days has been the discovery of

All that move in the Waters.

the oil-springs of the earth, on which some observations have already been made. Thus there is reason for thankfulness when we reflect that, although one source is likely to be impaired, others are gradually opening up to us through the never-failing providence of Our Father.

Praised be the Lord daily; even the God who helpeth us, and poureth His benefits upon us. — Ps. lxviii.

In the brief space that remains for the further consideration of "all that move in the waters," more cannot be done than merely to give a rapid glance at some interesting points connected with the habits and general structure of fishes.

It is a pleasant sight to watch the finny tribes as they swim about in the transparent waters. The whole fish is an instrument of progression, the very ideal of easy, graceful movement. The filmy, waving fins implanted on its sides and back balance, stop, and steer, besides aiding somewhat in slight changes of position, but the chief propelling power is in the tail. The entire body forms an animated scull, of which the bony vertebral column is the stem and the tail-fin the blade, while the powerful muscles grouped advantageously along both sides ply it with vigor, and urge the fish forward with a dexterity and effect which no artificial sculling can rival. The body of the fish is solidly massed in front to afford a firm support from which the scull may work, and the head is joined on to it without any intervening neck in order that it may offer a stiffer wedge in cleaving through the water. How smoothly and with how little effort fishes glide gently against the current, or poise themselves nearly motionless with head to stream, waiting patiently for their food to float down toward them. But, if suddenly alarmed, the whole water is thrown into commotion, as with a few vigorous tail-strokes they dart away with the quickness of an arrow. When fishes leap into the air, they gain the required impulse by a sudden blow with the tail against the resisting water. Even the feats of the, so-called, flying-fish are really not flights, but immense bounds produced by a jerk of the tail. The large pectoral fins are never used as wings, although they act as parachutes in breaking the force of the fall back into the water.

The covering of fishes is admirably adapted to the medium in which they live. To resist the macerating action of the water they are, as it were, tiled over, like the roof of a house, with impermeable scales; and the direction in which these lie and overlap is the one which offers the least impediment in swimming. Scales present much variety of form in different fishes. They are pretty objects when viewed in the microscope, and are manufactured into many kinds of useful ornaments. Popularly they are regarded as a mere external epiderm, but in reality they are developed within the substance of the skin, and are themselves covered by the cuticle as well as by a layer to which they owe their color. In structure they approach more or less to the nature of bone.

In a few fishes, as in the slender pipe-fish and the burly trunk-fish, the scales are neatly joined together like a piece of finely tesselated pavement, and have very much the character of plates of bone covered with a layer of enamel. This kind of scale-armor, though rare in existing fishes, was common among the older races, and universal among those that swam in the most ancient waters of the globe. The nearest approach to an external bony skeleton among the fishes of this country is found in the sturgeon. This ungainly creature is the scavenger of European rivers, routing with its snout among the mud and stones that form their bed, and it is probably to guard against the pressure and rough blows which such an occupation involves that it is provided with this shield.

To diminish friction during rapid movement, and for protection against the macerating action of the water,

Nature has taken care that the scales shall be well lubricated. Birds, as is elsewhere noticed, make their plumage impermeable to water by diffusing an oily matter over it by means of their bills; but as the want of a flexible neck in fishes precludes any analogous action, the same result is obtained by a beautifully designed modification of structure. Thus the lubricating glands, instead of being gathered together, as in birds, so as to form what may be termed an "oil-bottle" near the tail, are arranged in a row along either side of the body, where with their investing scales they exhibit the conspicuous "lateral line." Through openings in these scales the lubricating fluid exudes, and is subsequently applied over the surface by the diffusing action of the water during the movements of the fish.

Lying under the spinal column in most fishes there is a sac, containing a mixture of nitrogen and oxygen gas, to which the term swim-bladder is given by physiologists, but which is familiarly known to most persons as "the sounds." The weight of the body of a fish, bulk for bulk, is so nearly the same as water, that the mere distension or collapse of this air-bladder often makes the difference between floating and sinking. All fishes are not supplied with a swim-bladder. As might be anticipated, there is none in the plaice, turbot, sole, and many other flat fishes habitually living near the bottom of the water. But it was not to have been expected that some fishes which are usually found near the surface, as the red mullet and the mackerel, are equally destitute of it; while the eel, which generally frequents the muddy bottom of rivers, has a well-developed swim-bladder. On the whole, therefore, it may be inferred that, although the flotation influence of this sac must be considerable, it probably serves for other purposes also.

Fishes possess little power either of touch or taste. The scaliness of the skin, indeed, precludes the former; while the latter would be unnecessary, as the food is for the most part merely seized and gorged or gulped down into the stomach, without previously undergoing any thing that can be called mastication. In some fishes, as in the barbel and rockling, there are flexible feelers appended to the mouth, which must be considered as organs of touch of considerable delicacy, fitted to aid them in the selection of their food. Fishes also possess, in a slight degree, the sense of smell. Hence they are sometimes caught by persons who have smeared their hands with strongly scented matters; and Mr. Jesse relates that certain fishes which he kept in a pond gave the preference to bait that had been perfumed. Hearing is a sense of more importance to fishes, and, although there is no external opening or ear, the essential parts of the organ are found internally. There can be no doubt, therefore, that they possess this sense, though not acutely. In corroboration it may be mentioned that in China tame fish are sometimes called together for feeding by means of a whistle; some have been taught to pay attention to the ringing of a bell; while others have been seen to be startled at the sound of a gun. In the latter case, however, the effect may have been produced by the concussion communicated to the water.

Vision, on the other hand, is of high importance to fishes; accordingly the nerve of seeing is largely developed, and the optical apparatus of the eye is admirably adapted to the medium in which they live. Fishes do not possess a lachrymal gland, and it is obvious that tears cannot be required to moisten the eyes of animals living in the water. Where the obscurity is so great as to afford no light, eyes are of course useless, and they are reduced by thrifty Nature to a merely rudimentary condition. From this cause fishes living in the dark lakelets of the "Mammoth Cave" of Kentucky, which has been traced for ten miles underground and is known to extend much further, are destitute of organs which they cannot turn to account.

But, as a compensation for this visual defect, they are endowed with wonderful acuteness of hearing.

Fishes are preëminently omnivorous, and they can deal with every thing, from a soft jelly-like medusa up to hard lobsters and masses of stony corals. A few browse peacefully on tender sea-weed or fresh-water plants, but the majority are ravenously carnivorous, and prey upon one another. It is not to be wondered at, therefore, that the variety observed in the number, shape, and position of the teeth should be greater in fishes than in any other class of animals. The sturgeon and a few others have no teeth. Some have only three or four; while in many they are so numerous that they cannot be counted. Some teeth are so fine that they resemble the pile on velvet, as in the perch; other teeth are like bristles, or cones, or blades for cutting, or saws, or grinders. The mouth of a shark bristles with the most cruel-looking teeth. Of these some are obviously designed for stabbing and cutting, others for tearing and sawing. The wolf-fish has powerful front teeth for seizing, branching outward like grappling-hooks, and, as it finds its chief nourishment in lobsters, whelks, and other shell-protected creatures, it is likewise supplied with some massive blocks of teeth between which the shells are crunched into fragments. A harder diet still forms the favorite food of the scarus, or parrot-fish, of the Pacific, which, as Owen observes, "literally browses upon the corals clothing the bottom of the sea, as with a richly tinted-carpet, just as the ruminant quadrupeds crop the herbage of the dry land." Its object is, of course, to get at the minute polypes; but as these, when disturbed, shrink into their cells, the parrot-fish can only reach them by grinding down the coral mass; for which purpose its strong, broad jaws are laid with teeth consolidated together like a pavement.

The voracity of fishes is, of course, no sign of cruelty, but only the means appointed by Nature for carrying out her plans for the general welfare, in which man himself is interested more than any other creature. Considering the amazing fecundity of fishes, it was essential that some check should be set to guard against their undue increase. An idea of the rate at which fishes, if unchecked, would multiply may be formed from the circumstance that nine millions of eggs are estimated to exist in a single cod's roe, and two hundred and eighty thousand in that of a perch. Six hundred thousand have been computed in the roe of a carp weighing nine pounds. The roe of a herring contains between three and four thousand ova; and it was a speculation of the sagacious Buffon that a pair of them, if left undisturbed for twenty years, would produce a progeny whose bulk would equal that of the entire globe. Sprats are so abundant that many hundred tons of them are annually used as manure. The profusion of life contained in the roe is intended not only to stock the sea, but also to feed its inhabitants. The small fry yield an abundance of food to fishes of larger growth, and these last in their turn contribute, more abundantly, perhaps, than any other sub-kingdom of Nature, to the support of mankind. If fishes were not voracious, and if they did not prey on one another, the vast shoals that people the ocean could not be fed. With insufficient nourishment their numbers would necessarily fall off, and the abundant supply now granted to man would thus be inevitably curtailed.

It has been ascertained that in many fishes, among which may be mentioned the pike, carp, tench, and eel, a regurgitation of food takes place which is analogous to rumination in quadrupeds. The matters thus chewed are most frequently of an animal nature. Fishes, it is true, have no grinders fixed along the jaws; but, on the other hand, various parts about the top of the gullet are often densely crowded with teeth, by which the food is torn, comminuted, and otherwise prepared for digestion. Until the discovery of rumination in fishes was made, the existence of these teeth toward the back of the throat was an enigma to physiologists.

Every angler has stories to tell of the voracity of fishes. They live for the most part by preying on each other. That pleasant naturalist, Mr. Jesse, mentions that on one occasion he had an opportunity of ascertaining that eight pike, weighing five pounds each, consumed nearly eight hundred gudgeon in three weeks. We will here allude only to one other evidence of voracity which was exhibited at a public lecture in Dublin. It consisted of the "skeleton of a frog-fish, two and a half feet in length, in whose stomach the skeleton of a cod two feet long was found. Within the cod were contained two whitings of the ordinary size, while in the stomach of each whiting were found numerous half-digested fishes which were too small and broken down to admit of preservation.

On the other hand, Nature has set checks to the voracity of the tyrants of the deep, and the weaker fishes have not been left altogether without the means of escape or defense. Flat fishes partly owe their safety to the sameness of color subsisting between them and the bottom of the sea or river on which they usually lie. We know by experience how difficult it is to detect them so long as they remain motionless and half-buried in the mud. Hence, as fishes hunt by sight, they readily escape being seen; and the same inconspicuous color which protects them from their enemies, favors the unsuspecting approach of the creatures on which they prey. So important does color appear to be, that ground fishes are invariably found to have the same general tint as the bottom soil, whatever that may be; and, indeed, it is affirmed that fishes have to a certain extent the power of gradually changing their color, and assimilating it to that produced by alterations from any cause in the color of the bed itself.

Many fishes, as sticklebacks and perch, have strong sharp spines implanted on the ridge of the back, which under the excitement of fear or anger are erected like bayonets, so as to be equally available for attack or defense. The Diodon, or Globe-fish of the Brazil coast, has a very singular means of baffling its enemies. This creature, by swallowing air, is able to puff itself out like a ball, during which operation the sharp spines by which its body is beset all over are brought into an erect position. It may be easily supposed that a fish thus stuck round with daggers, like a sea hedgehog, has no attraction for even the most voracious of its enemies. It sometimes happens, however, that a shark snaps it up before it has had time to inflate itself; but no sooner does it reach the stomach than it begins, if the shark's teeth have left any life in it, to blow itself up into a very awkward morsel. Not only has the Diodon been found in this situation inflated and bristling, but it is asserted that it has been known actually to eat its way out of prison.

The saw-fish is so called, because it has the upper jaw prolonged into a most formidable bony weapon, from which teeth project on either side so as to give it somewhat the general appearance of a saw. The sword-fish has the jaw lengthened out into a round spear three or four feet in length, of great strength, and finely tapered to a point. Men have been stabbed to death by this fatal weapon. The sword-fish has, it is said, a strong antipathy to the whale, and has been known to run full tilt at ships under the erroneous idea, as it is thought, that it was charging one of its natural enemies. The shock of the blow on these occasions is sometimes so great as to lead the crew to suppose that their ship has struck upon a rock. It is believed that ships have been sunk by the water rushing in through the hole thus made; but more frequently the "spear" itself is broken off from the violence of the thrust, and the end which is left behind acts as an efficient plug.

Among the various means of attack and defense possessed by fishes, the power which a few possess of discharging an electric shock at their enemies is, perhaps, the most remarkable. Such animated batteries are observed in various fishes, but are chiefly developed in the Silurus of the Nile; the Torpedo, a kind of Ray found in the seas of Southern Europe; and in the Gymnotus, or electric eel, which is peculiar to some of the rivers of South America. These fishes appear to have the power not only of exciting electricity in their batteries, but also of partially regulating the direction in which it is to pass off from their bodies. The capture of the Gymnotus, as it is carried on in South America, has been graphically described by Humboldt. Acting on the fact that these creatures exhaust their electrical power, and become innocuous after repeated discharges, the natives forcibly drive horses into the waters where they abound; and after the horses, to their extreme terror as well as suffering, have received all the shocks which can be given at that time, the owners quietly step in, and secure the spent eels as prizes.

The instincts and powers with which the Creator has endowed fishes for the purpose of meeting certain local or climatic difficulties are really wonderful. In Ceylon many reservoirs and streams well stocked with fish dry up during the hot season. In circumstances so desperate one would think that the fate of the fishes was sealed, but they habitually rescue themselves by migrating across fields and forests in quest of water. The most extraordinary part of the case is that, if there should happen to be a pool still remaining in the neighborhood, they seem to divine its situation by a kind of instinct, and make for it as straight as a crow could fly. Sir J. E. Tennent gives a curious vignette in which a troop of fishes are seen *en route* on one of these occasions, and considering they are almost as devoid of legs as serpents, without having been formed like them for crawling, it is wonderful what distances they traverse in their journeys. They have the instinct always to set out by night, or in the early dawn, so that they may have the advantage of the dew then lying heavy on the ground. As a special provision against the drought of the climate, some of these fishes are supplied with a peculiar structure near the top of the gullet, dependent on an expansion of the pharyngeal bones, which enables them to retain for a time as much water as is sufficient to keep the gills moist during their venturesome journeys. In our own country eels occasionally travel short distances across meadows. Within the tropics some fishes escape death from starvation by burying themselves in the mud on the approach of the dry season. The famous Lepidosiren of the Gambia forms for itself a cell or chamber in the soft mud, which soon becomes baked hard over it, and there it remains in a torpid state until the return of the floods. Some fishes in Ceylon insert their head into the mud, and bore in with the whole body until they come to a sufficiently moist layer, in which they bury themselves. The sun then bakes the superjacent clay, and seals them up as in a bottle, where they remain torpid until liberated by the loosening of the mud on the return of the rainy season. In India, Siam, Guiana, and elsewhere, there are many migratory and burrowing fishes, and such probably exist to a greater or less extent in all tropical countries subject to droughts.

In higher latitudes, on the other hand, fishes sometimes bury themselves on the approach of cold weather. Eels for the most part descend from the shallow rivulets to deeper water, but many occasionally get caught by the frost and are sealed up in the mud. It is said that in some parts of England the country people are in the habit of digging up half-frozen, torpid eels in the winter time. On the coast of Coromandel there is a kind of perch which not only makes excursions inland in search of food, but which actually pursues its prey, a small crustacean, up tall trees, and is provided for the purpose with a climbing apparatus appended to its fins.

There is not much to be said in praise of the parental tenderness of fishes. They strive with the persevering energy of instinct to ascend rivers, approach shallow coasts, or get into other situations favorable for the deposition of their spawn; but with this act their cares seem to end, and the eggs are left to take their chance. To this rule, however, there are a few exceptions. A shrewd naturalist of ancient times, Aristotle, affirmed that in the Mediterranean there was a fish which built a sort of nest or house, in which it laid its spawn; and modern observation has not only confirmed this statement, but has shown that while the *Phycis* is attending to her maternal duties in the nest, her companion mounts guard outside and protects her against intrusion.

In the muddy streamlets of Guiana a fish is found abundantly which the inhabitants highly prize as food. It is locally called Hassar, but it has received from naturalists the name of Callichthys — beautiful fish — as a tribute to its scaly splendor. It builds a kind of nest with the more delicate shreds of plants growing in the water; and the fishermen, knowing the assiduity with which the parents hover near their spawn, are accustomed to slip a net under the place where the nest is situated, and then by suddenly raising it up out of the water rarely fail to secure them.

One of the most genuine instances of parental and, perhaps we may add, conjugal affection observed in fishes, is to be found in the bright little stickleback with which the boyish recollections of many of us are associated. Neither is it surpassed, perhaps not equaled, by any other fish in the skill with which it constructs its habitation. Out of stray bits of grass or straws blown into the river, or the most delicate of the neighboring plants, a nest is built, in shape not unlike a diminutive barrel, with an opening at each end to facilitate easy ingress and egress; and round this castle the brave little stickleback mounts faithful guard, and tolerates no intruders. Where these fishes are numerous such castles abound, although from their color, closely resembling that of the other plantal surfaces around, it is not easy to distinguish them. There is something almost ludicrous in the bravery of this minute champion — this *preux chevalier* — among fishes. The Rev. J. G. Wood tells us that "his boldness is astonishing, for he will dash at a fish ten times his size, and, by dint of his fierce onset, and his bristly spears, drive the enemy away. Even if a stick be placed within the sacred circle, he will dart at it, repeating the assault as often as the stick may trespass upon his domains."

I will think of all Thy works; and my talking shall be of Thy doings. — Ps. lxxvii.

SUCH are a few illustrations of the Power, Wisdom, and Goodness of God, which a cursory glance at Nature brings most readily to our thoughts; but the field is boundless, and, did space permit, might be profitably surveyed from other parts. Below the higher ranks of the Animal Kingdom more especially noticed in this book, countless tribes exist, the contemplation of whose habits and structure is not less interesting to us, or less glorifying to the Creator. It has often occurred to me that, amid the various branches of education which compete for the time of youth, Natural History is still too much neglected. What solid, enduring advantages would result were it an established study, instead of being a mere accident, of school-life! Would it not also be better in every point of view, if more attention were directed toward it in institutions designed for the improvement of the working-classes, even though it trenched a little on the time frequently devoted to politics or critical discussion? A profound acquaintance with Natural History, it is obvious, can only be attained by few; but every body in these days, at the cost of a little reading of the most agreeable kind, may prepare himself with knowledge amply sufficient to crowd his walks with pleasure.

And not with pleasure only! While leading its followers among the "green things upon the earth," the pursuit of Natural History strengthens both mind and body, and awakens trains of thought that are well calculated to serve as a shield against the temptation of grosser pleasures. Not many persons, perhaps, habitually realize the extent to which devotional feelings may be roused by the contemplation of surrounding objects. Yet we cannot doubt that these objects are placed there for that very purpose; and when we reflect how much they are interwoven with our happiness, and the relief of our wants, do they not naturally excite us to greater love, and suggest to us greater thankfulness? Thus were they wisely used by the Three Children in their hymn. Nature is a book written by the finger of God Himself, and of which every page is filled to overflowing with illustrations of His wisdom; it is a picture in which His Goodness is painted in colors of perfect truth; it is a sculpturing in which His Power is expressed in marvels of form and harmony. Who does not long to be able to read this book, to view with appreciation this picture, to study with intelligence the wonders of this sculpturing? Next to the knowledge which saves, what more precious knowledge can there be than this?

It is never too early to instill tenderness toward all creatures into the young heart, and it almost seems as if the attractive lessons of Natural History courted our notice in order that they might be used for the purpose. Such teaching should not depend exclusively upon appeals to feeling, for though a good guide in the main, it sometimes leads astray, and prompts to destroy as well as to save. Feeling, therefore, stands itself in need of correction, and has to learn its own lesson. With feeling must be associated some of that knowledge which causes interest to spring up in the young mind; but, above all, it must be imbued with the principle of *respect for the life which God has created*. It is our lofty privilege to be intrusted with dominion over every living thing; but, as stewards of His providence, we are bound to carry out His rule of government, and carefully to distinguish between checking life that is injurious, and wantonly destroying life that does no harm. All animals live by the same title as ourselves — the Will of the Creator; and, when unoffending, they have the same right to existence. Let the child, therefore, be taught to regard life as sacred for the Creator's sake. God made it. Cruelty in the young is for the most part only a repulsive form of thoughtlessness, and a really cruel child is a rare phenomenon. It is an outrage upon that innocence of heart in which we delight to think Nature has enshrined the opening days of life. It is a sight that perplexes almost as much as it distresses us. The remembrance of it haunts us like an evil dream, and casts a gloom over the rest of the day.

On the other hand, how pleasing it is to see childhood on good terms with all God's creatures — to watch the little one in whose gentle vocabulary words of disgust and hatred find no place — whose face brightens with sympathy toward all living things — whose eyes sparkle with laughter at the merry ways of dumb dependents, and fill with tears when they die. How pleasing to see the little hand that plunges fearlessly among the favorites of the vivarium, to grasp with tenderest care some fragile life and hold it up for our admiration. How pleasing to see the child which neither strikes down butterfly after butterfly with thoughtless caprice for the sake of gazing for an instant at their beauty, nor stamps its tiny foot with fury on a beetle or a worm on account of its fancied ugliness. The heart softened betimes will never afterward be sullied by cruelty. On the contrary, the germs of kindliness thus early planted will surely grow and ripen, until they cover with their protection every inoffensive living thing that God has created.

At the beginning of this commentary it was mentioned that a few verses of the hymn would be omitted, not from their being unsuited to arouse devotional feelings, but because they were scarcely adapted to the kind of illustration which has here been followed. I cannot, however, pass from the subject without at least some allusion to them. One verse carries our thoughts back to the marvelous things that were done in olden time for the sake of the people whom God had chosen; another calls to our remembrance the fiery furnace at Babylon, and the ordeal through which the Three Children passed in safety, because they were upheld by the power of the Lord. In one verse, they who are specially set apart for the sacred service, and are placed among us as the ministers and stewards of its mysteries, are called on to join in the work of praise; in another, we are reminded of that higher and purer worship which angels and the spirits of just men made perfect are privileged to offer to the Throne. In the appeal to the holy and humble men of heart, we recognize the fitness with which holiness and humility are ever associated together as the best preparation for approaching the footstool of Infinite Power. Lastly, in the invocation addressed to the servants of the Lord, and to all the children of men we feel the hymn brought home more especially to ourselves, and we join heartily in the chant raised throughout the universe in honor of the Great Creator.

It has been my aim to point out that the beauty in which "all the works of the Lord" are enshrined is not a mere garnish on which we are only to expend criticism or praise, but a substantial blessing expressly created for our enjoyment, and for which we ought to be thankful. With what gratitude ought we not to mark that all Nature is molded, grouped, and combined in endless varieties of loveliness, so as most fully to gratify that longing after beauty with which we alone among earthly beings have been endowed! Can it be right habitually to treat this privilege with neglect, or to pass coldly on without appreciation or acknowledgment? This sense of beauty is to be viewed as the overflow of the riches of our Father's love. After all our wants have been satisfied, — after we have been fed and clothed, housed and warmed, — this good gift has been added over and above, as an ever-blooming flower laid upon our path through life, to be enjoyed and acknowledged with adoring thankfulness.

It has likewise been my aim to combat that apathy which freezes the springs of gratitude, and, which being satisfied with general acknowledgments, makes no effort to understand the details of providential design that knit us so lovingly to our Father. Truly there is nothing more chilling to adoration than that indifference which hardly seems to be conscious of the atmosphere of blessings in the midst of which our lives are passed, and which accepts these blessings as if they were the results of aimless accident, rather than guided specially toward our individual selves by the hand of God. How much more happiness-bringing is it to cherish that sensitiveness of disposition which is ever on the alert to discover new evidences of heavenly love! Every fresh illustration, as it flashes upon the mind, will then surely touch a chord within which will send up adoration from the heart. To "praise the Lord with understanding" is the height to which the Psalmist exhorts us to aspire, but it can only be reached through knowledge and reflection. To the mind thus prepared the words of the Benedicite are replete with meaning, and never fail to call forth the honoring worship they are intended to awaken. Where shall we find a hymn in which the Creator is more loftily portrayed as the Father who blesses us — as the All-wise Architect whose work is worthy to be praised — and as the mighty Ruler of the universe, to be magnified for ever!

May I venture on a word of appeal to those who fancy they see a snare in the exaltation of the material works of God, and suppose that the adoration which springs from the contemplation of them detracts in some way from that other adoration which is the fruit of Christian faith :— as if the worship resulting from the contemplation of God the Father and Creator were antagonistic to that arising from the contemplation of the work of God the Son and Redeemer. It is difficult to imagine a greater error. Our Father lays no such snares against the good of his children; if there be a doubter let him look round and watch His ways. Natural Theology and Christian Theology can never be really opposed or antagonistic; on the contrary, they only serve to strengthen and confirm each other. Let each occupy in our thoughts its proper place, and then neither of them can be too much cherished.

In whatever direction we survey the universe, we see that nothing is isolated, and no one thing exists without being adjusted to other things. All is in the most perfect harmony. Nothing that could be added, or that could be withdrawn, would make creation more perfect than it is. In tracing the tender care lavished upon every living thing, the conviction sinks deeply into our hearts that inexhaustible benevolence constitutes the design of God to all. It is written everywhere, and on every thing. Trustingly, contentedly, hopefully, therefore, we look upward to our Father. The comfort of such thoughts is unspeakable. Our Father makes every thing, plans every thing, cares for, feeds, clothes, and protects every thing; and if the all-wise laws which govern the world do sometimes bring a passing sorrow upon its inhabitants, how little does this appear when compared with the blessings which at every instant are showered upon them. May it not even be said, that the physical evils attendant upon fallen nature are often so tempered through our Father's mercy that they seem to change their very nature, and to be converted into blessings?

There is something which irresistibly draws us on to contemplate the attributes of the Deity, even although conscious that we can never fully comprehend them. His Omnipotence fascinates our thoughts. Though ever baffled, we return to it again and again; — hopeless to fathom, yet eager to see more. At other times we try to grasp more largely the idea of His Omnipresence. Again our efforts falter and break down. But, though we cannot elevate our understanding to the level of such ideas, there is nothing in the material world which lifts us higher or brings us nearer to success than the marvels of Natural Theology. Through it we see His presence, power, and government proclaimed by every star that glimmers in the depths of space, and we feel that we have thus won for ourselves a loftier and clearer view of Him than we had before. Or if we turn to the opposite end of the material world, we trace the same mighty finger shaping with exquisite skill the microscopic particles of matter, and the perception that every atom in creation is in contact with Omnipresence becomes more real and practical than it was before. Well might the Psalmist ask, — Whither shall I go from Thy presence? It is as distinct and palpable at the pole of minuteness as it is at the pole of immensity.

A great Prophet — a man after God's own heart, and who spoke with the authority of inspiration — has left in The Book of Psalms a standard by which in all coming time we may learn how the Lord is to be praised. As the direct work of the Holy Spirit, it has inherently a weight to which nothing merely human can lay claim, and it is instructive to mark the general agreement that subsists between the last three Psalms of David and the Song of the

Three Children. There is in both the same flood-like pouring forth of praise, and the same earnest striving that every thing in every possible way should serve to swell the voice of universal adoration. The Lord is to be praised "in the sanctuary" and "in the firmament of His power," or throughout the realms of infinite space. He is to be praised with trumpets, psaltery, and harp; with timbrel and dance; with stringed instruments and organs, and high-sounding cymbals. How emphatically music is here indicated as an aid in the outward expression of devotional feeling, and how vain it is to affect to contemn as sensuous a means which thus comes to us not only sanctioned, but enjoined, by the inspired Psalmist. Ages change, and we are changed in them, but the principle that was originally good never yet became evil merely through the lapse of time or the force of accidental association. Music is, after all, only one of the ways by which emotion seeks to give itself utterance, and when it falls on sympathizing ears it sometimes succeeds in helping to rouse or soften where words alone might fail. Listen to the strains in which the Psalmist of Israel calls upon the whole universe of being — intelligent and unintelligent — to join in one glorious hymn of praise in honor of their Lord and Creator: —

Praise ye the Lord from the heavens: praise Him in the heights.

Praise ye Him, all His angels: praise ye Him, all His hosts.

Praise ye Him, sun and moon: praise Him, all ye stars of light.

Praise Him, ye heaven of heavens, and ye waters that be above the heavens.

Let them praise the name of the Lord: for He commanded, and they were created.

He hath also stablished them for ever and ever: He hath made a decree which shall not pass.

Praise the Lord from the earth, ye dragons and all deeps:

Fire and hail; snow and vapors; stormy wind fulfilling His word:

Mountains and all hills; fruitful trees and all cedars;

Beasts and all cattle; creeping things and flying fowl:

Kings of the earth, and all people; princes, and all judges of the earth:

Both young men and maidens; old men and children:

Let them praise the name of the Lord: for His name alone is excellent; His glory is above the earth and heaven.

Let every thing that hath breath praise the Lord. — Ps. cl.

INDEX.

A.

AIR-CELLS of birds, 307.
All that swim in the waters, 351.
Aluminium and Alumina, 236.
Animalcules, microscopic, 211; their use, 214.
Animals, their structure perfect in relation to their habits and functions, 216.
Ant-eater of South America, 297.
Aral, Sea of, balance maintained between evaporation and supply, 154.
Ararat, Mount, 221.
Asteroids, 34.
Astronomy, the Father of sciences, 24.
Atmosphere, distributes light, 91; reflects light, 93; purified by plants acted on by light, 92; causes of deterioration, 91; absorbs moisture, 101; capacity for vapor varies according to temperature, 101; necessity for atmospheric moisture, 103; atmosphere described, 158.
Aye-aye, the, 298.

B.

BENEDICITE, THE, 12; its meaning sometimes misunderstood, 14; its fitness as an aid to adoration, 15.
BEASTS AND CATTLE, 286; the horse, 287; camel, 287; llama, 289; elephant, 289; reindeer, 289; dog, 291; sheep, 292; kangaroo, 292; buffalo, bison, mammoth, 293; animal scavengers, 296; ant-eater, 298.
Babylon, present and past, 7.
Baltic, the, supplied with salt from the North Sea, 150.
Barometer, 160.
Beak of birds, 310.
Birds, the song of, 300; plumage, 302; wings, 303; buoyancy in flight how secured, 307; temperature of blood, 308; air-cells, 307; diving, 309; beak, 310; vision, 312; digestion, 312; habits, 318; affection of, 320.
Blubber of whale, 343.
Bones of birds, 307.
Buffalo and bison, 293.

C.

CATTLE; see Beasts and Cattle.
COLD, 182; see Frost and Cold.
Camel, the, 287.
Carbonic acid gas in the atmosphere, 91; removed by plants, 92.

Caspian Sea, balance maintained between evaporation and supply, 154.
Centrifugal force, 29.
Chalk, 228.
Chemical force, a "Power of the Lord," 205.
Christmas, 83.
Church-building and decoration, 241.
Circulation, capillary, of the ocean, 148; in whales and fishes, 341.
Clay, 236.
Climate, 76; advantages of diversity of, 80; Great Britain, 82, 118.
Clouds; see Waters above the Firmament.
Coal, 174.
Colors, from coal-tar, 207.
Cotton, 254.
Craigleith quarry, 239.
Cuckoo, the, 323.
Currents of the ocean, 141.

D.

DARKNESS, 88; see Light and Darkness.
DAYS, 85; see Nights and Days.
Deserts, from absence of rain, 117.
Dew, 118; cause of, 119; in the East, 119.
Diving, of birds, 309; of whales, 345.
Dog, the, 291.

E.

EARTH, the, 230; glass, 232; pottery, 234; metals, 237; rocks, 238; church-building, 241; and decoration, 243.
Earthquakes dependent on subterranean fire, 204.
Earthshine, 48.
Easter, time of, determined by the moon, 50.
Egg, the, of birds, 334.
Eider-down, 306.
Electricity and lightning, 106; in fishes, 359.
Elephant, the Siberian, 293.
Elevation and subsidence of land, 203.
Eye, the, 88.

F.

FIRE AND HEAT, 171; fuel, 172; coal, 174; petroleum, 178.
FLOODS, 134; see Seas and Floods.
FOWLS OF THE AIR, 300; see Birds.
FROST AND COLD, 182; snow and ice, 183; snow-huts, 186; cold temperatures, 187; freezing of water, 188; glaciers, 191; icebergs, 195.
Feathers, 303.
Ferocity in animals bestowed in mercy, 294.
Fishes, 351; scales of, 352; organs of sense, 353; teeth, 355; fecundity, 356; rumination, 356; electrical, 359; torpidity, 360; nest-building, 361.
Flax-plant, 254.
Flight of birds, 303.
Forests of ancient Britain, 172, 272.
Friction, 199.

Index.

Fruit, temperature of, 282.
Furnace, the burning fiery, 10.

G.

GREEN THINGS UPON THE EARTH, 251; adjustments to climate and physical conditions, 251; flax and cotton, 254; out of labor comes a blessing, 257; variety of useful products from same plant, 258; tropical vegetation, 258; polar, 261; seed, 263; "green things" in town, 267; trees, 269; the sap, 273; leaves, 275; wood, 280; medicinal plants, 283; leaves form mold, 284.
Gibraltar, currents at Straits of, 150.
Gizzard, the, in birds, 312.
Glaciers, their color, 183; described, 191; ancient glaciers in Britain, 195; Great Greenland glacier, 196; supply rivers in summer, 225.
Glass, 233.
Golden image, the, 10.
Gravity, solar and terrestrial, 198.
Gulf Stream, 139.
Gullet of whale, 346.
Gymnotus electricus, 359.

H.

HEAVENS, THE, 20; Astronomy one of the most exact of sciences, 21; see sun, moon, stars, etc.
HEAT, 171; see Fire and Heat.
Heat, internal, of earth, 201.
Herdsmen, in the Bible, 299.
Hibernation of fishes, 360.

I.

INTRODUCTION, 7.
ICE, 182; see Frost and Cold.
Icebergs, 195.
Inland climates, 77.
Iron, manufacture of, 173.

J.

Jupiter, 34.

K.

Kangaroo, the, 292.
Khamsin, the, 169.
Killers, in Australian seas, enemy of the whale, 349.

L.

LIGHT AND DARKNESS, 88; the eye, 88; light, distributed by atmosphere, 91; action on plants, 92; importance to health, 96; the organized world dependent on it, 98.
LIGHTNING AND CLOUDS, 106; artificial conductors, 108; natural, 109.
Lakes, ancient, dried up, 155; use of, near river sources, 155.
Leaves the lungs of plants, 275; purify atmosphere, 92, 275; absorb moisture, 277; conversion into mold, 284.
Life, principle of, 210; abundance in the sea, 137.
Limestone rocks, caves and rivers in, 127.

M.

MOON, 43; appearance of, 45; has

no atmosphere or water, 47; uses of, 49.
MOUNTAINS AND HILLS, 220; Bible hills, 221; height, 222; influence on vegetation, 224; sanatoria, 227; often the evidence of ancient convulsions, 227; and former abundance of life, 228.
Marbles, 243.
Maritime climates, 77.
Mars, 33.
Mediterranean, color of, 139; dependent on ocean currents, 149.
Mercury, 32.
Metals, 237.
Migration of birds, 329.
Moisture in the atmosphere, 101.
Monsoons, 167.
Mountains in the sun, 31; in the moon, 46.
Mouth of whale, 346; of fishes, 355.

N.

NIGHTS AND DAYS, 85; dependent on rotation of the earth, 85; polar night, 96.
Natural History, 362.
Nautical Almanac, 21.
Navigation, accuracy of modern, 152.
Nebuchadnezzar, 9.
Nebulæ, 63.
Neptune, discovery of the planet, 22.
Nests of birds, 327; of fishes, 361.
Nightingale, the, 329.
Northwest passage, discovered by a whale, 347.
Nutrition, the succession of, 98.

O.

Ocean, bed of, described, 136; currents, 141; distributes heat, 145.
Oil of whale, 350; other oils, 350; in birds, 314.

P.

POWERS OF THE LORD, 198; gravitation, 198; friction, 199; chemical power, 205; vital power, 210; the evils they sometimes bring are small in comparison to the blessings, 217.
Painting, in churches, 246.
Pelican, the, 319.
Planets, are they inhabited? 38.
Plants, medicinal, 283; see "Green Things."
Plumage, 302.
Polar vegetation, 261.
Pottery, 234.

Q.

Quails, the Israelites fed with, 316.

R.

Rain, former and latter, 111; its uses, 112; carried from tropical to higher latitudes, 113; rainy seasons in tropics, 115; associated with fertility, 116.
Raven, the, 328.
Red Sea, dependent for water on Indian Ocean, 150.
Reflection of light, 90.
Refraction of light, 93.
Reindeer, 289.

Index.

Representative plants in different climates, 80.
Reservoir of water, the crust of the earth is a, 126; reservoirs of blood in the whale, 341.
Rocks, 238.
Rumination in fishes, 356.

S.

SEAS AND FLOODS, 134; bed of the sea, 136; color, 139; phosphorescence and saltness, 140; profusion of life in, 137; desolate regions, 138; currents, 142; distribute heat, 145.
SHOWERS AND DEW, 111; see Rain and Dew.
SNOW, 182; see Frost and Cold.
STARS, the, 51; number, 52, 67; arrangement, 52; binary and multiple, 53; parallax, 55; gauging the heavens, 61; cannot be magnified, 65; size, 65; velocity, 66; Milky Way, 67; Nebulæ, 67; nature of, 69.
SUN, the, 27; attraction of, 28; distance, 30; diameter and bulk, 30; temperature, 31; atmosphere, 32; light of, 32; movement and position in space, 68; in polar regions, 96.
Sap, circulation of, 273.
Saturn, 35.
Scales of fishes, 352.
Scavengers, animal, 214, 296.
Sculpture, in churches, 244.
Sea-reed, its use, 278.
Seasons, 72; tropical, 78; see Winter and Summer.
Seed, the, 263, 266.
Sheep, the, 292.
Skylark, the, 301.

Solar space, excursion through, 32; the frontiers of, 35, 67.
Spiracle of whale, 343.
Springs, 122; see Wells.
Stickleback, the, 361.
Stork, the, 319.
Swimming of fishes, 351; swim-bladder, 353.
Symbolism, 249.

T.

Teeth of fishes, 355.
Temperature of earth in different latitudes, 76.
Text scrolls, in churches, 247.
Tides, 150; their height, 151.
Torpidity of fishes, 360.
Trade-winds, 163.
Trees, 269; size, 270; age, 270.
Tropical vegetation, described, 258.
Twilight, 94.

U.

Uranus, 35.

V.

Vapor in the atmosphere, 101; gathered in tropical seas to be carried to higher latitudes, where it supplies heat and rain, 113.
Vegetable principles, conversion of, 208.
Venus, 33.
Volcanic action, 201.
Voracity of fishes, 357.
Vulture, the; its use, 325; sagacity, 327.

W.

WATERS ABOVE THE FIRMAMENT, 100; clouds, their use, 100; formation, 101.

WELLS, 122; their importance in the East, 122; early appearance of, in coral islands, 124; in England, 127; Artesian, 128; spouting, 129; mineral, 131.

WHALES, 338; the whale not a fish, 338, 341; size, 339; circulation of, 342; spiracle, 343; blubber, 343; power of the tail, 345; narrow gullet, 346; the mouth and the whalebone, 346; a whale's feast, 346; discovery of Northwest passage, 347; former distribution, 348; its enemies, 348; tenderness to its young, 349; oil, 350.

WINDS, 158; circulation, 158; upper and lower currents, 162; land and sea breeze, 163; Trades, 164; Monsoons, 167; use of winds, 169.

WINTER AND SUMMER, cause of, 72; correspond to dry and wet seasons within tropics, 78; summer in polar regions, 79.

Wasps, destruction of, in autumn, 295.

Water, action of "cold" on, 188; its circulation, essential to organized existence, 157.

Wings of birds, 303.

Wood, various properties of, 269; concentric rings in, 281; sapwood and heart-wood, 282.

THE END.

www.ingramcontent.com/pod-product-compliance
Lightning Source LLC
Chambersburg PA
CBHW030402230426
43664CB00007BB/717